A Compilation of Selected

Homeland Security Related Laws

Volume 3

I0092676

Including:

★ United States-Israel Advanced Research Partnership Act of 2016
★ Strengthening State and Local Cyber Crime Fighting Act of 2017
★ Cybersecurity and Infrastructure Security Agency Act of 2018
★ Chemical Facility Anti-Terrorism Standards Program Extension
Act ★ Protecting and Securing Chemical Facilities from Terrorist
Attacks Act of 2014 ★ Internet of Things Cybersecurity Improve-
ment Act of 2020 ★ Cyber Response and Recovery Act ★ Pro-
visions of the National Defense Authorization Act for Fiscal Year
2022 ★ National Cybersecurity Preparedness Consortium Act of
2021 ★ State and Local Government Cybersecurity Act of 2021 ★
Consolidated Appropriations Act, 2021

Updated through Public Law 118-19,
enacted on October 6, 2023

Compiled by M. Twinchek

Forward

The following is a compilation of selected sections of the U.S. Code or public laws that either do not appear in the U.S. Code or have been classified to a title of the U.S. Code that has not been enacted into positive law. Each Statute Compilation incorporates the amendments made to the underlying statute since it was originally enacted. When legislation cites or amends a statutory provision that is not part of a positive law title of the U.S. Code, the citation or amendment must be to the underlying statute, not to the U.S. Code. Statute Compilations are a useful drafting aid in these circumstances.

This compilation is created from publicly available information provided by the U.S. House of Representatives, Office of the Legislative Counsel and the Office of the Law Revision Counsel.

The statutes are current as of the date and law indicated.

This compilation is not an official document and should not be cited as evidence of the law. The official version of Federal law is found in the United States Statutes at Large and in the U.S. Code, the legal effect of which is established in sections 112 and 204, respectively, of title 1, United States Code.

Contents

United States-Israel Advanced Research Partnership Act of 2016

PUBLIC LAW 114-304

United States-Israel Advanced Research Partnership Act of 2016

[(Public Law 114–304)]

[This law has not been amended]

[Currency: This publication is a compilation of the text of Public Law 114–304. It was last amended by the public law listed in the As Amended Through note above and below at the bottom of each page of the pdf version and reflects current law through the date of the enactment of the public law listed at https://www.govinfo.gov/app/collection/comps/]

AN ACT To amend the Homeland Security Act of 2002 and the United States-Israel Strategic Partnership Act of 2014 to promote cooperative homeland security research and antiterrorism programs relating to cybersecurity, and for other purposes.

Be it enacted by the Senate and House of Representatives of the United States of America in Congress assembled,

SECTION 1. [6 U.S.C. 101 note] SHORT TITLE.

This Act may be cited as the "United States-Israel Advanced Research Partnership Act of 2016".

SEC. 2. COOPERATIVE HOMELAND SECURITY RESEARCH AND ANTITERRORISM PROGRAMS RELATING TO CYBERSECURITY.

(a) HOMELAND SECURITY ACT OF 2002.—Section 317 of the Homeland Security Act of 2002 (6 U.S.C. 195c) is amended—

(1) in subsection (e)—

(A) in paragraph (1), by striking "and" after the semicolon;

(B) in paragraph (2), by striking the period at the end and inserting "; and"; and

(C) by inserting after paragraph (2) the following new paragraphs:

"(3) for international cooperative activities identified in the previous reporting period, a status update on the progress of such activities, including whether goals were realized, explaining any lessons learned, and evaluating overall success; and

"(4) a discussion of obstacles encountered in the course of forming, executing, or implementing agreements for international cooperative activities, including administrative, legal, or diplomatic challenges or resource constraints."

;

(2) by redesignating subsections (g) and (h) as subsections (h) and (i), respectively; and

(3) by inserting after subsection (f) the following new subsection:

"(g) CYBERSECURITY.—As part of the international cooperative activities authorized in this section, the Under Secretary, in coordination with the Department of State and appropriate Federal officials, may enter into cooperative research activities with Israel to strengthen preparedness against cyber threats and enhance capabilities in cybersecurity."

.

(b) UNITED STATES-ISRAEL STRATEGIC PARTNERSHIP ACT OF 2014.—Subsection (c) of section 7 of the United States-Israel Strategic Partnership Act of 2014 (Public Law 113-296; 22 U.S.C. 8606) is amended—

(1) in the heading, by striking "Pilot";

(2) in the matter preceding paragraph (1), by striking "pilot";

(3) in paragraph (2), by striking "and" at the end;

(4) in paragraph (3), by striking the period at the end and inserting "; and"; and

(5) by adding at the end the following new paragraph:

"(4) cybersecurity."

.

SEC. 3. PROHIBITION ON ADDITIONAL FUNDING.

No additional funds are authorized to be appropriated to carry out this Act or the amendments made by this Act.

Strengthening State and Local Cyber Crime Fighting Act of 2017

PUBLIC LAW 115-76

Strengthening State and Local Cyber Crime Fighting Act of 2017

[(Public Law 115–76)]

[This law has not been amended]

[Currency: This publication is a compilation of the text of Public Law 115-76. It was last amended by the public law listed in the As Amended Through note above and below at the bottom of each page of the pdf version and reflects current law through the date of the enactment of the public law listed at https://www.govinfo.gov/app/collection/comps/]

AN ACT To amend the Homeland Security Act of 2002 to authorize the National Computer Forensics Institute, and for other purposes.

Be it enacted by the Senate and House of Representatives of the United States of America in Congress assembled,

SECTION 1. [34 U.S.C. 10101 note] SHORT TITLE.

This Act may be cited as the "Strengthening State and Local Cyber Crime Fighting Act of 2017".

SEC. 2. AUTHORIZATION OF THE NATIONAL COMPUTER FORENSICS INSTITUTE OF THE DEPARTMENT OF HOMELAND SECURITY.

(a) IN GENERAL.—Subtitle C of title VIII of the Homeland Security Act of 2002 (6 U.S.C. 381 et seq.) is amended by adding at the end the following new section:

"SEC. 822. [6 U.S.C. 383] NATIONAL COMPUTER FORENSICS INSTITUTE

"(a) IN GENERAL.—There is authorized for fiscal years 2017

through 2022 within the United States Secret Service a National Computer Forensics Institute (in this section referred to as the 'Institute'). The Institute shall disseminate information related to the investigation and prevention of cyber and electronic crime and related threats, and educate, train, and equip State, local, tribal, and territorial law enforcement officers, prosecutors, and judges.

"(b) FUNCTIONS.—The functions of the Institute shall include the following:

"(1) Educating State, local, tribal, and territorial law enforcement officers, prosecutors, and judges on current—

"(A) cyber and electronic crimes and related threats;

"(B) methods for investigating cyber and electronic crime and related threats and conducting computer and mobile device forensic examinations; and

"(C) prosecutorial and judicial challenges related to cyber and electronic crime and related threats, and computer and mobile device forensic examinations.

"(2) Training State, local, tribal, and territorial law enforcement officers to—

"(A) conduct cyber and electronic crime and related threat investigations;

"(B) conduct computer and mobile device forensic examinations; and

"(C) respond to network intrusion incidents.

"(3) Training State, local, tribal, and territorial law enforcement officers, prosecutors, and judges on methods to obtain, process, store, and admit digital evidence in court.

"(c) PRINCIPLES.—In carrying out the functions specified in subsection (b), the Institute shall ensure, to the extent practicable, that timely, actionable, and relevant expertise and information related to cyber and electronic crime and related threats is shared with State, local, tribal, and territorial law enforcement officers and prosecutors.

"(d) EQUIPMENT.—The Institute may provide State, local, tribal, and territorial law enforcement officers with computer equipment, hardware, software, manuals, and tools necessary to conduct cyber and electronic crime and related threat investigations and computer and mobile device forensic examinations.

"(e) ELECTRONIC CRIME TASK FORCES.—The Institute shall facilitate the expansion of the network of Electronic Crime Task Forces of the United States Secret Service through the addition of State, local, tribal, and territorial law enforcement officers educated and trained at the Institute.

"(f) SAVINGS PROVISION.—All authorized activities and functions carried out by the Institute at any location as of the day before the date of the enactment of this section are authorized to continue to be carried out at any such location on and after such date."

.

(b) FUNDING.—For each of fiscal years 2018 through 2022, amounts appropriated for United States Secret Service, Operations and Support, may be used to carry out this Act and the amendments made by this Act.

(c) CLERICAL AMENDMENT.—The table of contents in section 1(b) of the Homeland Security Act of 2002 (6 U.S.C. 101 et seq.) is amended by inserting after the item relating to section 821 the following new item:

"Sec. 822. National Computer Forensics Institute."

.

SEC. 3. PREVENTION, INVESTIGATION, AND PROSECUTION OF ECONOMIC, HIGH TECHNOLOGY, INTERNET, AND OTHER WHITE COLLAR CRIME.

(a) IN GENERAL.—Title I of the Omnibus Crime Control and Safe Streets Act of 1968 (34 U.S.C. 10101 et seq.) is amended by adding at the end the following:

"PART MM—PREVENTION, INVESTIGATION, AND PROSECUTION OF WHITE COLLAR CRIME

"SEC. 3030. SHORT TITLE

"This part may be cited as the 'National White Collar Crime Control Act of 2017'.

"SEC. 3031. [34 U.S.C. 10721 note] ESTABLISHMENT OF GRANT PROGRAM

"(a) AUTHORIZATION.—The Director of the Bureau of Justice Assistance is authorized to enter into a cooperative agreement with or make a grant to an eligible entity for the purpose of improving the identification, investigation, and prosecution of white collar crime (including each category of such crimes set forth in paragraphs (1) through (3) of subsection (b)) by providing comprehensive, direct, and practical training and technical assistance to law enforcement officers, investigators, auditors and prosecutors in States and units of local government.

"(b) WHITE COLLAR CRIME DEFINED.—For purposes of this part, the term 'white collar crime' includes—

"(1) high-tech crime, including cyber and electronic crime and related threats;

"(2) economic crime, including financial fraud and mortgage fraud; and

"(3) Internet-based crime against children and child pornography.

"SEC. 3032. [34 U.S.C. 10722 note] PURPOSES
"The purposes of this part include the following:

"(1) To ensure that training is available for State, local, tribal and territorial law enforcement agencies and officers nationwide to support local efforts to identify, prevent, investigate, and prosecute cyber and financial crimes, including those crimes facilitated via computer networks and other electronic means, and crimes involving financial and economic impacts such as intellectual property crimes.

"(2) To deliver training to State, local, tribal, and territorial law enforcement officers, and other criminal justice professionals concerning the use of proven methodologies to prevent, detect, and respond to such crimes, recognize emerging issues, manage electronic and financial crime evidence and to improve local criminal justice agency responses to such threats.

"(3) To provide operational and technical assistance and training concerning tools, products, resources, guidelines, and procedures to aid and enhance criminal intelligence analysis, conduct cyber crime and financial crime investigations, and related justice information sharing at the local and State levels.

"(4) To provide appropriate training on protections for

12

privacy, civil rights, and civil liberties in the conduct of criminal intelligence analysis and cyber and electronic crime and financial crime investigations, including in the development of policies, guidelines, and procedures by State, local, tribal, and territorial law enforcement agencies to protect and enhance privacy, civil rights, and civil liberties protections and identify weaknesses and gaps in the protection of privacy, civil rights, and civil liberties.

"SEC. 3033. [34 U.S.C. 10723 note] AUTHORIZED PROGRAMS

"A grant or cooperative agreement awarded under this part may be made only for the following programs, with respect to the prevention, investigation, and prosecution of certain criminal activities:

"(1) Programs to provide a nationwide support system for State and local criminal justice agencies.

"(2) Programs to assist State and local criminal justice agencies to develop, establish, and maintain intelligence-focused policing strategies and related information sharing.

"(3) Programs to provide training and investigative support services to State and local criminal justice agencies to provide such agencies with skills and resources needed to investigate and prosecute such criminal activities and related criminal activities.

"(4) Programs to provide research support, to establish partnerships, and to provide other resources to aid State and local criminal justice agencies to prevent, investigate, and prosecute such criminal activities and related problems.

"(5) Programs to provide information and research to the general public to facilitate the prevention of such criminal activities.

"(6) Programs to establish or support national training and research centers regionally to provide training and research services for State and local criminal justice agencies.

"(7) Programs to provide training and oversight to State and local criminal justice agencies to develop and comply with applicable privacy, civil rights, and civil liberties related policies, procedures, rules, laws, and guidelines.

"(8) Any other programs specified by the Attorney General

as furthering the purposes of this part.

"SEC. 3034. [34 U.S.C. 10724 note] APPLICATION

"To be eligible for an award of a grant or cooperative agreement under this part, an entity shall submit to the Director of the Bureau of Justice Assistance an application in such form and manner, and containing such information, as required by the Director of the Bureau of Justice Assistance.

"SEC. 3035. [34 U.S.C. 10725 note] ELIGIBILITY

"States, units of local government, not-for-profit entities, and institutions of higher-education with demonstrated capacity and experience in delivering training, technical assistance and other resources including direct, practical laboratory training to law enforcement officers, investigators, auditors and prosecutors in States and units of local government and over the Internet shall be eligible to receive an award under this part.

"SEC. 3036. [34 U.S.C. 10726 note] RULES AND REGULATIONS

"The Director of the Bureau of Justice Assistance shall promulgate such rules and regulations as are necessary to carry out this part, including rules and regulations for submitting and reviewing applications under section 3035."

.

(b) AUTHORIZATION OF APPROPRIATIONS.—There are authorized to be appropriated $13,000,000 for each of fiscal years 2018 through 2022 to carry out—

(1) part MM of title I of the Omnibus Crime Control and Safe Streets Act of 1968, as added by subsection (a); and

(2) section 401(b) of the Prioritizing Resources and Organization for Intellectual Property Act of 2008 (34 U.S.C. 30103(b)).

Cybersecurity and Infrastructure Security Agency Act of 2018

PUBLIC LAW 115-278

Cybersecurity and Infrastructure Security Agency Act of 2018

[(Public Law 115–278)]

[This law has not been amended]

[Currency: This publication is a compilation of the text of Public Law 115-278. It was last amended by the public law listed in the As Amended Through note above and below at the bottom of each page of the pdf version and reflects current law through the date of the enactment of the public law listed at https://www.govinfo.gov/app/collection/comps/]

AN ACT To amend the Homeland Security Act of 2002 to authorize the Cybersecurity and Infrastructure Security Agency of the Department of Homeland Security, and for other purposes.

Be it enacted by the Senate and House of Representatives of the United States of America in Congress assembled,

SECTION 1. [6 U.S.C. 101 note] SHORT TITLE.

This Act may be cited as the "Cybersecurity and Infrastructure Security Agency Act of 2018".

SEC. 2. CYBERSECURITY AND INFRASTRUCTURE SECURITY AGENCY.

(a) IN GENERAL.—The Homeland Security Act of 2002 (6 U.S.C. 101 et seq.) is amended by adding at the end the following:

"TITLE XXII—CYBERSECURITY AND INFRASTRUCTURE SECURITY AGENCY

"Subtitle A—Cybersecurity and Infrastructure Security

"SEC. SEC. 2201. [6 U.S.C. 651] DEFINITIONS

"In this subtitle:

"(1) CRITICAL INFRASTRUCTURE INFORMATION.—The term 'critical infrastructure information' has the meaning given the term in section 2222.

"(2) CYBERSECURITY RISK.—The term 'cybersecurity risk' has the meaning given the term in section 2209.

"(3) CYBERSECURITY THREAT.—The term 'cybersecurity threat' has the meaning given the term in section 102(5) of the Cybersecurity Act of 2015 (contained in division N of the Consolidated Appropriations Act, 2016 (Public Law 114-113; 6 U.S.C. 1501)).

"(4) NATIONAL CYBERSECURITY ASSET RESPONSE ACTIVITIES.—The term 'national cybersecurity asset response activities' means—

"(A) furnishing cybersecurity technical assistance to entities affected by cybersecurity risks to protect assets, mitigate vulnerabilities, and reduce impacts of cyber incidents;

"(B) identifying other entities that may be at risk of an incident and assessing risk to the same or similar vulnerabilities;

"(C) assessing potential cybersecurity risks to a sector or region, including potential cascading effects, and developing courses of action to mitigate such risks;

"(D) facilitating information sharing and operational coordination with threat response; and

"(E) providing guidance on how best to utilize Federal resources and capabilities in a timely, effective manner to speed recovery from cybersecurity risks.

"(5) SECTOR-SPECIFIC AGENCY.—The term 'Sector-Specific Agency' means a Federal department or agency, designated by law or presidential directive, with responsibility for providing institutional knowledge and specialized expertise of a sector, as well as leading, facilitating, or supporting programs and associated activities of its designated critical infrastructure sector in the all hazards environment in coordination with the Department.

"(6) SHARING.—The term 'sharing' has the meaning given the term in section 2209.

"SEC. SEC. 2202. [6 U.S.C. 652] CYBERSECURITY AND INFRASTRUCTURE SECURITY AGENCY

"(a) REDESIGNATION.—

"(1) IN GENERAL.—The National Protection and Programs Directorate of the Department shall, on and after the date of the enactment of this subtitle, be known as the 'Cybersecurity and Infrastructure Security Agency' (in this subtitle referred to as the 'Agency').

"(2) REFERENCES.—Any reference to the National Protection and Programs Directorate of the Department in any law, regulation, map, document, record, or other paper of the United States shall be deemed to be a reference to the Cybersecurity and Infrastructure Security Agency of the Department.

"(b) DIRECTOR.—

"(1) IN GENERAL.—The Agency shall be headed by a Director of Cybersecurity and Infrastructure Security (in this subtitle referred to as the 'Director'), who shall report to the Secretary.

"(2) REFERENCE.—Any reference to an Under Secretary responsible for overseeing critical infrastructure protection, cybersecurity, and any other related program of the Department as described in section 103(a)(1)(H) as in effect on the day before the date of enactment of this subtitle in any law, regulation, map, document, record, or other paper of the United States shall be deemed to be a reference to the Director of Cybersecurity and Infrastructure Security of the Department.

"(c) RESPONSIBILITIES.—The Director shall—

"(1) lead cybersecurity and critical infrastructure security programs, operations, and associated policy for the Agency, including national cybersecurity asset response activities;

"(2) coordinate with Federal entities, including Sector-Specific Agencies, and non-Federal entities, including international entities, to carry out the cybersecurity and critical infrastructure activities of the Agency, as appropriate;

"(3) carry out the responsibilities of the Secretary to secure Federal information and information systems consistent with law, including subchapter II of chapter 35 of title 44, United States Code, and the Cybersecurity Act of 2015 (contained in division N of the Consolidated Appropriations Act, 2016 (Public Law 114-113));

"(4) coordinate a national effort to secure and protect against critical infrastructure risks, consistent with subsection (e)(1)(E);

"(5) upon request, provide analyses, expertise, and other technical assistance to critical infrastructure owners and operators and, where appropriate, provide those analyses, expertise, and other technical assistance in coordination with Sector-Specific Agencies and other Federal departments and agencies;

"(6) develop and utilize mechanisms for active and frequent collaboration between the Agency and Sector-Specific Agencies to ensure appropriate coordination, situational awareness, and communications with Sector-Specific Agencies;

"(7) maintain and utilize mechanisms for the regular and ongoing consultation and collaboration among the Divisions of the Agency to further operational coordination, integrated situational awareness, and improved integration across the Agency in accordance with this Act;

"(8) develop, coordinate, and implement—

"(A) comprehensive strategic plans for the activities of the Agency; and

"(B) risk assessments by and for the Agency;

"(9) carry out emergency communications responsibilities, in accordance with title XVIII;

"(10) carry out cybersecurity, infrastructure security, and emergency communications stakeholder outreach and engagement and coordinate that outreach and engagement with critical infrastructure Sector-Specific Agencies, as appropriate; and

"(11) carry out such other duties and powers prescribed by

law or delegated by the Secretary.

"(d) DEPUTY DIRECTOR.—There shall be in the Agency a Deputy Director of Cybersecurity and Infrastructure Security who shall—

"(1) assist the Director in the management of the Agency; and

"(2) report to the Director.

"(e) CYBERSECURITY AND INFRASTRUCTURE SECURITY AUTHORITIES OF THE SECRETARY.—

"(1) IN GENERAL.—The responsibilities of the Secretary relating to cybersecurity and infrastructure security shall include the following:

"(A) To access, receive, and analyze law enforcement information, intelligence information, and other information from Federal Government agencies, State, local, tribal, and territorial government agencies, including law enforcement agencies, and private sector entities, and to integrate that information, in support of the mission responsibilities of the Department, in order to—

"(i) identify and assess the nature and scope of terrorist threats to the homeland;

"(ii) detect and identify threats of terrorism against the United States; and

"(iii) understand those threats in light of actual and potential vulnerabilities of the homeland.

"(B) To carry out comprehensive assessments of the vulnerabilities of the key resources and critical infrastructure of the United States, including the performance of risk assessments to determine the risks posed by particular types of terrorist attacks within the United States, including an assessment of the probability of success of those attacks and the feasibility and potential efficacy of various countermeasures to those attacks. At the discretion of the Secretary, such assessments may be carried out in coordination with Sector-Specific Agencies.

"(C) To integrate relevant information, analysis, and vulnerability assessments, regardless of whether the information, analysis, or assessments are provided or produced by the Department, in order to make recommendations, including prioritization, for protective and support measures by the Department, other Federal Government agencies, State, local, tribal, and territorial government agencies and authorities, the private sector, and other entities regarding terrorist and other threats to homeland security.

"(D) To ensure, pursuant to section 202, the timely and efficient access by the Department to all information necessary to discharge the responsibilities under this title, including obtaining that information from other Federal Government agencies.

"(E) To develop, in coordination with the Sector-Specific Agencies with available expertise, a comprehensive national plan for securing the key resources and critical infrastructure of the United States, including power production, generation, and distribution systems, information technology and telecommunications systems (including satellites), electronic financial and property record storage and transmission systems, emergency communications systems, and the physical and technological assets that support those systems.

"(F) To recommend measures necessary to protect the key resources and critical infrastructure of the United States in coordination with other Federal Government agencies, including Sector-Specific Agencies, and in cooperation with State, local, tribal, and territorial government agencies and authorities, the private sector, and other entities.

"(G) To review, analyze, and make recommendations for improvements to the policies and procedures governing the sharing of information relating to homeland security within the Federal Government and between Federal Government agencies and State, local, tribal, and territorial government agencies and authorities.

"(H) To disseminate, as appropriate, information analyzed by the Department within the Department to other Federal Government agencies with responsibilities relating to homeland security and to State, local, tribal, and territorial government agencies and private sector entities with those responsibilities in order to assist in the deterrence, prevention, or preemption of, or response to, terrorist attacks against the United States.

"(I) To consult with State, local, tribal, and territorial government agencies and private sector entities to ensure appropriate exchanges of information, including law enforcement-related information, relating to threats of terrorism against the United States.

"(J) To ensure that any material received pursuant to this Act is protected from unauthorized disclosure and handled and used only for the performance of official duties.

"(K) To request additional information from other Federal Government agencies, State, local, tribal, and territorial government agencies, and the private sector relating to threats of terrorism in the United States, or relating to other areas of responsibility assigned by the Secretary, including the entry into cooperative agreements through the Secretary to obtain such information.

"(L) To establish and utilize, in conjunction with the Chief Information Officer of the Department, a secure communications and information technology infrastructure, including data-mining and other advanced analytical tools, in order to access, receive, and analyze data and information in furtherance of the responsibilities under this section, and to disseminate information acquired and analyzed by the Department, as appropriate.

"(M) To coordinate training and other support to the elements and personnel of the Department, other Federal Government agencies, and State, local, tribal, and territorial government agencies that provide information to the Department, or are consumers of information provided by the Department, in order to facilitate the identification and sharing of information revealed in their ordinary duties and the optimal utilization of information received from the Department.

"(N) To coordinate with Federal, State, local, tribal, and territorial law enforcement agencies, and the private sector, as appropriate.

"(O) To exercise the authorities and oversight of the

functions, personnel, assets, and liabilities of those components transferred to the Department pursuant to section 201(g).

"(P) To carry out the functions of the national cybersecurity and communications integration center under section 2209.

"(Q) To carry out the requirements of the Chemical Facility Anti-Terrorism Standards Program established under title XXI and the secure handling of ammonium nitrate program established under subtitle J of title VIII, or any successor programs.

"(2) REALLOCATION.—The Secretary may reallocate within the Agency the functions specified in sections 2203(b) and 2204(b), consistent with the responsibilities provided in paragraph (1), upon certifying to and briefing the appropriate congressional committees, and making available to the public, at least 60 days prior to the reallocation that the reallocation is necessary for carrying out the activities of the Agency.

"(3) STAFF.—

"(A) IN GENERAL.—The Secretary shall provide the Agency with a staff of analysts having appropriate expertise and experience to assist the Agency in discharging the responsibilities of the Agency under this section.

"(B) PRIVATE SECTOR ANALYSTS.—Analysts under this subsection may include analysts from the private sector.

"(C) SECURITY CLEARANCES.—Analysts under this subsection shall possess security clearances appropriate for their work under this section.

"(4) DETAIL OF PERSONNEL.—

"(A) IN GENERAL.—In order to assist the Agency in discharging the responsibilities of the Agency under this section, personnel of the Federal agencies described in subparagraph (B) may be detailed to the Agency for the performance of analytic functions and related duties.

"(B) AGENCIES.—The Federal agencies described in this subparagraph are—

"(i) the Department of State;

"(ii) the Central Intelligence Agency;

"(iii) the Federal Bureau of Investigation;

"(iv) the National Security Agency;

"(v) the National Geospatial-Intelligence Agency;

"(vi) the Defense Intelligence Agency;

"(vii) Sector-Specific Agencies; and

"(viii) any other agency of the Federal Government that the President considers appropriate.

"(C) INTERAGENCY AGREEMENTS.—The Secretary and the head of a Federal agency described in subparagraph (B) may enter into agreements for the purpose of detailing personnel under this paragraph.

"(D) BASIS.—The detail of personnel under this paragraph may be on a reimbursable or non-reimbursable basis.

"(f) COMPOSITION.—The Agency shall be composed of the following divisions:

"(1) The Cybersecurity Division, headed by an Assistant Director.

"(2) The Infrastructure Security Division, headed by an Assistant Director.

"(3) The Emergency Communications Division under title XVIII, headed by an Assistant Director.

"(g) CO-LOCATION.—

"(1) IN GENERAL.—To the maximum extent practicable, the Director shall examine the establishment of central locations in geographical regions with a significant Agency presence.

"(2) COORDINATION.—When establishing the central locations described in paragraph (1), the Director shall coordinate with component heads and the Under Secretary for Management to co-locate or partner on any new real property leases, renewing any occupancy agreements for existing leases, or agreeing to extend or newly occupy any Federal space or new construction.

"(h) PRIVACY.—

"(1) IN GENERAL.—There shall be a Privacy Officer of the Agency with primary responsibility for privacy policy and compliance for the Agency.

"(2) RESPONSIBILITIES.—The responsibilities of the Privacy Officer of the Agency shall include—

"(A) assuring that the use of technologies by the Agency sustain, and do not erode, privacy protections relating to the use, collection, and disclosure of personal information;

"(B) assuring that personal information contained in systems of records of the Agency is handled in full compliance as specified in section 552a of title 5, United States Code (commonly known as the 'Privacy Act of 1974');

"(C) evaluating legislative and regulatory proposals involving collection, use, and disclosure of personal information by the Agency; and

"(D) conducting a privacy impact assessment of proposed rules of the Agency on the privacy of personal information, including the type of personal information collected and the number of people affected.

"(i) SAVINGS.—Nothing in this title may be construed as affecting in any manner the authority, existing on the day before the date of enactment of this title, of any other component of the Department or any other Federal department or agency, including the authority provided to the Sector-Specific Agency specified in section 61003(c) of division F of the Fixing America's Surface Transportation Act (6 U.S.C. 121 note; Public Law 114-94).

"SEC. SEC. 2203. [6 U.S.C. 653] CYBERSECURITY DIVISION

"(a) ESTABLISHMENT.—

"(1) IN GENERAL.—There is established in the Agency a Cybersecurity Division.

"(2) ASSISTANT DIRECTOR.—The Cybersecurity Division shall be headed by an Assistant Director for Cybersecurity (in this section referred to as the 'Assistant Director'), who shall—

"(A) be at the level of Assistant Secretary within the Department;

"(B) be appointed by the President without the advice and consent of the Senate; and

"(C) report to the Director.

"(3) REFERENCE.—Any reference to the Assistant Secretary for Cybersecurity and Communications in any law, regulation, map, document, record, or other paper of the United States shall be deemed to be a reference to the Assistant Director for Cybersecurity.

"(b) FUNCTIONS.—The Assistant Director shall—

"(1) direct the cybersecurity efforts of the Agency;

"(2) carry out activities, at the direction of the Director, related to the security of Federal information and Federal information systems consistent with law, including subchapter II of chapter 35 of title 44, United States Code, and the Cybersecurity Act of 2015 (contained in division N of the Consolidated Appropriations Act, 2016 (Public Law 114-113));

"(3) fully participate in the mechanisms required under section 2202(c)(7); and

"(4) carry out such other duties and powers as prescribed by the Director.

"SEC. SEC. 2204. [6 U.S.C. 654] INFRASTRUCTURE SECURITY DIVISION

"(a) ESTABLISHMENT.—

"(1) IN GENERAL.—There is established in the Agency an Infrastructure Security Division.

"(2) ASSISTANT DIRECTOR.—The Infrastructure Security Division shall be headed by an Assistant Director for Infrastructure Security (in this section referred to as the 'Assistant Director'), who shall—

"(A) be at the level of Assistant Secretary within the Department;

"(B) be appointed by the President without the advice and consent of the Senate; and

"(C) report to the Director.

"(3) REFERENCE.—Any reference to the Assistant Secretary for Infrastructure Protection in any law, regulation, map, document, record, or other paper of the United States shall be deemed to be a reference to the Assistant Director for Infrastructure Security.

"(b) FUNCTIONS.—The Assistant Director shall—

"(1) direct the critical infrastructure security efforts of the Agency;

"(2) carry out, at the direction of the Director, the Chemical Facilities Anti-Terrorism Standards Program established under title XXI and the secure handling of ammonium nitrate program established under subtitle J of title VIII, or any successor programs;

"(3) fully participate in the mechanisms required under section 2202(c)(7); and

"(4) carry out such other duties and powers as prescribed by the Director."

(b) TREATMENT OF CERTAIN POSITIONS.—

(1) [6 U.S.C. 652 note] UNDER SECRETARY.—The individual serving as the Under Secretary appointed pursuant to section 103(a)(1)(H) of the Homeland Security Act of 2002 (6 U.S.C. 113(a)(1)(H)) of the Department of Homeland Security on the day before the date of enactment of this Act may continue to serve as the Director of Cybersecurity and Infrastructure Security of the Department on and after such date.

(2) [6 U.S.C. 571 note] DIRECTOR FOR EMERGENCY COMMUNICATIONS.—The individual serving as the Director for Emergency Communications of the Department of Homeland Security on the day before the date of enactment of this Act may continue to serve as the Assistant Director for Emergency Communications of the Department on and after such date.

(3) [6 U.S.C. 653 note] ASSISTANT SECRETARY FOR CYBERSECURITY AND COMMUNICATIONS.—The individual serving as the Assistant Secretary for Cybersecurity and Communications on the day before the date of enactment of this Act may continue to serve as the Assistant Director for Cybersecurity on and after such date.

(4) [6 U.S.C. 654 note] ASSISTANT SECRETARY FOR INFRASTRUCTURE PROTECTION.—The individual serving as the Assistant Secretary for Infrastructure Protection on the day before the date of enactment of this Act may continue to serve as the Assistant Director for Infrastructure Security on and after such date.

(c) [6 U.S.C. 571 note] REFERENCE.—Any reference to—

(1) the Office of Emergency Communications in any law, regulation, map, document, record, or other paper of the United States shall be deemed to be a reference to the Emergency Communications Division; and

(2) the Director for Emergency Communications in any law, regulation, map, document, record, or other paper of the United States shall be deemed to be a reference to the Assistant Director for Emergency Communications.

(d) OVERSIGHT.—The Director of Cybersecurity and Infrastructure Security of the Department of Homeland Security shall provide to Congress, in accordance with the deadlines specified in paragraphs (1) through (6), information on the following:

(1) Not later than 60 days after the date of enactment of this Act, a briefing on the activities of the Agency relating to the development and use of the mechanisms required pursuant to section 2202(c)(6) of the Homeland Security Act of 2002 (as added by subsection (a)).

(2) Not later than 1 year after the date of the enactment of this Act, a briefing on the activities of the Agency relating to the use and improvement by the Agency of the mechanisms required pursuant to section 2202(c)(6) of the Homeland Security Act of 2002 and how such activities have impacted coordination, situational awareness, and communications with Sector-Specific Agencies.

(3) Not later than 90 days after the date of the enactment of this Act, information on the mechanisms of the Agency for regular and ongoing consultation and collaboration, as required pursuant to section 2202(c)(7) of the Homeland Security Act of 2002 (as added by subsection (a)).

(4) Not later than 1 year after the date of the enactment of this Act, information on the activities of the consultation and collaboration mechanisms of the Agency as required pursuant to section 2202(c)(7) of the Homeland Security Act of 2002, and how such mechanisms have impacted operational coordination, situational awareness, and integration across the Agency.

(5) Not later than 180 days after the date of enactment of this Act, information, which shall be made publicly available and updated as appropriate, on the mechanisms and structures of the Agency responsible for stakeholder outreach and

engagement, as required under section 2202(c)(10) of the Homeland Security Act of 2002 (as added by subsection (a)).

(e) CYBER WORKFORCE.—Not later than 90 days after the date of enactment of this Act, the Director of the Cybersecurity and Infrastructure Security Agency of the Department of Homeland Security, in coordination with the Director of the Office of Personnel Management, shall submit to Congress a report detailing how the Agency is meeting legislative requirements under the Cybersecurity Workforce Assessment Act (Public Law 113-246; 128 Stat. 2880) and the Homeland Security Cybersecurity Workforce Assessment Act (enacted as section 4 of the Border Patrol Agent Pay Reform Act of 2014; Public Law 113-277) to address cyber workforce needs.

(f) FACILITY.—Not later than 180 days after the date of enactment of this Act, the Director of the Cybersecurity and Infrastructure Security Agency of the Department of Homeland Security shall report to Congress on the most efficient and effective methods of consolidating Agency facilities, personnel, and programs to most effectively carry out the Agency's mission.

(g) TECHNICAL AND CONFORMING AMENDMENTS TO THE HOMELAND SECURITY ACT OF 2002.—The Homeland Security Act of 2002 (6 U.S.C. 101 et seq.) is amended—

(1) by amending section 103(a)(1)(H) (6 U.S.C. 113(a)(1)(H)) to read as follows:

"(H) A Director of the Cybersecurity and Infrastructure Security Agency."

;

(2) in title II (6 U.S.C. 121 et seq.)—

(A) in the title heading, by striking "AND INFRASTRUCTURE PROTECTION";

(B) in the subtitle A heading, by striking "and Infrastructure Protection";

(C) in section 201 (6 U.S.C. 121)—

(i) in the section heading, by striking "and infrastructure protection";

(ii) in subsection (a)—

(I) in the subsection heading, by striking "and Infrastructure Protection"; and

(II) by striking "and an Office of

Infrastructure Protection";

(iii) in subsection (b)—

(I) in the subsection heading, by striking "and Assistant Secretary for Infrastructure Protection"; and

(II) by striking paragraph (3);

(iv) in subsection (c)—

(I) by striking "and infrastructure protection"; and

(II) by striking "or the Assistant Secretary for Infrastructure Protection, as appropriate";

(v) in subsection (d)—

(I) in the subsection heading, by striking "and Infrastructure Protection";

(II) in the matter preceding paragraph (1), by striking "and infrastructure protection";

(III) by striking paragraphs (5), (6), and (25);

(IV) by redesignating paragraphs (7) through (24) as paragraphs (5) through (22), respectively;

(V) by redesignating paragraph (26) as paragraph (23); and

(VI) in paragraph (23)(B)(i), as so redesignated, by striking "section 319" and inserting "section 320";

(vi) in subsection (e)(1), by striking "and the Office of Infrastructure Protection"; and

(vii) in subsection (f)(1), by striking "and the Office of Infrastructure Protection";

(D) in section 202 (6 U.S.C. 122)—

(i) in subsection (c), in the matter preceding paragraph (1), by striking "Director of Central Intelligence" and inserting "Director of National Intelligence"; and

(ii) in subsection (d)(2), by striking "Director of Central Intelligence" and inserting "Director of National Intelligence";

(E) in section 204 (6 U.S.C. 124a)—

(i) in subsection (c)(1), in the matter preceding subparagraph (A), by striking "Assistant Secretary for Infrastructure Protection" and inserting "Director of the Cybersecurity and Infrastructure Security Agency"; and

(ii) in subsection (d)(1), in the matter preceding subparagraph (A), by striking "Assistant Secretary for Infrastructure Protection" and inserting "Director of the Cybersecurity and Infrastructure Security Agency";

(F) in section 210A(c)(2)(B) (6 U.S.C. 124h(c)(2)(B)), by striking "Office of Infrastructure Protection" and inserting "Cybersecurity and Infrastructure Security Agency";

(G) [6 U.S.C. 664] by redesignating section 210E (6 U.S.C. 124l) as section 2214 and transferring such section to appear after section 2213 (as redesignated by subparagraph (I));

(H) [6 U.S.C. 671-674] in subtitle B, by redesignating sections 211 through 215 (6 U.S.C. 101 note, and 131 through 134) as sections 2221 through 2225, respectively, and transferring such subtitle, including the enumerator and heading of subtitle B and such sections, to appear after section 2214 (as redesignated by subparagraph (G));

(I) [6 U.S.C. 655-663] by redesignating sections 223 through 230 (6 U.S.C. 143 through 151) as sections 2205 through 2213, respectively, and transferring such sections to appear after section 2204, as added by this Act;

(J) [6 U.S.C. 124m] by redesignating section 210F as section 210E; and

(K) by redesignating subtitles C and D as subtitles B and C, respectively;

(3) in title III (6 U.S.C. 181 et seq.)—

(A) in section 302 (6 U.S.C. 182)—

(i) by striking "biological,," each place that term appears and inserting "biological,"; and

(ii) in paragraph (3), by striking "Assistant Secretary for Infrastructure Protection" and inserting

"Director of the Cybersecurity and Infrastructure Security Agency";

(B) by redesignating the second section 319 (6 U.S.C. 195f) (relating to EMP and GMD mitigation research and development) as section 320; and

(C) in section 320(c)(1), as so redesignated, by striking "Section 214" and inserting "Section 2224";

(4) in title V (6 U.S.C. 311 et seq.)—

(A) in section 508(d)(2)(D) (6 U.S.C. 318(d)(2)(D)), by striking "The Director of the Office of Emergency Communications of the Department of Homeland Security" and inserting "The Assistant Director for Emergency Communications";

(B) in section 514 (6 U.S.C. 321c)—

(i) by striking subsection (b); and

(ii) by redesignating subsection (c) as subsection (b); and

(C) in section 523 (6 U.S.C. 321l)—

(i) in subsection (a), in the matter preceding paragraph (1), by striking "Assistant Secretary for Infrastructure Protection" and inserting "Director of Cybersecurity and Infrastructure Security"; and

(ii) in subsection (c), by striking "Assistant Secretary for Infrastructure Protection" and inserting "Director of Cybersecurity and Infrastructure Security";

(5) in title VIII (6 U.S.C. 361 et seq.)—

(A) in section 884(d)(4)(A)(ii) (6 U.S.C. 464(d)(4)(A)(ii)), by striking "Under Secretary responsible for overseeing critical infrastructure protection, cybersecurity, and other related programs of the Department" and inserting "Director of Cybersecurity and Infrastructure Security"; and

(B) in section 899B(a) (6 U.S.C. 488a(a)), by adding at the end the following: "Such regulations shall be carried out by the Cybersecurity and Infrastructure Security Agency.";

(6) in title XVIII (6 U.S.C. 571 et seq.)—

(A) in section 1801 (6 U.S.C. 571)—

(i) in the section heading, by striking "office of emergency communications" and inserting "emergency communications division";

(ii) in subsection (a)—

(I) by striking "Office of Emergency Communications" and inserting "Emergency Communications Division"; and

(II) by adding at the end the following: "The Division shall be located in the Cybersecurity and Infrastructure Security Agency.";

(iii) by amending subsection (b) to read as follows:

"(b) ASSISTANT DIRECTOR.—The head of the Division shall be the Assistant Director for Emergency Communications. The Assistant Director shall report to the Director of Cybersecurity and Infrastructure Security. All decisions of the Assistant Director that entail the exercise of significant authority shall be subject to the approval of the Director of Cybersecurity and Infrastructure Security."

;

(iv) in subsection (c)—

(I) in the matter preceding paragraph (1), by inserting "Assistant" before "Director";

(II) in paragraph (14), by striking "and" at the end;

(III) in paragraph (15), by striking the period at the end and inserting "; and"; and

(IV) by inserting after paragraph (15) the following:

"(16) fully participate in the mechanisms required under section 2202(c)(7)."

;

(v) in subsection (d), in the matter preceding paragraph (1), by inserting "Assistant" before "Director"; and

(vi) in subsection (e), in the matter preceding

paragraph (1), by inserting "Assistant" before "Director";

(B) in sections 1802 through 1805 (6 U.S.C. 572 through 575), by striking "Director for Emergency Communications" each place that term appears and inserting "Assistant Director for Emergency Communications";

(C) in section 1809 (6 U.S.C. 579)—

(i) by striking "Director of Emergency Communications" each place that term appears and inserting "Assistant Director for Emergency Communications";

(ii) in subsection (b)—

(I) by striking "Director for Emergency Communications" and inserting "Assistant Director for Emergency Communications"; and

(II) by striking "Office of Emergency Communications" and inserting "Emergency Communications Division";

(iii) in subsection (e)(3), by striking "the Director" and inserting "the Assistant Director"; and

(iv) in subsection (m)(1)—

(I) by striking "The Director" and inserting "The Assistant Director";

(II) by striking "the Director determines" and inserting "the Assistant Director determines"; and

(III) by striking "Office of Emergency Communications" and inserting "Cybersecurity and Infrastructure Security Agency";

(D) in section 1810 (6 U.S.C. 580)—

(i) in subsection (a)(1), by striking "Director of the Office of Emergency Communications (referred to in this section as the 'Director')" and inserting "Assistant Director for Emergency Communications (referred to in this section as the 'Assistant Director')";

(ii) in subsection (c), by striking "Office of Emergency Communications" and inserting "Emergency Communications Division"; and

(iii) by striking "Director" each place that term appears and inserting "Assistant Director";

(7) in title XX (6 U.S.C. 601 et seq.)—

(A) in paragraph (4)(A)(iii)(II) of section 2001 (6 U.S.C. 601), by striking "section 210E(a)(2)" and inserting "section 2214(a)(2)";

(B) in section 2008(a)(3) (6 U.S.C. 609(a)(3)), by striking "section 210E(a)(2)" and inserting "section 2214(a)(2)"; and

(C) in section 2021 (6 U.S.C. 611)—

(i) by striking subsection (c); and

(ii) by redesignating subsection (d) as subsection (c);

(8) in title XXI (6 U.S.C. 621 et seq.)—

(A) in section 2102(a)(1) (6 U.S.C. 622(a)(1)), by inserting ", which shall be located in the Cybersecurity and Infrastructure Security Agency" before the period at the end; and

(B) in section 2104(c)(2) (6 U.S.C. 624(c)(2)), by striking "Under Secretary responsible for overseeing critical infrastructure protection, cybersecurity, and other related programs of the Department appointed under section 103(a)(1)(H)" and inserting "Director of Cybersecurity and Infrastructure Security"; and

(9) in title XXII, as added by this Act—

(A) in subtitle A—

(i) in section 2205, as so redesignated—

(I) in the matter preceding paragraph (1)—

(aa) by striking "section 201" and inserting "section 2202"; and

(bb) by striking "Under Secretary appointed under section 103(a)(1)(H)" and inserting "Director of Cybersecurity and Infrastructure Security"; and

(II) in paragraph (1)(B), by striking "and" at the end;

(ii) in section 2206, as so redesignated, by striking

"Assistant Secretary for Infrastructure Protection" and inserting "Director of Cybersecurity and Infrastructure Security";

(iii) in section 2209, as so redesignated—

(I) by striking "Under Secretary appointed under section 103(a)(1)(H)" each place that term appears and inserting "Director";

(II) in subsection (a)(4), by striking "section 212(5)" and inserting "section 2222(5)";

(III) in subsection (b), by adding at the end the following: "The Center shall be located in the Cybersecurity and Infrastructure Security Agency. The head of the Center shall report to the Assistant Director for Cybersecurity."; and

(IV) in subsection (c)(11), by striking "Office of Emergency Communications" and inserting "Emergency Communications Division";

(iv) in section 2210, as so redesignated—

(I) by striking "section 227" each place that term appears and inserting "section 2209"; and

(II) in subsection (c)—

(aa) by striking "Under Secretary appointed under section 103(a)(1)(H)" and inserting "Director of Cybersecurity and Infrastructure Security"; and

(bb) by striking "section 212(5)" and inserting "section 2222(5)";

(v) in section 2211(b)(2)(A), as so redesignated, by striking "the section 227" and inserting "section 2209";

(vi) in section 2212, as so redesignated, by striking "section 212(5)" and inserting "section 2222(5)";

(vii) in section 2213(a), as so redesignated—

(I) in paragraph (3), by striking "section 228" and inserting "section 2210"; and

(II) in paragraph (4), by striking "section 227" and inserting "section 2209"; and

(viii) in section 2214, as so redesignated—

(I) by striking subsection (e); and

(II) by redesignating subsection (f) as subsection (e); and

(B) in subtitle B—

(i) in section 2222(8), as so redesignated, by striking "section 227" and inserting "section 2209"; and

(ii) in section 2224(h), as so redesignated, by striking "section 213" and inserting "section 2223";

(h) TECHNICAL AND CONFORMING AMENDMENTS TO OTHER LAWS.—

(1) CYBERSECURITY ACT OF 2015.—The Cybersecurity Act of 2015 (6 U.S.C. 1501 et seq.) is amended—

(A) in section 202(2) (6 U.S.C. 131 note)—

(i) by striking "section 227" and inserting "section 2209"; and

(ii) by striking ", as so redesignated by section 223(a)(3) of this division";

(B) in section 207(2) (Public Law 114-113; 129 Stat. 2962)—

(i) by striking "section 227" and inserting "section 2209"; and

(ii) by striking ", as redesignated by section 223(a) of this division,";

(C) in section 208 (Public Law 114-113; 129 Stat. 2962), by striking "Under Secretary appointed under section 103(a)(1)(H) of the Homeland Security Act of 2002 (6 U.S.C. 113(a)(1)(H))" and inserting "Director of Cybersecurity and Infrastructure Security of the Department";

(D) in section 222 (6 U.S.C. 1521)—

(i) in paragraph (2)—

(I) by striking "section 228" and inserting "section 2210"; and

(II) by striking ", as added by section 223(a)(4) of this division"; and

(ii) in paragraph (4)—

(I) by striking "section 227" and inserting

"section 2209"; and

(II) by striking ", as so redesignated by section 223(a)(3) of this division";

(E) in section 223(b) (6 U.S.C. 151 note)—

(i) by striking "section 230(b)(1) of the Homeland Security Act of 2002, as added by subsection (a)" each place that term appears and inserting "section 2213(b)(1) of the Homeland Security Act of 2002"; and

(ii) in paragraph (1)(B), by striking "section 230(b)(2) of the Homeland Security Act of 2002, as added by subsection (a)" and inserting "section 2213(b)(2) of the Homeland Security Act of 2002";

(F) in section 226 (6 U.S.C. 1524)—

(i) in subsection (a)—

(I) in paragraph (1)—

(aa) by striking "section 230" and inserting "section 2213"; and

(bb) by striking ", as added by section 223(a)(6) of this division";

(II) in paragraph (4)—

(aa) by striking "section 228(b)(1)" and inserting "section 2210(b)(1)"; and

(bb) by striking ", as added by section 223(a)(4) of this division"; and

(III) in paragraph (5)—

(aa) by striking "section 230(b)" and inserting "section 2213(b)"; and

(bb) by striking ", as added by section 223(a)(6) of this division"; and

(ii) in subsection (c)(1)(A)(vi)—

(I) by striking "section 230(c)(5)" and inserting "section 2213(c)(5)"; and

(II) by striking ", as added by section 223(a)(6) of this division";

(G) in section 227 (6 U.S.C. 1525)—

(i) in subsection (a)—

(I) by striking "section 230" and inserting "section 2213"; and

(II) by striking ", as added by section 223(a)(6) of this division,"; and

(ii) in subsection (b)—

(I) by striking "section 230(d)(2)" and inserting "section 2213(d)(2)"; and

(II) by striking ", as added by section 223(a)(6) of this division,"; and

(H) in section 404 (6 U.S.C. 1532)—

(i) by striking "Director for Emergency Communications" each place that term appears and inserting "Assistant Director for Emergency Communications"; and

(ii) in subsection (a)—

(I) by striking "section 227" and inserting "section 2209"; and

(II) by striking ", as redesignated by section 223(a)(3) of this division,".

(2) SMALL BUSINESS ACT.—Section 21(a)(8)(B) of the Small Business Act (15 U.S.C. 648(a)(8)(B)) is amended by striking "section 227(a) of the Homeland Security Act of 2002 (6 U.S.C. 148(a))" and inserting "section 2209(a) of the Homeland Security Act of 2002".

(3) TITLE 5.—Subchapter II of chapter 53 of title 5, United States Code, is amended—

(A) in section 5314, by inserting after "Under Secretaries, Department of Homeland Security." the following:"Director, Cybersecurity and Infrastructure Security Agency."; and

(B) in section 5315, by inserting after "Assistant Secretaries, Department of Homeland Security." the following:"Assistant Director for Cybersecurity, Cybersecurity and Infrastructure Security Agency. Assistant Director for Infrastructure Security, Cybersecurity and Infrastructure Security Agency.".

(i) TABLE OF CONTENTS AMENDMENTS.—The table of contents in section 1(b) of the Homeland Security Act of 2002 (Public Law

107-296; 116 Stat. 2135) is amended—

(1) by striking the item relating to title II and inserting the following:

""TITLE II—INFORMATION ANALYSIS";"

(2) by striking the item relating to subtitle A of title II and inserting the following:

""Subtitle A—Information and Analysis; Access to Information";"

(3) by striking the item relating to section 201 and inserting the following:

""Sec. 201. Information and analysis.";"

(4) by striking the items relating to sections 210E and 210F and inserting the following:

""Sec. 210E. Classified Information Advisory Officer.";"

(5) by striking the items relating to subtitle B of title II and sections 211 through 215;

(6) by striking the items relating to section 223 through section 230;

(7) by striking the item relating to subtitle C and inserting the following:

""Subtitle B—Information Security";"

(8) by striking the item relating to subtitle D and inserting the following:

""Subtitle C—Office of Science and Technology";"

(9) by striking the items relating to sections 317, 319, 318, and 319 and inserting the following:

""Sec. 317. Promoting antiterrorism through international cooperation program.
""Sec. 318. Social media working group.

""Sec. 319. Transparency in research and development.
""Sec. 320. EMP and GMD mitigation research and development.";"

(10) by striking the item relating to section 1801 and inserting the following:

""Sec. 1801. Emergency Communications Division."; and"

(11) by adding at the end the following:

""TITLE XXII—CYBERSECURITY AND INFRASTRUCTURE SECURITY AGENCY

""Subtitle A—Cybersecurity and Infrastructure Security

""Sec. 2201. Definitions.
""Sec. 2202. Cybersecurity and Infrastructure Security Agency.
""Sec. 2203. Cybersecurity Division.
""Sec. 2204. Infrastructure Security Division.
""Sec. 2205. Enhancement of Federal and non-Federal cybersecurity.
""Sec. 2206. Net guard.
""Sec. 2207. Cyber Security Enhancement Act of 2002.
""Sec. 2208. Cybersecurity recruitment and retention.
""Sec. 2209. National cybersecurity and communications integration center.
""Sec. 2210. Cybersecurity plans.
""Sec. 2211. Cybersecurity strategy.
""Sec. 2212. Clearances.
""Sec. 2213. Federal intrusion detection and prevention system.
""Sec. 2214. National Asset Database.

""Subtitle B—Critical Infrastructure Information

""Sec. 2221. Short title.
""Sec. 2222. Definitions.
""Sec. 2223. Designation of critical infrastructure protection program.
""Sec. 2224. Protection of voluntarily shared critical infrastructure information.
""Sec. 2225. No private right of action."."

SEC. 3. [6 U.S.C. 452 note] TRANSFER OF OTHER ENTITIES.

(a) OFFICE OF BIOMETRIC IDENTITY MANAGEMENT.—The Office of Biometric Identity Management of the Department of Homeland Security located in the National Protection and Programs Directorate of the Department of Homeland Security on the day before the date of enactment of this Act is hereby transferred to the Management Directorate of the Department.

(b) FEDERAL PROTECTIVE SERVICE.—

(1) IN GENERAL.—Not later than 90 days after the completion of the Government Accountability Office review of the organizational placement of the Federal Protective Service (authorized under section 1315 of title 40, United States Code), the Secretary of Homeland Security shall determine the appropriate placement of the Service within the Department of Homeland Security and commence the transfer of the Service to such component, directorate, or other office of the Department that the Secretary so determines appropriate.

(2) EXCEPTION.—If the Secretary of Homeland Security determines pursuant to paragraph (1) that no component, directorate, or other office of the Department of Homeland Security is an appropriate placement for the Federal Protective Service, the Secretary shall—

(A) provide to the Committee on Homeland Security and the Committee on Transportation and Infrastructure of the House of Representatives and the Committee on Homeland Security and Governmental Affairs of the Senate and the Office of Management and Budget a detailed explanation, in writing, of the reason for such determination that includes—

(i) information on how the Department considered the Government Accountability Office review described in such paragraph;

(ii) a list of the components, directorates, or other offices of the Department that were considered for such placement; and

(iii) information on why each such component, directorate, or other office of the Department was determined to not be an appropriate placement for the Service;

(B) not later than 120 days after the completion of the Government Accountability Office review described in such paragraph, develop and submit to the committees specified in subparagraph (A) and the Office of Management and Budget a plan to coordinate with other appropriate Federal agencies, including the General Services Administration, to determine a more appropriate placement for the Service; and

(C) not later than 180 days after the completion of such Government Accountability Office review, submit to such committees and the Office of Management and Budget a recommendation regarding the appropriate placement of the Service within the executive branch of the Federal Government.

SEC. 4. DHS REPORT ON CLOUD-BASED CYBERSECURITY.

(a) DEFINITION.—In this section, the term "Department" means the Department of Homeland Security.

(b) REPORT.—Not later than 120 days after the date of enactment of this Act, the Secretary of Homeland Security, in coordination with the Director of the Office of Management and Budget and the Administrator of General Services, shall submit to the Committee on Homeland Security and Governmental Affairs of the Senate and the Committee on Oversight and Government Reform and the Committee on Homeland Security of the House of Representatives a report on the leadership role of the Department in cloud-based cybersecurity deployments for civilian Federal departments and agencies, which shall include—

(1) information on the plan of the Department for ensuring access to a security operations center as a service capability in accordance with the December 19, 2017 Report to the President on Federal IT Modernization issued by the American Technology Council;

(2) information on what service capabilities under paragraph (1) the Department will prioritize, including—

(A) criteria the Department will use to evaluate capabilities offered by the private sector; and

(B) how Federal government- and private sector-provided capabilities will be integrated to enable visibility and consistency of such capabilities across all cloud and on premise environments, as called for in the report described in paragraph (1); and

(3) information on how the Department will adapt the current capabilities of, and future enhancements to, the intrusion detection and prevention system of the Department and the Continuous Diagnostics and Mitigation Program of the Department to secure civilian Federal government networks in a cloud environment.

SEC. 5. [6 U.S.C. 651 note] RULE OF CONSTRUCTION.

Nothing in this Act or an amendment made by this Act may be construed as—

(1) conferring new authorities to the Secretary of Homeland Security, including programmatic, regulatory, or enforcement authorities, outside of the authorities in existence on the day before the date of enactment of this Act;

(2) reducing or limiting the programmatic, regulatory, or enforcement authority vested in any other Federal agency by statute; or

(3) affecting in any manner the authority, existing on the day before the date of enactment of this Act, of any other Federal agency or component of the Department of Homeland Security.

SEC. 6. PROHIBITION ON ADDITIONAL FUNDING.

No additional funds are authorized to be appropriated to carry out this Act or the amendments made by this Act. This Act and the amendments made by this Act shall be carried out using amounts otherwise authorized.

Chemical Facility Anti-Terrorism Standards Program Extension Act

PUBLIC LAW 116-2

Chemical Facility Anti-Terrorism Standards Program Extension Act

[(Public Law 116–2)]

[This law has not been amended]

[Currency: This publication is a compilation of the text of Public Law 116–2. It was last amended by the public law listed in the As Amended Through note above and below at the bottom of each page of the pdf version and reflects current law through the date of the enactment of the public law listed at https://www.govinfo.gov/app/collection/comps/]

[Note: While this publication does not represent an official version of any Federal statute, substantial efforts have been made to ensure the accuracy of its contents. The official version of Federal law is found in the United States Statutes at Large and in the United States Code. The legal effect to be given to the Statutes at Large and the United States Code is established by statute (1 U.S.C. 112, 204).]

AN ACT To extend by 15 months the Chemical Facility Anti-Terrorism Standards Program of the Department of Homeland Security, and for other purposes.

Be it enacted by the Senate and House of Representatives of the United States of America in Congress assembled,

SECTION 1. [6 U.S.C. 101 note] SHORT TITLE.

This Act may be cited as the "Chemical Facility Anti-Terrorism Standards Program Extension Act".

SEC. 2. EXTENSION OF CHEMICAL FACILITY ANTI-TERRORISM STANDARDS PROGRAM OF THE DEPARTMENT OF HOMELAND SECURITY.

Section 5 of the Protecting and Securing Chemical Facilities from Terrorist Attacks Act of 2014 (Public Law 113-254; 6 U.S.C. 621 note) is amended by striking "4 years" and inserting "5 years and 3 months".

Protecting and Securing Chemical Facilities from Terrorist Attacks Act of 2014

PUBLIC LAW 113-150, AMENDED

Protecting and Securing Chemical Facilities from Terrorist Attacks Act of 2014

[(Public Law 113–254)]

[As Amended Through P.L. 116–150, Enacted July 22, 2020]

[Currency: This publication is a compilation of the text of Public Law 113–254. It was last amended by the public law listed in the As Amended Through note above and below at the bottom of each page of the pdf version and reflects current law through the date of the enactment of the public law listed at https://www.govinfo.gov/app/collection/comps/]

[Note: While this publication does not represent an official version of any Federal statute, substantial efforts have been made to ensure the accuracy of its contents. The official version of Federal law is found in the United States Statutes at Large and in the United States Code. The legal effect to be given to the Statutes at Large and the United States Code is established by statute (1 U.S.C. 112, 204).]

AN ACT To recodify and reauthorize the Chemical Facility Anti-Terrorism Standards Program.

Be it enacted by the Senate and House of Representatives of the United States of America in Congress assembled,

SECTION 1. [6 U.S.C. 101 note] SHORT TITLE.

This Act may be cited as the "Protecting and Securing Chemical Facilities from Terrorist Attacks Act of 2014".

SEC. 2. CHEMICAL FACILITY ANTI-TERRORISM STANDARDS PROGRAM.

(a) IN GENERAL.—The Homeland Security Act of 2002 (6 U.S.C. 101 et seq.) is amended by adding at the end the following:

"TITLE XXI—CHEMICAL FACILITY ANTI-TERRORISM STANDARDS

"SEC. 2101. [6 U.S.C. 621] DEFINITIONS

"In this title—

"(1) the term 'CFATS regulation' means—

"(A) an existing CFATS regulation; and

"(B) any regulation or amendment to an existing CFATS regulation issued pursuant to the authority under section 2107;

"(2) the term 'chemical facility of interest' means a facility that—

"(A) holds, or that the Secretary has a reasonable basis to believe holds, a chemical of interest, as designated under Appendix A to part 27 of title 6, Code of Federal Regulations, or any successor thereto, at a threshold quantity set pursuant to relevant risk-related security principles; and

"(B) is not an excluded facility;

"(3) the term 'covered chemical facility' means a facility that—

"(A) the Secretary—

"(i) identifies as a chemical facility of interest; and

"(ii) based upon review of the facility's Top-Screen, determines meets the risk criteria developed under section 2102(e)(2)(B); and

"(B) is not an excluded facility;

"(4) the term 'excluded facility' means—

"(A) a facility regulated under the Maritime Transportation Security Act of 2002 (Public Law 107-295; 116 Stat. 2064);

"(B) a public water system, as that term is defined in section 1401 of the Safe Drinking Water Act (42 U.S.C. 300f);

"(C) a Treatment Works, as that term is defined in section 212 of the Federal Water Pollution Control Act (33 U.S.C. 1292);

"(D) a facility owned or operated by the Department of Defense or the Department of Energy; or

"(E) a facility subject to regulation by the Nuclear Regulatory Commission, or by a State that has entered into an agreement with the Nuclear Regulatory Commission under section 274 b. of the Atomic Energy Act of 1954 (42 U.S.C. 2021(b)) to protect against unauthorized access of any material, activity, or structure licensed by the Nuclear Regulatory Commission;

"(5) the term 'existing CFATS regulation' means—

"(A) a regulation promulgated under section 550 of the Department of Homeland Security Appropriations Act, 2007 (Public Law 109-295; 6 U.S.C. 121 note) that is in effect on the day before the date of enactment of the Protecting and Securing Chemical Facilities from Terrorist Attacks Act of 2014; and

"(B) a Federal Register notice or other published guidance relating to section 550 of the Department of Homeland Security Appropriations Act, 2007 that is in effect on the day before the date of enactment of the Protecting and Securing Chemical Facilities from Terrorist Attacks Act of 2014;

"(6) the term 'expedited approval facility' means a covered chemical facility for which the owner or operator elects to submit a site security plan in accordance with section 2102(c)(4);

"(7) the term 'facially deficient', relating to a site security plan, means a site security plan that does not support a certification that the security measures in the plan address the security vulnerability assessment and the risk-based performance standards for security for the facility, based on a review of—

"(A) the facility's site security plan;

"(B) the facility's Top-Screen;

"(C) the facility's security vulnerability assessment; or

"(D) any other information that—

"(i) the facility submits to the Department; or

"(ii) the Department obtains from a public source or other source;

"(8) the term 'guidance for expedited approval facilities' means the guidance issued under section 2102(c)(4)(B)(i);

"(9) the term 'risk assessment' means the Secretary's

55

application of relevant risk criteria identified in section 2102(e)(2)(B);

"(10) the term 'terrorist screening database' means the terrorist screening database maintained by the Federal Government Terrorist Screening Center or its successor;

"(11) the term 'tier' has the meaning given the term in section 27.105 of title 6, Code of Federal Regulations, or any successor thereto;

"(12) the terms 'tiering' and 'tiering methodology' mean the procedure by which the Secretary assigns a tier to each covered chemical facility based on the risk assessment for that covered chemical facility;

"(13) the term 'Top-Screen' has the meaning given the term in section 27.105 of title 6, Code of Federal Regulations, or any successor thereto; and

"(14) the term 'vulnerability assessment' means the identification of weaknesses in the security of a chemical facility of interest.

"SEC. 2102. [6 U.S.C. 22] CHEMICAL FACILITY ANTI-TERRORISM STANDARDS PROGRAM

"(a) PROGRAM ESTABLISHED.—

"(1) IN GENERAL.—There is in the Department a Chemical Facility Anti-Terrorism Standards Program.

"(2) REQUIREMENTS.—In carrying out the Chemical Facility Anti-Terrorism Standards Program, the Secretary shall—

"(A) identify—

"(i) chemical facilities of interest; and

"(ii) covered chemical facilities;

"(B) require each chemical facility of interest to submit a Top-Screen and any other information the Secretary determines necessary to enable the Department to assess the security risks associated with the facility;

"(C) establish risk-based performance standards designed to address high levels of security risk at covered chemical facilities; and

"(D) require each covered chemical facility to—

"(i) submit a security vulnerability assessment; and

"(ii) develop, submit, and implement a site security plan.

"(b) SECURITY MEASURES.—

"(1) IN GENERAL.—A facility, in developing a site security plan as required under subsection (a), shall include security measures that, in combination, appropriately address the security vulnerability assessment and the risk-based performance standards for security for the facility.

"(2) EMPLOYEE INPUT.—To the greatest extent practicable, a facility's security vulnerability assessment and site security plan shall include input from at least 1 facility employee and, where applicable, 1 employee representative from the bargaining agent at that facility, each of whom possesses, in the determination of the facility's security officer, relevant knowledge, experience, training, or education as pertains to matters of site security.

"(c) APPROVAL OR DISAPPROVAL OF SITE SECURITY PLANS.—

"(1) IN GENERAL.—

"(A) REVIEW.—Except as provided in paragraph (4), the Secretary shall review and approve or disapprove each site security plan submitted pursuant to subsection (a).

"(B) BASES FOR DISAPPROVAL.—The Secretary—

"(i) may not disapprove a site security plan based on the presence or absence of a particular security measure; and

"(ii) shall disapprove a site security plan if the plan fails to satisfy the risk-based performance standards established pursuant to subsection (a)(2)(C).

"(2) ALTERNATIVE SECURITY PROGRAMS.—

"(A) AUTHORITY TO APPROVE.—

"(i) IN GENERAL.—The Secretary may approve an alternative security program established by a private sector entity or a Federal, State, or local authority or under other applicable laws, if the Secretary determines that the requirements of the program meet the requirements under this section.

"(ii) ADDITIONAL SECURITY MEASURES.—If the requirements of an alternative security program do not meet the requirements under this section, the Secretary may recommend additional security measures to the program that will enable the Secretary to approve the program.

"(B) SATISFACTION OF SITE SECURITY PLAN REQUIREMENT.—A covered chemical facility may satisfy the site security plan requirement under subsection (a) by adopting an alternative security program that the Secretary has—

"(i) reviewed and approved under subparagraph (A); and

"(ii) determined to be appropriate for the operations and security concerns of the covered chemical facility.

"(3) SITE SECURITY PLAN ASSESSMENTS.—

"(A) RISK ASSESSMENT POLICIES AND PROCEDURES.—In approving or disapproving a site security plan under this subsection, the Secretary shall employ the risk assessment policies and procedures developed under this title.

"(B) PREVIOUSLY APPROVED PLANS.—In the case of a covered chemical facility for which the Secretary approved a site security plan before the date of enactment of the Protecting and Securing Chemical Facilities from Terrorist Attacks Act of 2014, the Secretary may not require the facility to resubmit the site security plan solely by reason of the enactment of this title.

"(4) EXPEDITED APPROVAL PROGRAM.—

"(A) IN GENERAL.—A covered chemical facility assigned to tier 3 or 4 may meet the requirement to develop and submit a site security plan under subsection (a)(2)(D) by developing and submitting to the Secretary—

"(i) a site security plan and the certification described in subparagraph (C); or

"(ii) a site security plan in conformance with a template authorized under subparagraph (H).

"(B) GUIDANCE FOR EXPEDITED APPROVAL FACILITIES.—

"(i) IN GENERAL.—Not later than 180 days after the date of enactment of the Protecting and Securing Chemical Facilities from Terrorist Attacks Act of 2014, the Secretary shall issue guidance for expedited approval facilities that identifies specific security measures that are sufficient to meet the risk-based performance standards.

"(ii) MATERIAL DEVIATION FROM GUIDANCE.—If a security measure in the site security plan of an expedited approval facility materially deviates from a security measure in the guidance for expedited approval facilities, the site security plan shall include an explanation of how such security measure meets the risk-based performance standards.

"(iii) APPLICABILITY OF OTHER LAWS TO DEVELOPMENT AND ISSUANCE OF INITIAL GUIDANCE.—During the period before the Secretary has met the deadline under clause (i), in developing and issuing, or amending, the guidance for expedited approval facilities under this subparagraph and in collecting information from expedited approval facilities, the Secretary shall not be subject to—

"(I) section 553 of title 5, United States Code;

"(II) subchapter I of chapter 35 of title 44, United States Code; or

"(III) section 2107(b) of this title.

"(C) CERTIFICATION.—The owner or operator of an expedited approval facility shall submit to the Secretary a certification, signed under penalty of perjury, that—

"(i) the owner or operator is familiar with the requirements of this title and part 27 of title 6, Code of Federal Regulations, or any successor thereto, and the site security plan being submitted;

"(ii) the site security plan includes the security measures required by subsection (b);

"(iii)(I) the security measures in the site security plan do not materially deviate from the guidance for expedited approval facilities except where indicated in the site security plan;

"(II) any deviations from the guidance for expedited approval facilities in the site security plan meet the risk-based performance standards for the tier to which the facility is assigned; and

"(III) the owner or operator has provided an explanation of how the site security plan meets the risk-based performance standards for any material deviation;

"(iv) the owner or operator has visited, examined, documented, and verified that the expedited approval facility meets the criteria set forth in the site security plan;

"(v) the expedited approval facility has implemented all of the required performance measures outlined in the site security plan or set out planned measures that will be implemented within a reasonable time period stated in the site security plan;

"(vi) each individual responsible for implementing the site security plan has been made aware of the requirements relevant to the individual's responsibility contained in the site security plan and has demonstrated competency to carry out those requirements;

"(vii) the owner or operator has committed, or, in the case of planned measures will commit, the necessary resources to fully implement the site security plan; and

"(viii) the planned measures include an adequate procedure for addressing events beyond the control of the owner or operator in implementing any planned measures.

"(D) DEADLINE.—

"(i) IN GENERAL.—Not later than 120 days after the date described in clause (ii), the owner or operator of an expedited approval facility shall submit to the Secretary the site security plan and the certification described in subparagraph (C).

"(ii) DATE.—The date described in this clause is—

"(I) for an expedited approval facility that was

assigned to tier 3 or 4 under existing CFATS regulations before the date of enactment of the Protecting and Securing Chemical Facilities from Terrorist Attacks Act of 2014, the date that is 210 days after the date of enactment of that Act; and

"(II) for any expedited approval facility not described in subclause (I), the later of—

"(aa) the date on which the expedited approval facility is assigned to tier 3 or 4 under subsection (e)(2)(A); or

"(bb) the date that is 210 days after the date of enactment of the Protecting and Securing Chemical Facilities from Terrorist Attacks Act of 2014.

"(iii) NOTICE.—An owner or operator of an expedited approval facility shall notify the Secretary of the intent of the owner or operator to certify the site security plan for the expedited approval facility not later than 30 days before the date on which the owner or operator submits the site security plan and certification described in subparagraph (C).

"(E) COMPLIANCE.—

"(i) IN GENERAL.—For an expedited approval facility submitting a site security plan and certification in accordance with subparagraphs (A), (B), (C), and (D)—

"(I) the expedited approval facility shall comply with all of the requirements of its site security plan; and

"(II) the Secretary—

"(aa) except as provided in subparagraph (G), may not disapprove the site security plan; and

"(bb) may audit and inspect the expedited approval facility under subsection (d) to verify compliance with its site security plan.

"(ii) NONCOMPLIANCE.—If the Secretary determines an expedited approval facility is not in compliance with the requirements of the site security plan or is otherwise in violation of this title, the Secretary may enforce compliance in accordance with section 2104.

"(F) AMENDMENTS TO SITE SECURITY PLAN.—

"(i) REQUIREMENT.—

"(I) IN GENERAL.—If the owner or operator of an expedited approval facility amends a site security plan submitted under subparagraph (A), the owner or operator shall submit the amended site security plan and a certification relating to the amended site security plan that contains the information described in subparagraph (C).

"(II) TECHNICAL AMENDMENTS.—For purposes of this clause, an amendment to a site security plan includes any technical amendment to the site security plan.

"(ii) AMENDMENT REQUIRED.—The owner or operator of an expedited approval facility shall amend the site security plan if—

"(I) there is a change in the design, construction, operation, or maintenance of the expedited approval facility that affects the site security plan;

"(II) the Secretary requires additional security measures or suspends a certification and recommends additional security measures under subparagraph (G); or

"(III) the owner or operator receives notice from the Secretary of a change in tiering under subsection (e)(3).

"(iii) DEADLINE.—An amended site security plan and certification shall be submitted under clause (i)—

"(I) in the case of a change in design, construction, operation, or maintenance of the expedited approval facility that affects the security plan, not later than 120 days after the date on which the change in design, construction, operation, or maintenance occurred;

"(II) in the case of the Secretary requiring additional security measures or suspending a certification and recommending additional security measures under subparagraph (G), not later than 120 days after the date on which the owner or operator receives notice of the requirement for additional security measures or suspension of the certification and recommendation of additional security measures; and

"(III) in the case of a change in tiering, not later than 120 days after the date on which the owner or operator receives notice under subsection (e)(3).

"(G) FACIALLY DEFICIENT SITE SECURITY PLANS.—

"(i) PROHIBITION.—Notwithstanding subparagraph (A) or (E), the Secretary may suspend the authority of a covered chemical facility to certify a site security plan if the Secretary—

"(I) determines the certified site security plan or an amended site security plan is facially deficient; and

"(II) not later than 100 days after the date on which the Secretary receives the site security plan and certification, provides the covered chemical facility with written notification that the site security plan is facially deficient, including a clear explanation of each deficiency in the site security plan.

"(ii) ADDITIONAL SECURITY MEASURES.—

"(I) IN GENERAL.—If, during or after a compliance inspection of an expedited approval facility, the Secretary determines that planned or implemented security measures in the site security plan of the facility are insufficient to meet the risk-based performance standards based on misrepresentation, omission, or an inadequate description of the site, the Secretary may—

"(aa) require additional security

measures; or

"(bb) suspend the certification of the facility.

"(II) RECOMMENDATION OF ADDITIONAL SECURITY MEASURES.—If the Secretary suspends the certification of an expedited approval facility under subclause (I), the Secretary shall—

"(aa) recommend specific additional security measures that, if made part of the site security plan by the facility, would enable the Secretary to approve the site security plan; and

"(bb) provide the facility an opportunity to submit a new or modified site security plan and certification under subparagraph (A).

"(III) SUBMISSION; REVIEW.—If an expedited approval facility determines to submit a new or modified site security plan and certification as authorized under subclause (II)(bb)—

"(aa) not later than 90 days after the date on which the facility receives recommendations under subclause (II)(aa), the facility shall submit the new or modified plan and certification; and

"(bb) not later than 45 days after the date on which the Secretary receives the new or modified plan under item (aa), the Secretary shall review the plan and determine whether the plan is facially deficient.

"(IV) DETERMINATION NOT TO INCLUDE ADDITIONAL SECURITY MEASURES.—

"(aa) REVOCATION OF CERTIFICATION.—If an expedited approval facility does not agree to include in its site security plan specific additional security measures recommended by the Secretary under subclause (II)(aa), or does not submit a new or modified site security plan in accordance with subclause (III), the Secretary may revoke the certification of the facility by issuing an order under section 2104(a)(1)(B).

"(bb) EFFECT OF REVOCATION.—If the Secretary revokes the certification of an expedited approval facility under item (aa) by issuing an order under section 2104(a)(1)(B)—

"(AA) the order shall require the owner or operator of the facility to submit a site security plan or alternative security program for review by the Secretary review under subsection (c)(1); and

"(BB) the facility shall no longer be eligible to certify a site security plan under this paragraph.

"(V) FACIAL DEFICIENCY.—If the Secretary determines that a new or modified site security plan submitted by an expedited approval facility under subclause (III) is facially deficient—

"(aa) not later than 120 days after the date of the determination, the owner or operator of the facility shall submit a site security plan or alternative security program for review by the Secretary under subsection (c)(1); and

"(bb) the facility shall no longer be eligible to certify a site security plan under this paragraph.

"(H) TEMPLATES.—

"(i) IN GENERAL.—The Secretary may develop prescriptive site security plan templates with specific security measures to meet the risk-based performance standards under subsection (a)(2)(C) for adoption and certification by a covered chemical facility assigned to tier 3 or 4 in lieu of developing and certifying its own plan.

"(ii) APPLICABILITY OF OTHER LAWS TO DEVELOPMENT AND ISSUANCE OF INITIAL SITE SECURITY PLAN TEMPLATES AND RELATED GUIDANCE.—During the period before the Secretary has met the deadline under subparagraph (B)(i), in developing and issuing, or amending, the site security plan templates under this subparagraph, in issuing guidance for implementation of the templates, and in collecting information from expedited approval facilities, the Secretary shall not be subject to—

"(I) section 553 of title 5, United States Code;

"(II) subchapter I of chapter 35 of title 44, United States Code; or

"(III) section 2107(b) of this title.

"(iii) RULE OF CONSTRUCTION.—Nothing in this subparagraph shall be construed to prevent a covered chemical facility from developing and certifying its own security plan in accordance with subparagraph (A).

"(I) EVALUATION.—

"(i) IN GENERAL.—Not later than 18 months after the date of enactment of the Protecting and Securing Chemical Facilities from Terrorist Attacks Act of 2014, the Secretary shall take any appropriate action necessary for a full evaluation of the expedited approval program authorized under this paragraph, including conducting an appropriate number of inspections, as authorized under subsection (d), of expedited approval facilities.

"(ii) REPORT.—Not later than 18 months after the date of enactment of the Protecting and Securing Chemical Facilities from Terrorist Attacks Act of 2014, the Secretary shall submit to the Committee on Homeland Security and Governmental Affairs of the Senate and the Committee on Homeland Security and the Committee on Energy and Commerce of the House of Representatives a report that contains—

"(I)(aa) the number of eligible facilities using the expedited approval program authorized under this paragraph; and

"(bb) the number of facilities that are eligible for the expedited approval program but are using the standard process for developing and submitting a site security plan under subsection (a)(2)(D);

"(II) any costs and efficiencies associated with the expedited approval program;

"(III) the impact of the expedited approval program on the backlog for site security plan approval and authorization inspections;

"(IV) an assessment of the ability of expedited approval facilities to submit facially sufficient site security plans;

"(V) an assessment of any impact of the expedited approval program on the security of chemical facilities; and

"(VI) a recommendation by the Secretary on the frequency of compliance inspections that may be required for expedited approval facilities.

"(d) COMPLIANCE.—

"(1) AUDITS AND INSPECTIONS.—

"(A) DEFINITIONS.—In this paragraph—

"(i) the term 'nondepartmental'—

"(I) with respect to personnel, means personnel that is not employed by the Department; and

"(II) with respect to an entity, means an entity that is not a component or other authority of the Department; and

"(ii) the term 'nongovernmental'—

"(I) with respect to personnel, means personnel that is not employed by the Federal Government; and

"(II) with respect to an entity, means an entity that is not an agency, department, or other authority of the Federal Government.

"(B) AUTHORITY TO CONDUCT AUDITS AND INSPECTIONS.—The Secretary shall conduct audits or inspections under this title using—

"(i) employees of the Department;

"(ii) nondepartmental or nongovernmental personnel approved by the Secretary; or

"(iii) a combination of individuals described in clauses (i) and (ii).

"(C) SUPPORT PERSONNEL.—The Secretary may use nongovernmental personnel to provide administrative and logistical services in support of audits and inspections under this title.

"(D) REPORTING STRUCTURE.—

"(i) NONDEPARTMENTAL AND NONGOVERNMENTAL AUDITS AND INSPECTIONS.—Any audit or inspection conducted by an individual employed by a nondepartmental or nongovernmental entity shall be assigned in coordination with a regional supervisor with responsibility for supervising inspectors within the Infrastructure Security Compliance Division of the Department for the region in which the audit or inspection is to be conducted.

"(ii) REQUIREMENT TO REPORT.—While an individual employed by a nondepartmental or nongovernmental entity is in the field conducting an audit or inspection under this subsection, the individual shall report to the regional supervisor with responsibility for supervising inspectors within the Infrastructure Security Compliance Division of the Department for the region in which the individual is operating.

"(iii) APPROVAL.—The authority to approve a site security plan under subsection (c) or determine if a covered chemical facility is in compliance with an approved site security plan shall be exercised solely by the Secretary or a designee of the Secretary within the Department.

"(E) STANDARDS FOR AUDITORS AND INSPECTORS.—The Secretary shall prescribe standards for the training and retraining of each individual used by the Department as an auditor or inspector, including each individual employed by the Department and all nondepartmental or nongovernmental personnel, including—

"(i) minimum training requirements for new auditors and inspectors;

"(ii) retraining requirements;

"(iii) minimum education and experience levels;

"(iv) the submission of information as required by the Secretary to enable determination of whether the auditor or inspector has a conflict of interest;

"(v) the proper certification or certifications necessary to handle chemical-terrorism vulnerability information (as defined in section 27.105 of title 6, Code of Federal Regulations, or any successor thereto);

"(vi) the reporting of any issue of non-compliance with this section to the Secretary within 24 hours; and

"(vii) any additional qualifications for fitness of duty as the Secretary may require.

"(F) CONDITIONS FOR NONGOVERNMENTAL AUDITORS AND INSPECTORS.—If the Secretary arranges for an audit or inspection under subparagraph (B) to be carried out by a nongovernmental entity, the Secretary shall—

"(i) prescribe standards for the qualification of the individuals who carry out such audits and inspections that are commensurate with the standards for similar Government auditors or inspectors; and

"(ii) ensure that any duties carried out by a nongovernmental entity are not inherently governmental functions.

"(2) PERSONNEL SURETY.—

"(A) PERSONNEL SURETY PROGRAM.—For purposes of this title, the Secretary shall establish and carry out a Personnel Surety Program that—

"(i) does not require an owner or operator of a covered chemical facility that voluntarily participates in the program to submit information about an individual more than 1 time;

"(ii) provides a participating owner or operator of a covered chemical facility with relevant information about an individual based on vetting the individual against the terrorist screening database, to the extent

69

that such feedback is necessary for the facility to be in compliance with regulations promulgated under this title; and

"(iii) provides redress to an individual—

"(I) whose information was vetted against the terrorist screening database under the program; and

"(II) who believes that the personally identifiable information submitted to the Department for such vetting by a covered chemical facility, or its designated representative, was inaccurate.

"(B) PERSONNEL SURETY PROGRAM IMPLEMENTATION.—To the extent that a risk-based performance standard established under subsection (a) requires identifying individuals with ties to terrorism—

"(i) a covered chemical facility—

"(I) may satisfy its obligation under the standard by using any Federal screening program that periodically vets individuals against the terrorist screening database, or any successor program, including the Personnel Surety Program established under subparagraph (A); and

"(II) shall—

"(aa) accept a credential from a Federal screening program described in subclause (I) if an individual who is required to be screened presents such a credential; and

"(bb) address in its site security plan or alternative security program the measures it will take to verify that a credential or documentation from a Federal screening program described in subclause (I) is current;

"(ii) visual inspection shall be sufficient to meet the requirement under clause (i)(II)(bb), but the facility should consider other means of verification, consistent with the facility's assessment of the threat posed by acceptance of such credentials; and "(iii) the Secretary may not require a covered chemical facility to submit any information about an individual unless the individual—

"(I) is to be vetted under the Personnel Surety Program; or

"(II) has been identified as presenting a terrorism security risk.

"(C) RIGHTS UNAFFECTED.—Nothing in this section shall supersede the ability—

"(i) of a facility to maintain its own policies regarding the access of individuals to restricted areas or critical assets; or

"(ii) of an employing facility and a bargaining agent, where applicable, to negotiate as to how the results of a background check may be used by the facility with respect to employment status.

"(3) AVAILABILITY OF INFORMATION.—The Secretary shall share with the owner or operator of a covered chemical facility any information that the owner or operator needs to comply with this section.

"(e) RESPONSIBILITIES OF THE SECRETARY.—

"(1) IDENTIFICATION OF CHEMICAL FACILITIES OF INTEREST.—In carrying out this title, the Secretary shall consult with the heads of other Federal agencies, States and political subdivisions thereof, relevant business associations, and public and private labor organizations to identify all chemical facilities of interest.

"(2) RISK ASSESSMENT.—

"(A) IN GENERAL.—For purposes of this title, the Secretary shall develop a security risk assessment approach and corresponding tiering methodology for covered chemical facilities that incorporates the relevant elements of risk, including threat, vulnerability, and consequence.

"(B) CRITERIA FOR DETERMINING SECURITY RISK.—The criteria for determining the security risk of terrorism associated with a covered chemical facility shall take into account—

"(i) relevant threat information;

"(ii) potential severe economic consequences and the potential loss of human life in the event of the facility being subject to attack, compromise, infiltration, or exploitation by terrorists; and

"(iii) vulnerability of the facility to attack, compromise, infiltration, or exploitation by terrorists.

"(3) CHANGES IN TIERING.—

"(A) MAINTENANCE OF RECORDS.—The Secretary shall document the basis for each instance in which—

"(i) tiering for a covered chemical facility is changed; or

"(ii) a covered chemical facility is determined to no longer be subject to the requirements under this title.

"(B) REQUIRED INFORMATION.—The records maintained under subparagraph (A) shall include information on whether and how the Secretary confirmed the information that was the basis for the change or determination described in subparagraph (A).

"(4) SEMIANNUAL PERFORMANCE REPORTING.—Not later than 6 months after the date of enactment of the Protecting and Securing Chemical Facilities from Terrorist Attacks Act of 2014, and not less frequently than once every 6 months thereafter, the Secretary shall submit to the Committee on Homeland Security and Governmental Affairs of the Senate and the Committee on Homeland Security and the Committee on Energy and Commerce of the House of Representatives a report that includes, for the period covered by the report—

"(A) the number of covered chemical facilities in the United States;

"(B) information—

"(i) describing—

"(I) the number of instances in which the Secretary—

"(aa) placed a covered chemical facility in a lower risk tier; or

"(bb) determined that a facility that had previously met the criteria for a covered chemical facility under section 2101(3) no longer met the criteria; and

"(II) the basis, in summary form, for each action or determination under subclause (I); and

"(ii) that is provided in a sufficiently anonymized form to ensure that the information does not identify any specific facility or company as the source of the information when viewed alone or in combination with other public information;

"(C) the average number of days spent reviewing site security or an alternative security program for a covered chemical facility prior to approval;

"(D) the number of covered chemical facilities inspected;

"(E) the average number of covered chemical facilities inspected per inspector; and

"(F) any other information that the Secretary determines will be helpful to Congress in evaluating the performance of the Chemical Facility Anti-Terrorism Standards Program.

"SEC. 2103. [6 U.S.C. 623] PROTECTION AND SHARING OF INFORMATION

"(a) IN GENERAL.—Notwithstanding any other provision of law, information developed under this title, including vulnerability assessments, site security plans, and other security related information, records, and documents shall be given protections from public disclosure consistent with the protection of similar information under section 70103(d) of title 46, United States Code.

"(b) SHARING OF INFORMATION WITH STATES AND LOCAL GOVERNMENTS.—Nothing in this section shall be construed to prohibit the sharing of information developed under this title, as the Secretary determines appropriate, with State and local government officials possessing a need to know and the necessary security clearances, including law enforcement officials and first responders, for the purpose of carrying out this title, provided that such information may not be disclosed pursuant to any State or local law.

"(c) SHARING OF INFORMATION WITH FIRST RESPONDERS.—

"(1) REQUIREMENT.—The Secretary shall provide to State,

local, and regional fusion centers (as that term is defined in
section 210A(j)(1)) and State and local government officials,
as the Secretary determines appropriate, such information as
is necessary to help ensure that first responders are properly
prepared and provided with the situational awareness needed
to respond to security incidents at covered chemical facilities.

"(2) DISSEMINATION.—The Secretary shall disseminate
information under paragraph (1) through a medium or system
determined by the Secretary to be appropriate to ensure the
secure and expeditious dissemination of such information to
necessary selected individuals.

"(d) ENFORCEMENT PROCEEDINGS.—In any proceeding to
enforce this section, vulnerability assessments, site security plans,
and other information submitted to or obtained by the Secretary
under this title, and related vulnerability or security information,
shall be treated as if the information were classified information.

"(e) AVAILABILITY OF INFORMATION.—Notwithstanding any
other provision of law (including section 552(b)(3) of title 5, United
States Code), section 552 of title 5, United States Code (commonly
known as the 'Freedom of Information Act') shall not apply to
information protected from public disclosure pursuant to subsection
(a) of this section.

"(f) SHARING OF INFORMATION WITH MEMBERS OF
CONGRESS.—Nothing in this section shall prohibit the Secretary
from disclosing information developed under this title to a Member
of Congress in response to a request by a Member of Congress.

"SEC. 2104. [6 U.S.C. 624] CIVIL ENFORCEMENT

"(a) NOTICE OF NONCOMPLIANCE.—

"(1) NOTICE.—If the Secretary determines that a covered
chemical facility is not in compliance with this title, the
Secretary shall—

"(A) provide the owner or operator of the facility with—

"(i) not later than 14 days after date on which
the Secretary makes the determination, a written
notification of noncompliance that includes a clear
explanation of any deficiency in the security
vulnerability assessment or site security plan; and

"(ii) an opportunity for consultation with the

Secretary or the Secretary's designee; and

"(B) issue to the owner or operator of the facility an order to comply with this title by a date specified by the Secretary in the order, which date shall be not later than 180 days after the date on which the Secretary issues the order.

"(2) CONTINUED NONCOMPLIANCE.—If an owner or operator remains noncompliant after the procedures outlined in paragraph (1) have been executed, or demonstrates repeated violations of this title, the Secretary may enter an order in accordance with this section assessing a civil penalty, an order to cease operations, or both.

"(b) CIVIL PENALTIES.—

"(1) VIOLATIONS OF ORDERS.—Any person who violates an order issued under this title shall be liable for a civil penalty under section 70119(a) of title 46, United States Code.

"(2) NON-REPORTING CHEMICAL FACILITIES OF INTEREST.—Any owner of a chemical facility of interest who fails to comply with, or knowingly submits false information under, this title or the CFATS regulations shall be liable for a civil penalty under section 70119(a) of title 46, United States Code.

"(c) EMERGENCY ORDERS.—

"(1) IN GENERAL.—Notwithstanding subsection (a) or any site security plan or alternative security program approved under this title, if the Secretary determines that there is an imminent threat of death, serious illness, or severe personal injury, due to a violation of this title or the risk of a terrorist incident that may affect a chemical facility of interest, the Secretary—

"(A) shall consult with the facility, if practicable, on steps to mitigate the risk; and

"(B) may order the facility, without notice or opportunity for a hearing, effective immediately or as soon as practicable, to—

"(i) implement appropriate emergency security measures; or

"(ii) cease or reduce some or all operations, in

accordance with safe shutdown procedures, if the Secretary determines that such a cessation or reduction of operations is the most appropriate means to address the risk.

"(2) LIMITATION ON DELEGATION.—The Secretary may not delegate the authority under paragraph (1) to any official other than the Under Secretary responsible for overseeing critical infrastructure protection, cybersecurity, and other related programs of the Department appointed under section 103(a)(1)(H).

"(3) LIMITATION ON AUTHORITY.—The Secretary may exercise the authority under this subsection only to the extent necessary to abate the imminent threat determination under paragraph (1).

"(4) DUE PROCESS FOR FACILITY OWNER OR OPERATOR.—

"(A) WRITTEN ORDERS.—An order issued by the Secretary under paragraph (1) shall be in the form of a written emergency order that—

"(i) describes the violation or risk that creates the imminent threat;

"(ii) states the security measures or order issued or imposed; and

"(iii) describes the standards and procedures for obtaining relief from the order.

"(B) OPPORTUNITY FOR REVIEW.—After issuing an order under paragraph (1) with respect to a chemical facility of interest, the Secretary shall provide for review of the order under section 554 of title 5 if a petition for review is filed not later than 20 days after the date on which the Secretary issues the order.

"(C) EXPIRATION OF EFFECTIVENESS OF ORDER.—If a petition for review of an order is filed under subparagraph (B) and the review under that paragraph is not completed by the last day of the 30-day period beginning on the date on which the petition is filed, the order shall vacate automatically at the end of that period unless the Secretary determines, in writing, that the imminent threat providing a basis for the order continues to exist.

"(d) RIGHT OF ACTION.—Nothing in this title confers upon any person except the Secretary or his or her designee a right of action against an owner or operator of a covered chemical facility to enforce any provision of this title.

"SEC. 2105. [6 U.S.C. 625] WHISTLEBLOWER PROTECTIONS

"(a) PROCEDURE FOR REPORTING PROBLEMS.—

"(1) ESTABLISHMENT OF A REPORTING PROCEDURE.—Not later than 180 days after the date of enactment of the Protecting and Securing Chemical Facilities from Terrorist Attacks Act of 2014, the Secretary shall establish, and provide information to the public regarding, a procedure under which any employee or contractor of a chemical facility of interest may submit a report to the Secretary regarding a violation of a requirement under this title.

"(2) CONFIDENTIALITY.—The Secretary shall keep confidential the identity of an individual who submits a report under paragraph (1) and any such report shall be treated as a record containing protected information to the extent that the report does not consist of publicly available information.

"(3) ACKNOWLEDGMENT OF RECEIPT.—If a report submitted under paragraph (1) identifies the individual making the report, the Secretary shall promptly respond to the individual directly and shall promptly acknowledge receipt of the report.

"(4) STEPS TO ADDRESS PROBLEMS.—The Secretary—

"(A) shall review and consider the information provided in any report submitted under paragraph (1); and

"(B) may take action under section 2104 of this title if necessary to address any substantiated violation of a requirement under this title identified in the report.

"(5) DUE PROCESS FOR FACILITY OWNER OR OPERATOR.—

"(A) IN GENERAL.—If, upon the review described in paragraph (4), the Secretary determines that a violation of a provision of this title, or a regulation prescribed under this title, has occurred, the Secretary may—

"(i) institute a civil enforcement under section 2104(a) of this title; or

"(ii) if the Secretary makes the determination under section 2104(c), issue an emergency order.

"(B) WRITTEN ORDERS.—The action of the Secretary under paragraph (4) shall be in a written form that—

"(i) describes the violation;

"(ii) states the authority under which the Secretary is proceeding; and

"(iii) describes the standards and procedures for obtaining relief from the order.

"(C) OPPORTUNITY FOR REVIEW.—After taking action under paragraph (4), the Secretary shall provide for review of the action if a petition for review is filed within 20 calendar days of the date of issuance of the order for the action.

"(D) EXPIRATION OF EFFECTIVENESS OF ORDER.—If a petition for review of an action is filed under subparagraph (C) and the review under that subparagraph is not completed by the end of the 30-day period beginning on the date the petition is filed, the action shall cease to be effective at the end of such period unless the Secretary determines, in writing, that the violation providing a basis for the action continues to exist.

"(6) RETALIATION PROHIBITED.—

"(A) IN GENERAL.—An owner or operator of a chemical facility of interest or agent thereof may not discharge an employee or otherwise discriminate against an employee with respect to the compensation provided to, or terms, conditions, or privileges of the employment of, the employee because the employee (or an individual acting pursuant to a request of the employee) submitted a report under paragraph (1).

"(B) EXCEPTION.—An employee shall not be entitled to the protections under this section if the employee—

"(i) knowingly and willfully makes any false, fictitious, or fraudulent statement or representation; or

"(ii) uses any false writing or document knowing the writing or document contains any false, fictitious, or fraudulent statement or entry.

"(b) PROTECTED DISCLOSURES.—Nothing in this title shall be

construed to limit the right of an individual to make any disclosure—

"(1) protected or authorized under section 2302(b)(8) or 7211 of title 5, United States Code;

"(2) protected under any other Federal or State law that shields the disclosing individual against retaliation or discrimination for having made the disclosure in the public interest; or

"(3) to the Special Counsel of an agency, the inspector general of an agency, or any other employee designated by the head of an agency to receive disclosures similar to the disclosures described in paragraphs (1) and (2).

"(c) PUBLICATION OF RIGHTS.—The Secretary, in partnership with industry associations and labor organizations, shall make publicly available both physically and online the rights that an individual who discloses information, including security-sensitive information, regarding problems, deficiencies, or vulnerabilities at a covered chemical facility would have under Federal whistleblower protection laws or this title.

"(d) PROTECTED INFORMATION.—All information contained in a report made under this subsection (a) shall be protected in accordance with section 2103.

"SEC. 2106. [6 U.S.C. 626] RELATIONSHIP TO OTHER LAWS

"(a) OTHER FEDERAL LAWS.—Nothing in this title shall be construed to supersede, amend, alter, or affect any Federal law that—

"(1) regulates (including by requiring information to be submitted or made available) the manufacture, distribution in commerce, use, handling, sale, other treatment, or disposal of chemical substances or mixtures; or

"(2) authorizes or requires the disclosure of any record or information obtained from a chemical facility under any law other than this title.

"(b) STATES AND POLITICAL SUBDIVISIONS.—This title shall not preclude or deny any right of any State or political subdivision thereof to adopt or enforce any regulation, requirement, or standard of performance with respect to chemical facility security that is more stringent than a regulation, requirement, or standard of performance issued under this section, or otherwise impair any right or jurisdiction of any State with respect to chemical facilities within that State, unless there is an actual conflict between this section and the law of that State.

"SEC. 2107. [6 U.S.C. 627] CFATS REGULATIONS

"(a) GENERAL AUTHORITY.—The Secretary may, in accordance with chapter 5 of title 5, United States Code, promulgate regulations or amend existing CFATS regulations to implement the provisions under this title.

"(b) EXISTING CFATS REGULATIONS.—

"(1) IN GENERAL.—Notwithstanding section 4(b) of the Protecting and Securing Chemical Facilities from Terrorist Attacks Act of 2014, each existing CFATS regulation shall remain in effect unless the Secretary amends, consolidates, or repeals the regulation.

"(2) REPEAL.—Not later than 30 days after the date of enactment of the Protecting and Securing Chemical Facilities from Terrorist Attacks Act of 2014, the Secretary shall repeal any existing CFATS regulation that the Secretary determines is duplicative of, or conflicts with, this title.

"(c) AUTHORITY.—The Secretary shall exclusively rely upon authority provided under this title in—

"(1) determining compliance with this title;

"(2) identifying chemicals of interest; and

"(3) determining security risk associated with a chemical facility.

"SEC. 2108. [6 U.S.C. 628] SMALL COVERED CHEMICAL FACILITIES

"(a) DEFINITION.—In this section, the term 'small covered chemical facility' means a covered chemical facility that—

"(1) has fewer than 100 employees employed at the covered chemical facility; and

"(2) is owned and operated by a small business concern (as defined in section 3 of the Small Business Act (15 U.S.C. 632)).

"(b) ASSISTANCE TO FACILITIES.—The Secretary may provide guidance and, as appropriate, tools, methodologies, or computer software, to assist small covered chemical facilities in developing the physical security, cybersecurity, recordkeeping, and reporting procedures required under this title.

"(c) REPORT.—The Secretary shall submit to the Committee on Homeland Security and Governmental Affairs of the Senate and the Committee on Homeland Security and the Committee on Energy and Commerce of the House of Representatives a report on best practices that may assist small covered chemical facilities in development of physical security best practices.

"SEC. 2109. [6 U.S.C. 629] OUTREACH TO CHEMICAL FACILITIES OF INTEREST

"Not later than 90 days after the date of enactment of the Protecting and Securing Chemical Facilities from Terrorist Attacks Act of 2014, the Secretary shall establish an outreach implementation plan, in coordination with the heads of other appropriate Federal and State agencies, relevant business associations, and public and private labor organizations, to—

"(1) identify chemical facilities of interest; and

"(2) make available compliance assistance materials and information on education and training."

.

(b) CLERICAL AMENDMENT.—The table of contents in section 1(b) of the Homeland Security Act of 2002 (Public Law 107-196; 116 Stat. 2135) is amended by adding at the end the following:

"TITLE XXI—CHEMICAL FACILITY ANTI-TERRORISM STANDARDS

"Sec. 2101. Definitions.
"Sec. 2102. Chemical Facility Anti-Terrorism Standards Program.
"Sec. 2103. Protection and sharing of information.-
"Sec. 2104. Civil enforcement.
"Sec. 2105. Whistleblower protections.
"Sec. 2106. Relationship to other laws.
"Sec. 2107. CFATS regulations.
"Sec. 2108. Small covered chemical facilities.
"Sec. 2109. Outreach to chemical facilities of interest."

.

SEC. 3. ASSESSMENT; REPORTS.

(a) DEFINITIONS.—In this section—

(1) the term "Chemical Facility Anti-Terrorism Standards Program" means—

(A) the Chemical Facility Anti-Terrorism Standards program initially authorized under section 550 of the Department of Homeland Security Appropriations Act, 2007 (Public Law 109-295; 6 U.S.C. 121 note); and

(B) the Chemical Facility Anti-Terrorism Standards Program subsequently authorized under section 2102(a) of the Homeland Security Act of 2002, as added by section 2;

(2) the term "Department" means the Department of Homeland Security; and

(3) the term "Secretary" means the Secretary of Homeland Security.

(b) THIRD-PARTY ASSESSMENT.—Using amounts appropriated to the Department before the date of enactment of this Act, the Secretary shall commission a third-party study to assess vulnerabilities of covered chemical facilities, as defined in section 2101 of the Homeland Security Act of 2002 (as added by section 2), to acts of terrorism.

(c) REPORTS.—

(1) REPORT TO CONGRESS.—Not later than 18 months after the date of enactment of this Act, the Secretary shall submit to the Committee on Homeland Security and Governmental Affairs of the Senate and the Committee on Homeland Security and the Committee on Energy and Commerce of the House of Representatives a report on the Chemical Facility Anti-Terrorism Standards Program that includes—

(A) a certification by the Secretary that the Secretary has made significant progress in the identification of all chemical facilities of interest under section 2102(e)(1) of the Homeland Security Act of 2002, as added by section 2, including—

(i) a description of the steps taken to achieve that progress and the metrics used to measure the progress;

(ii) information on whether facilities that submitted Top-Screens as a result of the identification of chemical facilities of interest were tiered and in what tiers those facilities were placed; and

(iii) an action plan to better identify chemical facilities of interest and bring those facilities into compliance with title XXI of the Homeland Security Act of 2002, as added by section 2;

(B) a certification by the Secretary that the Secretary has developed a risk assessment approach and corresponding tiering methodology under section 2102(e)(2) of the Homeland Security Act of 2002, as added by section 2;

(C) an assessment by the Secretary of the implementation by the Department of the recommendations made by the Homeland Security Studies and Analysis Institute as outlined in the Institute's Tiering Methodology Peer Review (Publication Number: RP12-22-02); and

(D) a description of best practices that may assist small covered chemical facilities, as defined in section 2108(a) of the Homeland Security Act of 2002, as added by section 2, in the development of physical security best practices.

(2) ANNUAL GAO REPORT.—

(A) IN GENERAL.—During the 3-year period beginning on the date of enactment of this Act, the Comptroller General of the United States shall submit to Congress an annual report that assesses the implementation of this Act and the amendments made by this Act.

(B) INITIAL REPORT.—Not later than 180 days after the date of enactment of this Act, the Comptroller General shall submit to Congress the first report under subparagraph (A).

(C) SECOND ANNUAL REPORT.—Not later than 1 year after the date of the initial report required under subparagraph (B), the Comptroller General shall submit to Congress the second report under subparagraph (A), which shall include an assessment of the whistleblower protections provided under section 2105 of the Homeland Security Act of 2002, as added by section 2, and—

(i) describes the number and type of problems, deficiencies, and vulnerabilities with respect to which

SEC. 4. [6 U.S.C. 621 note] EFFECTIVE
DATE; CONFORMING REPEAL.

Protecting and Securing
Chemical Facilities from

reports have been submitted under such section 2105;

(ii) evaluates the efforts of the Secretary in addressing the problems, deficiencies, and vulnerabilities described in subsection (a)(1) of such section 2105; and

(iii) evaluates the efforts of the Secretary to inform individuals of their rights, as required under subsection (c) of such section 2105.

(D) THIRD ANNUAL REPORT.—Not later than 1 year after the date on which the Comptroller General submits the second report required under subparagraph (A), the Comptroller General shall submit to Congress the third report under subparagraph (A), which shall include an assessment of—

(i) the expedited approval program authorized under section 2102(c)(4) of the Homeland Security Act of 2002, as added by section 2; and

(ii) the report on the expedited approval program submitted by the Secretary under subparagraph (I)(ii) of such section 2102(c)(4).

SEC. 4. [6 U.S.C. 621 note] EFFECTIVE DATE; CONFORMING REPEAL.

(a) EFFECTIVE DATE.—This Act, and the amendments made by this Act, shall take effect on the date that is 30 days after the date of enactment of this Act.

(b) [6 U.S.C. 621 note] CONFORMING REPEAL.—Section 550 of the Department of Homeland Security Appropriations Act, 2007 (Public Law 109-295; 120 Stat. 1388), is repealed as of the effective date of this Act.

SEC. 5. [6 U.S.C. 621 note] TERMINATION.

The authority provided under title XXI of the Homeland Security Act of 2002, as added by section 2(a), shall terminate on July 27, 2023.

Internet of Things Cybersecurity Improvement Act of 2020

PUBLIC LAW 116-207, AMENDED

Internet of Things Cybersecurity Improvement Act of 2020

[(Public Law 116–207)]

[As Amended Through P.L. 117–263, Enacted December 23, 2022]

[Currency: This publication is a compilation of the text of Public Law 116-207. It was last amended by the public law listed in the As Amended Through note above and below at the bottom of each page of the pdf version and reflects current law through the date of the enactment of the public law listed at https://www.govinfo.gov/app/collection/comps/]

[Note: While this publication does not represent an official version of any Federal statute, substantial efforts have been made to ensure the accuracy of its contents. The official version of Federal law is found in the United States Statutes at Large and in the United States Code. The legal effect to be given to the Statutes at Large and the United States Code is established by statute (1 U.S.C. 112, 204).]

AN ACT To establish minimum security standards for Internet of Things devices owned or controlled by the Federal Government, and for other purposes.

Be it enacted by the Senate and House of Representatives of the United States of America in Congress assembled,

SECTION 1. [15 U.S.C. 271 note] SHORT TITLE.

This Act may be cited as the "Internet of Things Cybersecurity Improvement Act of 2020" or the "IoT Cybersecurity Improvement Act of 2020".

SEC. 2. [15 U.S.C. 278g-3a note] SENSE OF CONGRESS.

It is the sense of Congress that—

(1) ensuring the highest level of cybersecurity at agencies in the executive branch is the responsibility of the President, followed by the Director of the Office of Management and Budget, the Secretary of Homeland Security, and the head of each such agency;

(2) this responsibility is to be carried out by working

collaboratively within and among agencies in the executive branch, industry, and academia;

(3) the strength of the cybersecurity of the Federal Government and the positive benefits of digital technology transformation depend on proactively addressing cybersecurity throughout the acquisition and operation of Internet of Things devices by the Federal Government; and

(4) consistent with the second draft National Institute for Standards and Technology Interagency or Internal Report 8259 titled "Recommendations for IoT Device Manufacturers: Foundational Activities and Core Device Cybersecurity Capability Baseline", published in January 2020, Internet of Things devices are devices that—

(A) have at least one transducer (sensor or actuator) for interacting directly with the physical world, have at least one network interface, and are not conventional Information Technology devices, such as smartphones and laptops, for which the identification and implementation of cybersecurity features is already well understood; and

(B) can function on their own and are not only able to function when acting as a component of another device, such as a processor.

SEC. 3. [15 U.S.C. 278g-3a] DEFINITIONS.

In this Act:

(1) AGENCY.—The term "agency" has the meaning given that term in section 3502 of title 44, United States Code.

(2) DIRECTOR OF OMB.—The term "Director of OMB" means the Director of the Office of Management and Budget.

(3) DIRECTOR OF THE INSTITUTE.—The term "Director of the Institute" means the Director of the National Institute of Standards and Technology.

(4) INFORMATION SYSTEM.—The term "information system" has the meaning given that term in section 3502 of title 44, United States Code.

(5) NATIONAL SECURITY SYSTEM.—The term "national security system" has the meaning given that term in section 3552(b)(6) of title 44, United States Code.

(6) OPERATIONAL TECHNOLOGY.—The term "operational

technology" means hardware and software that detects or causes a change through the direct monitoring or control of physical devices, processes, and events in the enterprise.

(7) SECRETARY.—The term "Secretary" means the Secretary of Homeland Security.

(8) SECURITY VULNERABILITY.—The term "security vulnerability" has the meaning given that term in section 2200 of the Homeland Security Act of 2002.

SEC. 4. [15 U.S.C. 278g-3b] SECURITY STANDARDS AND GUIDELINES FOR AGENCIES ON USE AND MANAGEMENT OF INTERNET OF THINGS DEVICES.

(a) NATIONAL INSTITUTE OF STANDARDS AND TECHNOLOGY DEVELOPMENT OF STANDARDS AND GUIDELINES FOR USE OF INTERNET OF THINGS DEVICES BY AGENCIES.—

(1) IN GENERAL.—Not later than 90 days after the date of the enactment of this Act, the Director of the Institute shall develop and publish under section 20 of the National Institute of Standards and Technology Act (15 U.S.C. 278g-3) standards and guidelines for the Federal Government on the appropriate use and management by agencies of Internet of Things devices owned or controlled by an agency and connected to information systems owned or controlled by an agency, including minimum information security requirements for managing cybersecurity risks associated with such devices.

(2) CONSISTENCY WITH ONGOING EFFORTS.—The Director of the Institute shall ensure that the standards and guidelines developed under paragraph (1) are consistent with the efforts of the National Institute of Standards and Technology in effect on the date of the enactment of this Act—

(A) regarding—

(i) examples of possible security vulnerabilities of Internet of Things devices; and

(ii) considerations for managing the security vulnerabilities of Internet of Things devices; and

(B) with respect to the following considerations for Internet of Things devices:

(i) Secure Development.

(ii) Identity management.

(iii) Patching.

(iv) Configuration management.

(3) CONSIDERING RELEVANT STANDARDS.—In developing the standards and guidelines under paragraph (1), the Director of the Institute shall consider relevant standards, guidelines, and best practices developed by the private sector, agencies, and public-private partnerships.

(b) REVIEW OF AGENCY INFORMATION SECURITY POLICIES AND PRINCIPLES.—

(1) REQUIREMENT.—Not later than 180 days after the date on which the Director of the Institute completes the development of the standards and guidelines required under subsection (a), the Director of OMB shall review agency information security policies and principles on the basis of the standards and guidelines published under subsection (a) pertaining to Internet of Things devices owned or controlled by agencies (excluding agency information security policies and principles pertaining to Internet of Things of devices owned or controlled by agencies that are or comprise a national security system) for consistency with the standards and guidelines submitted under subsection (a) and issue such policies and principles as may be necessary to ensure those policies and principles are consistent with such standards and guidelines.

(2) REVIEW.—In reviewing agency information security policies and principles under paragraph (1) and issuing policies and principles under such paragraph, as may be necessary, the Director of OMB shall—

(A) consult with the Director of the Cybersecurity and Infrastructure Security Agency of the Department of Homeland Security; and

(B) ensure such policies and principles are consistent with the information security requirements under subchapter II of chapter 35 of title 44, United States Code.

(3) NATIONAL SECURITY SYSTEMS.—Any policy or principle issued by the Director of OMB under paragraph (1) shall not apply to national security systems.

(c) QUINQUENNIAL REVIEW AND REVISION.—

(1) REVIEW AND REVISION OF NIST STANDARDS AND GUIDELINES.—Not later than 5 years after the date on which the Director of the Institute publishes the standards and guidelines under subsection (a), and not less frequently than once every 5 years thereafter, the Director of the Institute, shall—

(A) review such standards and guidelines; and

(B) revise such standards and guidelines as appropriate.

(2) UPDATED OMB POLICIES AND PRINCIPLES FOR AGENCIES.—Not later than 180 days after the Director of the Institute makes a revision pursuant to paragraph (1), the Director of OMB, in consultation with the Director of the Cybersecurity and Infrastructure Security Agency of the Department of Homeland Security, shall update any policy or principle issued under subsection (b)(1) as necessary to ensure those policies and principles are consistent with the review and any revision under paragraph (1) under this subsection and paragraphs (2) and (3) of subsection (b).

(d) REVISION OF FEDERAL ACQUISITION REGULATION.—The Federal Acquisition Regulation shall be revised as necessary to implement any standards and guidelines promulgated in this section.

SEC. 5. [15 U.S.C. 278g-3c] GUIDELINES ON THE DISCLOSURE PROCESS FOR SECURITY VULNERABILITIES RELATING TO INFORMATION SYSTEMS, INCLUDING INTERNET OF THINGS DEVICES.

(a) IN GENERAL.—Not later than 180 days after the date of the enactment of this Act, the Director of the Institute, in consultation with such cybersecurity researchers and private sector industry experts as the Director considers appropriate, and in consultation with the Secretary, shall develop and publish under section 20 of the National Institute of Standards and Technology Act (15 U.S.C. 278g-3) guidelines—

(1) for the reporting, coordinating, publishing, and receiving of information about—

(A) a security vulnerability relating to information systems owned or controlled by an agency (including Internet of Things devices owned or controlled by an agency); and

(B) the resolution of such security vulnerability; and

(2) for a contractor providing to an agency an information system (including an Internet of Things device) and any subcontractor thereof at any tier providing such information system to such contractor, on—

(A) receiving information about a potential security vulnerability relating to the information system; and

(B) disseminating information about the resolution of a security vulnerability relating to the information system.

(b) ELEMENTS.—The guidelines published under subsection (a) shall—

(1) to the maximum extent practicable, be aligned with industry best practices and Standards 29147 and 30111 of the International Standards Organization (or any successor standard) or any other appropriate, relevant, and widely-used standard;

(2) incorporate guidelines on—

(A) receiving information about a potential security vulnerability relating to an information system owned or controlled by an agency (including an Internet of Things device); and

(B) disseminating information about the resolution of a security vulnerability relating to an information system owned or controlled by an agency (including an Internet of Things device); and

(3) be consistent with the policies and procedures produced under section 2009(m) of the Homeland Security Act of 2002 (6 U.S.C. 659(m)).

(c) INFORMATION ITEMS.—The guidelines published under subsection (a) shall include example content, on the information items that should be reported, coordinated, published, or received pursuant to this section by a contractor, or any subcontractor thereof at any tier, providing an information system (including Internet of Things device) to the Federal Government.

(d) OVERSIGHT.—The Director of OMB shall oversee the implementation of the guidelines published under subsection (a).

(e) OPERATIONAL AND TECHNICAL ASSISTANCE.—The Secretary, in consultation with the Director of OMB, shall administer the implementation of the guidelines published under subsection (a) and provide operational and technical assistance in implementing such guidelines.

SEC. 6. [15 U.S.C. 278g-3d] IMPLEMENTATION OF COORDINATED DISCLOSURE OF SECURITY VULNERABILITIES RELATING TO AGENCY INFORMATION SYSTEMS, INCLUDING INTERNET OF THINGS DEVICES.

(a) AGENCY GUIDELINES REQUIRED.—Not later than 2 years after the date of the enactment of this Act, the Director of OMB, in consultation with the Secretary, shall develop and oversee the implementation of policies, principles, standards, or guidelines as may be necessary to address security vulnerabilities of information systems (including Internet of Things devices).

(b) OPERATIONAL AND TECHNICAL ASSISTANCE.—Consistent with section 3553(b) of title 44, United States Code, the Secretary, in consultation with the Director of OMB, shall provide operational and technical assistance to agencies on reporting, coordinating, publishing, and receiving information about security vulnerabilities of information systems (including Internet of Things devices).

(c) CONSISTENCY WITH GUIDELINES FROM NATIONAL INSTITUTE OF STANDARDS AND TECHNOLOGY.—The Secretary shall ensure that the assistance provided under subsection (b) is consistent with applicable standards and publications developed by the Director of the Institute.

(d) REVISION OF FEDERAL ACQUISITION REGULATION.—The Federal Acquisition Regulation shall be revised as necessary to implement the provisions under this section.

SEC. 7. [15 U.S.C. 278g-3e] CONTRACTOR COMPLIANCE WITH COORDINATED DISCLOSURE OF SECURITY VULNERABILITIES RELATING TO AGENCY INTERNET OF THINGS DEVICES.

(a) PROHIBITION ON PROCUREMENT AND USE.—

(1) IN GENERAL.—The head of an agency is prohibited from procuring or obtaining, renewing a contract to procure or obtain, or using an Internet of Things device, if the Chief Information Officer of that agency determines during a review required by section 11319(b)(1)(C) of title 40, United States Code, of a contract for such device that the use of such device prevents compliance with the standards and guidelines developed under section 4 or the guidelines published under

section 5 with respect to such device.

(2) SIMPLIFIED ACQUISITION THRESHOLD.—Notwithstanding section 1905 of title 41, United States Code, the requirements under paragraph (1) shall apply to a contract or subcontract in amounts not greater than the simplified acquisition threshold.

(b) WAIVER.—

(1) AUTHORITY.—The head of an agency may waive the prohibition under subsection (a)(1) with respect to an Internet of Things device if the Chief Information Officer of that agency determines that—

(A) the waiver is necessary in the interest of national security;

(B) procuring, obtaining, or using such device is necessary for research purposes; or

(C) such device is secured using alternative and effective methods appropriate to the function of such device.

(2) AGENCY PROCESS.—The Director of OMB shall establish a standardized process for the Chief Information Officer of each agency to follow in determining whether the waiver under paragraph (1) may be granted.

(c) REPORTS TO CONGRESS.—

(1) REPORT.—Every 2 years during the 6-year period beginning on the date of the enactment of this Act, the Comptroller General of the United States shall submit to the Committee on Oversight and Reform of the House of Representatives, the Committee on Homeland Security of the House of Representatives, and the Committee on Homeland Security and Governmental Affairs of the Senate a report—

(A) on the effectiveness of the process established under subsection (b)(2);

(B) that contains recommended best practices for the procurement of Internet of Things devices; and

(C) that lists—

(i) the number and type of each Internet of Things device for which a waiver under subsection (b)(1) was granted during the 2-year period prior to the submission of the report; and

(ii) the legal authority under which each such waiver was granted, such as whether the waiver was granted pursuant to subparagraph (A), (B), or (C) of such subsection.

(2) CLASSIFICATION OF REPORT.—Each report submitted under this subsection shall be submitted in unclassified form, but may include a classified annex that contains the information described under paragraph (1)(C).

(d) EFFECTIVE DATE.—The prohibition under subsection (a)(1) shall take effect 2 years after the date of the enactment of this Act.

SEC. 8. GOVERNMENT ACCOUNTABILITY OFFICE REPORT ON CYBERSECURITY CONSIDERATIONS STEMMING FROM THE CONVERGENCE OF INFORMATION TECHNOLOGY, INTERNET OF THINGS, AND OPERATIONAL TECHNOLOGY DEVICES, NETWORKS, AND SYSTEMS.

(a) BRIEFING.—Not later than 1 year after the date of the enactment of this Act, the Comptroller General of the United States shall provide a briefing to the Committee on Oversight and Reform of the House of Representatives, the Committee on Homeland Security of the House of Representatives, and the Committee on Homeland Security and Governmental Affairs of the Senate on broader Internet of Things efforts, including projects designed to assist in managing potential security vulnerabilities associated with the use of traditional information technology devices, networks, and systems with—

(1) Internet of Things devices, networks, and systems; and

(2) operational technology devices, networks, and systems.

(b) REPORT.—Not later than 2 years after the date of enactment of this Act, the Comptroller General shall submit a report to the Committee on Oversight and Reform of the House of Representatives, the Committee on Homeland Security of the House of Representatives, and the Committee on Homeland Security and Governmental Affairs of the Senate on broader Internet of Things efforts addressed in subsection (a).

Cyber Response and Recovery Act

(Title VI of Division G of the Infrastructure Investment and Jobs Act)

PUBLIC LAW 117-58, AMENDED

Cyber Response and Recovery Act (Title VI of Division G of the Infrastructure Investment and Jobs Act)

[(Public Law 117–58)]

[As Amended Through P.L. 117–328, Enacted December 29, 2022]

[Currency: This publication is a compilation of Public Law 117-58. It was last amended by the public law listed in the As Amended Through note above and below at the bottom of each page of the pdf version and reflects current law through the date of the enactment of the public law listed at https://www.govinfo.gov/app/collection/comps/]

[Note: While this publication does not represent an official version of any Federal statute, substantial efforts have been made to ensure the accuracy of its contents. The official version of Federal law is found in the United States Statutes at Large and in the United States Code. The legal effect to be given to the Statutes at Large and the United States Code is established by statute (1 U.S.C. 112, 204).]

AN ACT To authorize funds for Federal-aid highways, highway safety programs, and transit programs, and for other purposes.

Be it enacted by the Senate and House of Representatives of the United States of America in Congress assembled,

SECTION 1. SHORT TITLE; TABLE OF CONTENTS.

(a) [23 U.S.C. 101 note] SHORT TITLE.—This Act may be cited as the "Infrastructure Investment and Jobs Act".

(b) TABLE OF CONTENTS.—The table of contents for this Act is as follows:

* * * * * * *

DIVISION G—OTHER AUTHORIZATIONS

TITLE VI— CYBERSECURITY

Subtitle A— Cyber Response and Recovery Act

* * * * * * *

SEC. 2. [1 U.S.C. 1 note] REFERENCES.

Except as expressly provided otherwise, any reference to "this Act" contained in any division of this Act shall be treated as referring only to the provisions of that division.

DIVISION G—OTHER AUTHORIZATIONS

* * * * * * *

TITLE VI— CYBERSECURITY

Subtitle A— Cyber Response and Recovery Act

SEC. 70601. [6 U.S.C. 101 note] SHORT TITLE.

This subtitle may be cited as the "Cyber Response and Recovery Act".

SEC. 70602. DECLARATION OF A SIGNIFICANT INCIDENT.

(a) IN GENERAL.— Title XXII of the Homeland Security Act of 2002 (6 U.S.C. 651 et seq.) is amended by adding at the end the following:

"Subtitle C— Declaration of a Significant Incident

"SEC. 2231. [6 U.S.C. 677] SENSE OF CONGRESS

"It is the sense of Congress that—

"(1) the purpose of this subtitle is to authorize the Secretary to declare that a significant incident has occurred and to establish the authorities that are provided under the declaration to respond to and recover from the significant incident; and

"(2) the authorities established under this subtitle are intended to enable the Secretary to provide voluntary assistance to non-Federal entities impacted by a significant incident.

"SEC. 2232. [6 U.S.C. 677a] DEFINITIONS
"For the purposes of this subtitle:

"(1) ASSET RESPONSE ACTIVITY.— The term 'asset response activity' means an activity to support an entity impacted by an incident with the response to, remediation of, or recovery from, the incident, including—

"(A) furnishing technical and advisory assistance to the entity to protect the assets of the entity, mitigate vulnerabilities, and reduce the related impacts;

"(B) assessing potential risks to the critical infrastructure sector or geographic region impacted by the incident, including potential cascading effects of the incident on other critical infrastructure sectors or geographic regions;

"(C) developing courses of action to mitigate the risks assessed under subparagraph (B);

"(D) facilitating information sharing and operational coordination with entities performing threat response activities; and

"(E) providing guidance on how best to use Federal resources and capabilities in a timely, effective manner to speed recovery from the incident.

"(2) DECLARATION.— The term 'declaration' means a declaration of the Secretary under section 2233(a)(1).

"(3) DIRECTOR.— The term 'Director' means the Director of the Cybersecurity and Infrastructure Security Agency.

"(4) FEDERAL AGENCY.— The term 'Federal agency' has the meaning given the term 'agency' in section 3502 of title 44, United States Code.

"(5) FUND.— The term 'Fund' means the Cyber Response and Recovery Fund established under section 2234(a).

"(6) INCIDENT.— The term 'incident' has the meaning given the term in section 3552 of title 44, United States Code.

"(7) RENEWAL.— The term 'renewal' means a renewal of a declaration under section 2233(d).

"(8) SIGNIFICANT INCIDENT.— The term 'significant incident'—

"(A) means an incident or a group of related incidents that results, or is likely to result, in demonstrable harm to—

"(i) the national security interests, foreign relations, or economy of the United States; or

"(ii) the public confidence, civil liberties, or public health and safety of the people of the United States; and

"(B) does not include an incident or a portion of a group of related incidents that occurs on—

"(i) a national security system (as defined in section 3552 of title 44, United States Code); or

"(ii) an information system described in paragraph (2) or (3) of section 3553(e) of title 44, United States Code.

"SEC. 2233. [6 U.S.C. 677b] DECLARATION

"(a) IN GENERAL.—

"(1) DECLARATION.— The Secretary, in consultation with the National Cyber Director, may make a declaration of a significant incident in accordance with this section for the purpose of enabling the activities described in this subtitle if the Secretary determines that—

"(A) a specific significant incident—

"(i) has occurred; or

"(ii) is likely to occur imminently; and

"(B) otherwise available resources, other than the Fund, are likely insufficient to respond effectively to, or to mitigate effectively, the specific significant incident described in subparagraph (A).

"(2) PROHIBITION ON DELEGATION.— The Secretary may not delegate the authority provided to the Secretary under paragraph (1).

"(b) ASSET RESPONSE ACTIVITIES.— Upon a declaration, the Director shall coordinate—

"(1) the asset response activities of each Federal agency in response to the specific significant incident associated with the declaration; and

"(2) with appropriate entities, which may include—

"(A) public and private entities and State and local governments with respect to the asset response activities of those entities and governments; and

"(B) Federal, State, local, and Tribal law enforcement agencies with respect to investigations and threat response activities of those law enforcement agencies; and

"(3) Federal, State, local, and Tribal emergency management and response agencies.

"(c) DURATION.— Subject to subsection (d), a declaration shall terminate upon the earlier of—

"(1) a determination by the Secretary that the declaration is no longer necessary; or

"(2) the expiration of the 120-day period beginning on the date on which the Secretary makes the declaration.

"(d) RENEWAL.— The Secretary, without delegation, may renew a declaration as necessary.

"(e) PUBLICATION.—

"(1) IN GENERAL.— Not later than 72 hours after a declaration or a renewal, the Secretary shall publish the declaration or renewal in the Federal Register.

"(2) PROHIBITION.— A declaration or renewal published under paragraph (1) may not include the name of any affected individual or private company.

"(f) ADVANCE ACTIONS.—

"(1) IN GENERAL.— The Secretary—

"(A) shall assess the resources available to respond to a potential declaration; and

"(B) may take actions before and while a declaration is in effect to arrange or procure additional resources for asset response activities or technical assistance the Secretary determines necessary, which may include entering into standby contracts with private entities for cybersecurity services or incident responders in the event of a declaration.

"(2) EXPENDITURE OF FUNDS.— Any expenditure from the Fund for the purpose of paragraph (1)(B) shall be made from amounts available in the Fund, and amounts available in the Fund shall be in addition to any other appropriations available to the Cybersecurity and Infrastructure Security Agency for such purpose.

"SEC. 2234. [6 U.S.C. 677c] CYBER RESPONSE AND RECOVERY FUND

"(a) IN GENERAL.— There is established a Cyber Response and Recovery Fund, which shall be available for—

"(1) the coordination of activities described in section 2233(b);

"(2) response and recovery support for the specific significant incident associated with a declaration to Federal, State, local, and Tribal, entities and public and private entities on a reimbursable or non-reimbursable basis, including through asset response activities and technical assistance, such as—

"(A) vulnerability assessments and mitigation;

"(B) technical incident mitigation;

"(C) malware analysis;

"(D) analytic support;

"(E) threat detection and hunting; and

"(F) network protections;

"(3) as the Director determines appropriate, grants for, or cooperative agreements with, Federal, State, local, and Tribal public and private entities to respond to, and recover from, the specific significant incident associated with a declaration, such as—

"(A) hardware or software to replace, update, improve, harden, or enhance the functionality of existing hardware, software, or systems; and

"(B) technical contract personnel support; and

"(4) advance actions taken by the Secretary under section

2233(f)(1)(B).

"(b) DEPOSITS AND EXPENDITURES.—

"(1) IN GENERAL.— Amounts shall be deposited into the Fund from—

"(A) appropriations to the Fund for activities of the Fund; and

"(B) reimbursement from Federal agencies for the activities described in paragraphs (1), (2), and (4) of subsection (a), which shall only be from amounts made available in advance in appropriations Acts for such reimbursement.

"(2) EXPENDITURES.— Any expenditure from the Fund for the purposes of this subtitle shall be made from amounts available in the Fund from a deposit described in paragraph (1), and amounts available in the Fund shall be in addition to any other appropriations available to the Cybersecurity and Infrastructure Security Agency for such purposes.

"(c) SUPPLEMENT NOT SUPPLANT.— Amounts in the Fund shall be used to supplement, not supplant, other Federal, State, local, or Tribal funding for activities in response to a declaration.

"(d) REPORTING.— The Secretary shall require an entity that receives amounts from the Fund to submit a report to the Secretary that details the specific use of the amounts.

"SEC. 2235. [6 U.S.C. 677d] NOTIFICATION AND REPORTING

"(a) NOTIFICATION.— Upon a declaration or renewal, the Secretary shall immediately notify the National Cyber Director and appropriate congressional committees and include in the notification—

"(1) an estimation of the planned duration of the declaration;

"(2) with respect to a notification of a declaration, the reason for the declaration, including information relating to the specific significant incident or imminent specific significant incident, including—

"(A) the operational or mission impact or anticipated impact of the specific significant incident on Federal and non-Federal entities;

"(B) if known, the perpetrator of the specific significant incident; and

"(C) the scope of the Federal and non-Federal entities impacted or anticipated to be impacted by the specific significant incident;

"(3) with respect to a notification of a renewal, the reason for the renewal;

"(4) justification as to why available resources, other than the Fund, are insufficient to respond to or mitigate the specific significant incident; and

"(5) a description of the coordination activities described in section 2233(b) that the Secretary anticipates the Director to perform.

"(b) REPORT TO CONGRESS.— Not later than 180 days after the date of a declaration or renewal, the Secretary shall submit to the appropriate congressional committees a report that includes—

"(1) the reason for the declaration or renewal, including information and intelligence relating to the specific significant incident that led to the declaration or renewal;

"(2) the use of any funds from the Fund for the purpose of responding to the incident or threat described in paragraph (1);

"(3) a description of the actions, initiatives, and projects undertaken by the Department and State and local governments and public and private entities in responding to and recovering from the specific significant incident described in paragraph (1);

"(4) an accounting of the specific obligations and outlays of the Fund; and

"(5) an analysis of—

"(A) the impact of the specific significant incident described in paragraph (1) on Federal and non-Federal entities;

"(B) the impact of the declaration or renewal on the response to, and recovery from, the specific significant incident described in paragraph (1); and

"(C) the impact of the funds made available from the Fund as a result of the declaration or renewal on the recovery from, and response to, the specific significant incident described in paragraph (1).

"(c) CLASSIFICATION.— Each notification made under subsection (a) and each report submitted under subsection (b)—

"(1) shall be in an unclassified form with appropriate markings to indicate information that is exempt from disclosure under section 552 of title 5, United States Code (commonly known as the 'Freedom of Information Act'); and

"(2) may include a classified annex.

"(d) CONSOLIDATED REPORT.— The Secretary shall not be required to submit multiple reports under subsection (b) for multiple declarations or renewals if the Secretary determines that the declarations or renewals substantively relate to the same specific significant incident.

"(e) EXEMPTION.— The requirements of subchapter I of chapter 35 of title 44 (commonly known as the 'Paperwork Reduction Act') shall not apply to the voluntary collection of information by the Department during an investigation of, a response to, or an immediate post-response review of, the specific significant incident leading to a declaration or renewal.

"SEC. 2236. [6 U.S.C. 677e] RULE OF CONSTRUCTION

"Nothing in this subtitle shall be construed to impair or limit the ability of the Director to carry out the authorized activities of the Cybersecurity and Infrastructure Security Agency.

"SEC. 2237. [6 U.S.C. 677f] AUTHORIZATION OF APPROPRIATIONS

"There are authorized to be appropriated to the Fund $20,000,000 for fiscal year 2022 and each fiscal year thereafter until September 30, 2028, which shall remain available until September 30, 2028.

"SEC. 2238. [6 U.S.C. 677g] SUNSET

"The authorities granted to the Secretary or the Director under this subtitle shall expire on the date that is 7 years after the date of enactment of this subtitle.".

(b) CLERICAL AMENDMENT.— The table of contents in section 1(b) of the Homeland Security Act of 2002 (Public Law 107-296; 116 Stat. 2135) is amended by adding at the end the following:

"Subtitle C— Declaration of a Significant Incident

"Sec. 2231. Sense of congress.
"Sec. 2232. Definitions.
"Sec. 2233. Declaration.
"Sec. 2234. Cyber response and recovery fund.
"Sec. 2235. Notification and reporting.
"Sec. 2236. Rule of construction.
"Sec. 2237. Authorization of appropriations.
"Sec. 2238. Sunset.".

Subtitle B— State and Local Cybersecurity Improvement Act

SEC. 70611. [6 U.S.C. 101 note] SHORT TITLE.

This subtitle may be cited as the "State and Local Cybersecurity Improvement Act".

SEC. 70612. STATE AND LOCAL CYBERSECURITY GRANT PROGRAM.

(a) IN GENERAL.— Subtitle A of title XXII of the Homeland Security Act of 2002 (6 U.S.C. 651 et seq.) is amended by adding at the end the following:

"SEC. 2218. [6 U.S.C. 665g] STATE AND LOCAL CYBERSECURITY GRANT PROGRAM

"(a) DEFINITIONS.— In this section:

"(1) APPROPRIATE COMMITTEES OF CONGRESS.— The term 'appropriate committees of Congress' means—

"(A) the Committee on Homeland Security and Governmental Affairs of the Senate; and

"(B) the Committee on Homeland Security of the House of Representatives.

"(2) CYBER THREAT INDICATOR.— The term 'cyber threat indicator' has the meaning given the term in section 102 of the Cybersecurity Act of 2015 (6 U.S.C. 1501).

"(3) CYBERSECURITY PLAN.— The term 'Cybersecurity Plan' means a plan submitted by an eligible entity under subsection (e)(1).

"(4) ELIGIBLE ENTITY.— The term 'eligible entity' means a—

"(A) State; or

"(B) Tribal government.

108

"(5) INCIDENT.— The term 'incident' has the meaning given the term in section 2209.

"(6) INFORMATION SHARING AND ANALYSIS ORGANIZATION.— The term 'information sharing and analysis organization' has the meaning given the term in section 2222.

"(7) INFORMATION SYSTEM.— The term 'information system' has the meaning given the term in section 102 of the Cybersecurity Act of 2015 (6 U.S.C. 1501).

"(8) MULTI-ENTITY GROUP.— The term 'multi-entity group' means a group of 2 or more eligible entities desiring a grant under this section.

"(9) ONLINE SERVICE.— The term 'online service' means any internet-facing service, including a website, email, virtual private network, or custom application.

"(10) RURAL AREA.— The term 'rural area' has the meaning given the term in section 5302 of title 49, United States Code.

"(11) STATE AND LOCAL CYBERSECURITY GRANT PROGRAM.— The term 'State and Local Cybersecurity Grant Program' means the program established under subsection (b).

"(12) TRIBAL GOVERNMENT.— The term 'Tribal government' means the recognized governing body of any Indian or Alaska Native Tribe, band, nation, pueblo, village, community, component band, or component reservation, that is individually identified (including parenthetically) in the most recent list published pursuant to Section 104 of the Federally Recognized Indian Tribe List Act of 1994 (25 U.S.C. 5131).

"(b) ESTABLISHMENT.—

"(1) IN GENERAL.— There is established within the Department a program to award grants to eligible entities to address cybersecurity risks and cybersecurity threats to information systems owned or operated by, or on behalf of, State, local, or Tribal governments.

"(2) APPLICATION.— An eligible entity desiring a grant under the State and Local Cybersecurity Grant Program shall submit to the Secretary an application at such time, in such manner, and containing such information as the Secretary may require.

"(c) ADMINISTRATION.— The State and Local Cybersecurity

Grant Program shall be administered in the same office of the Department that administers grants made under sections 2003 and 2004.

"(d) USE OF FUNDS.— An eligible entity that receives a grant under this section and a local government that receives funds from a grant under this section, as appropriate, shall use the grant to—

"(1) implement the Cybersecurity Plan of the eligible entity;

"(2) develop or revise the Cybersecurity Plan of the eligible entity;

"(3) pay expenses directly relating to the administration of the grant, which shall not exceed 5 percent of the amount of the grant;

"(4) assist with activities that address imminent cybersecurity threats, as confirmed by the Secretary, acting through the Director, to the information systems owned or operated by, or on behalf of, the eligible entity or a local government within the jurisdiction of the eligible entity; or

"(5) fund any other appropriate activity determined by the Secretary, acting through the Director.

"(e) CYBERSECURITY PLANS.—

"(1) IN GENERAL.— An eligible entity applying for a grant under this section shall submit to the Secretary a Cybersecurity Plan for review in accordance with subsection (i).

"(2) REQUIRED ELEMENTS.— A Cybersecurity Plan of an eligible entity shall—

"(A) incorporate, to the extent practicable—

"(i) any existing plans of the eligible entity to protect against cybersecurity risks and cybersecurity threats to information systems owned or operated by, or on behalf of, State, local, or Tribal governments; and

"(ii) if the eligible entity is a State, consultation and feedback from local governments and associations of local governments within the jurisdiction of the eligible entity;

"(B) describe, to the extent practicable, how the eligible entity will—

"(i) manage, monitor, and track information

systems, applications, and user accounts owned or operated by, or on behalf of, the eligible entity or, if the eligible entity is a State, local governments within the jurisdiction of the eligible entity, and the information technology deployed on those information systems, including legacy information systems and information technology that are no longer supported by the manufacturer of the systems or technology;

"(ii) monitor, audit, and, track network traffic and activity transiting or traveling to or from information systems, applications, and user accounts owned or operated by, or on behalf of, the eligible entity or, if the eligible entity is a State, local governments within the jurisdiction of the eligible entity;

"(iii) enhance the preparation, response, and resiliency of information systems, applications, and user accounts owned or operated by, or on behalf of, the eligible entity or, if the eligible entity is a State, local governments within the jurisdiction of the eligible entity, against cybersecurity risks and cybersecurity threats;

"(iv) implement a process of continuous cybersecurity vulnerability assessments and threat mitigation practices prioritized by degree of risk to address cybersecurity risks and cybersecurity threats on information systems, applications, and user accounts owned or operated by, or on behalf of, the eligible entity or, if the eligible entity is a State, local governments within the jurisdiction of the eligible entity;

"(v) ensure that the eligible entity and, if the eligible entity is a State, local governments within the jurisdiction of the eligible entity, adopt and use best practices and methodologies to enhance cybersecurity, such as—

"(I) the practices set forth in the cybersecurity framework developed by the National Institute of Standards and Technology;

"(II) cyber chain supply chain risk management best practices identified by the

National Institute of Standards and Technology; and

"(III) knowledge bases of adversary tools and tactics;

"(vi) promote the delivery of safe, recognizable, and trustworthy online services by the eligible entity and, if the eligible entity is a State, local governments within the jurisdiction of the eligible entity, including through the use of the .gov internet domain;

"(vii) ensure continuity of operations of the eligible entity and, if the eligible entity is a State, local governments within the jurisdiction of the eligible entity, in the event of a cybersecurity incident, including by conducting exercises to practice responding to a cybersecurity incident;

"(viii) use the National Initiative for Cybersecurity Education Workforce Framework for Cybersecurity developed by the National Institute of Standards and Technology to identify and mitigate any gaps in the cybersecurity workforces of the eligible entity and, if the eligible entity is a State, local governments within the jurisdiction of the eligible entity, enhance recruitment and retention efforts for those workforces, and bolster the knowledge, skills, and abilities of personnel of the eligible entity and, if the eligible entity is a State, local governments within the jurisdiction of the eligible entity, to address cybersecurity risks and cybersecurity threats, such as through cybersecurity hygiene training;

"(ix) if the eligible entity is a State, ensure continuity of communications and data networks within the jurisdiction of the eligible entity between the eligible entity and local governments within the jurisdiction of the eligible entity in the event of an incident involving those communications or data networks;

"(x) assess and mitigate, to the greatest degree possible, cybersecurity risks and cybersecurity threats relating to critical infrastructure and key resources, the degradation of which may impact the performance of information systems within the jurisdiction of the eligible entity;

"(xi) enhance capabilities to share cyber threat indicators and related information between the eligible entity and—

"(I) if the eligible entity is a State, local governments within the jurisdiction of the eligible entity, including by expanding information sharing agreements with the Department; and

"(II) the Department;

"(xii) leverage cybersecurity services offered by the Department;

"(xiii) implement an information technology and operational technology modernization cybersecurity review process that ensures alignment between information technology and operational technology cybersecurity objectives;

"(xiv) develop and coordinate strategies to address cybersecurity risks and cybersecurity threats in consultation with—

"(I) if the eligible entity is a State, local governments and associations of local governments within the jurisdiction of the eligible entity; and

"(II) as applicable—

"(aa) eligible entities that neighbor the jurisdiction of the eligible entity or, as appropriate, members of an information sharing and analysis organization; and

"(bb) countries that neighbor the jurisdiction of the eligible entity;

"(xv) ensure adequate access to, and participation in, the services and programs described in this subparagraph by rural areas within the jurisdiction of the eligible entity; and

"(xvi) distribute funds, items, services, capabilities, or activities to local governments under subsection (n)(2)(A), including the fraction of that distribution the eligible entity plans to distribute to rural areas under subsection (n)(2)(B);

"(C) assess the capabilities of the eligible entity relating to the actions described in subparagraph (B);

"(D) describe, as appropriate and to the extent practicable, the individual responsibilities of the eligible entity and local governments within the jurisdiction of the eligible entity in implementing the plan;

"(E) outline, to the extent practicable, the necessary resources and a timeline for implementing the plan; and

"(F) describe the metrics the eligible entity will use to measure progress towards—

"(i) implementing the plan; and

"(ii) reducing cybersecurity risks to, and identifying, responding to, and recovering from cybersecurity threats to, information systems owned or operated by, or on behalf of, the eligible entity or, if the eligible entity is a State, local governments within the jurisdiction of the eligible entity.

"(3) DISCRETIONARY ELEMENTS.— In drafting a Cybersecurity Plan, an eligible entity may—

"(A) consult with the Multi-State Information Sharing and Analysis Center;

"(B) include a description of cooperative programs developed by groups of local governments within the jurisdiction of the eligible entity to address cybersecurity risks and cybersecurity threats; and

"(C) include a description of programs provided by the eligible entity to support local governments and owners and operators of critical infrastructure to address cybersecurity risks and cybersecurity threats.

"(f) MULTI-ENTITY GRANTS.—

"(1) IN GENERAL.— The Secretary may award grants under this section to a multi-entity group to support multi-entity efforts to address cybersecurity risks and cybersecurity threats to information systems within the jurisdictions of the eligible entities that comprise the multi-entity group.

"(2) SATISFACTION OF OTHER REQUIREMENTS.— In order to

be eligible for a multi-entity grant under this subsection, each eligible entity that comprises a multi-entity group shall have—

"(A) a Cybersecurity Plan that has been reviewed by the Secretary in accordance with subsection (i); and

"(B) a cybersecurity planning committee established in accordance with subsection (g).

"(3) APPLICATION.—

"(A) IN GENERAL.— A multi-entity group applying for a multi-entity grant under paragraph (1) shall submit to the Secretary an application at such time, in such manner, and containing such information as the Secretary may require.

"(B) MULTI-ENTITY PROJECT PLAN.— An application for a grant under this section of a multi-entity group under subparagraph (A) shall include a plan describing—

"(i) the division of responsibilities among the eligible entities that comprise the multi-entity group;

"(ii) the distribution of funding from the grant among the eligible entities that comprise the multi-entity group; and

"(iii) how the eligible entities that comprise the multi-entity group will work together to implement the Cybersecurity Plan of each of those eligible entities.

"(g) PLANNING COMMITTEES.—

"(1) IN GENERAL.— An eligible entity that receives a grant under this section shall establish a cybersecurity planning committee to—

"(A) assist with the development, implementation, and revision of the Cybersecurity Plan of the eligible entity;

"(B) approve the Cybersecurity Plan of the eligible entity; and

"(C) assist with the determination of effective funding priorities for a grant under this section in accordance with subsections (d) and (j).

"(2) COMPOSITION.— A committee of an eligible entity established under paragraph (1) shall—

"(A) be comprised of representatives from—

"(i) the eligible entity;

"(ii) if the eligible entity is a State, counties, cities, and towns within the jurisdiction of the eligible entity; and

"(iii) institutions of public education and health within the jurisdiction of the eligible entity; and

"(B) include, as appropriate, representatives of rural, suburban, and high-population jurisdictions.

"(3) CYBERSECURITY EXPERTISE.— Not less than one-half of the representatives of a committee established under paragraph (1) shall have professional experience relating to cybersecurity or information technology.

"(4) RULE OF CONSTRUCTION REGARDING EXISTING PLANNING COMMITTEES.— Nothing in this subsection shall be construed to require an eligible entity to establish a cybersecurity planning committee if the eligible entity has established and uses a multijurisdictional planning committee or commission that—

"(A) meets the requirements of this subsection; or

"(B) may be expanded or leveraged to meet the requirements of this subsection, including through the formation of a cybersecurity planning subcommittee.

"(5) RULE OF CONSTRUCTION REGARDING CONTROL OF INFORMATION SYSTEMS OF ELIGIBLE ENTITIES.— Nothing in this subsection shall be construed to permit a cybersecurity planning committee of an eligible entity that meets the requirements of this subsection to make decisions relating to information systems owned or operated by, or on behalf of, the eligible entity.

"(h) SPECIAL RULE FOR TRIBAL GOVERNMENTS.— With respect to any requirement under subsection (e) or (g), the Secretary, in consultation with the Secretary of the Interior and Tribal governments, may prescribe an alternative substantively similar requirement for Tribal governments if the Secretary finds that the alternative requirement is necessary for the effective delivery and administration of grants to Tribal governments under this section.

"(i) REVIEW OF PLANS.—

"(1) REVIEW AS CONDITION OF GRANT.—

"(A) IN GENERAL.— Subject to paragraph (3), before an

eligible entity may receive a grant under this section, the Secretary, acting through the Director, shall—

"(i) review the Cybersecurity Plan of the eligible entity, including any revised Cybersecurity Plans of the eligible entity; and

"(ii) determine that the Cybersecurity Plan reviewed under clause (i) satisfies the requirements under paragraph (2).

"(B) DURATION OF DETERMINATION.— In the case of a determination under subparagraph (A)(ii) that a Cybersecurity Plan satisfies the requirements under paragraph (2), the determination shall be effective for the 2-year period beginning on the date of the determination.

"(C) ANNUAL RENEWAL.— Not later than 2 years after the date on which the Secretary determines under subparagraph (A)(ii) that a Cybersecurity Plan satisfies the requirements under paragraph (2), and annually thereafter, the Secretary, acting through the Director, shall—

"(i) determine whether the Cybersecurity Plan and any revisions continue to meet the criteria described in paragraph (2); and

"(ii) renew the determination if the Secretary, acting through the Director, makes a positive determination under clause (i).

"(2) PLAN REQUIREMENTS.— In reviewing a Cybersecurity Plan of an eligible entity under this subsection, the Secretary, acting through the Director, shall ensure that the Cybersecurity Plan—

"(A) satisfies the requirements of subsection (e)(2); and

"(B) has been approved by—

"(i) the cybersecurity planning committee of the eligible entity established under subsection (g); and

"(ii) the Chief Information Officer, the Chief Information Security Officer, or an equivalent official of the eligible entity.

"(3) EXCEPTION.— Notwithstanding subsection (e) and paragraph (1) of this subsection, the Secretary may award a

117

grant under this section to an eligible entity that does not
submit a Cybersecurity Plan to the Secretary for review before
September 30, 2023, if the eligible entity certifies to the
Secretary that—

"(A) the activities that will be supported by the grant
are—

"(i) integral to the development of the
Cybersecurity Plan of the eligible entity; or

"(ii) necessary to assist with activities described in
subsection (d)(4), as confirmed by the Director; and

"(B) the eligible entity will submit to the Secretary
a Cybersecurity Plan for review under this subsection by
September 30, 2023.

"(4) RULE OF CONSTRUCTION.— Nothing in this subsection
shall be construed to provide authority to the Secretary to—

"(A) regulate the manner by which an eligible entity
or local government improves the cybersecurity of the
information systems owned or operated by, or on behalf of,
the eligible entity or local government; or

"(B) condition the receipt of grants under this section
on—

"(i) participation in a particular Federal program;
or

"(ii) the use of a specific product or technology.

"(j) LIMITATIONS ON USES OF FUNDS.—

"(1) IN GENERAL.— Any entity that receives funds from a
grant under this section may not use the grant—

"(A) to supplant State or local funds;

"(B) for any recipient cost-sharing contribution;

"(C) to pay a ransom;

"(D) for recreational or social purposes; or

"(E) for any purpose that does not address
cybersecurity risks or cybersecurity threats on information
systems owned or operated by, or on behalf of, the eligible
entity that receives the grant or a local government within
the jurisdiction of the eligible entity.

"(2) COMPLIANCE OVERSIGHT.— In addition to any other

remedy available, the Secretary may take such actions as are necessary to ensure that a recipient of a grant under this section uses the grant for the purposes for which the grant is awarded.

"(3) RULE OF CONSTRUCTION.— Nothing in paragraph (1)(A) shall be construed to prohibit the use of funds from a grant under this section awarded to a State, local, or Tribal government for otherwise permissible uses under this section on the basis that the State, local, or Tribal government has previously used State, local, or Tribal funds to support the same or similar uses.

"(k) OPPORTUNITY TO AMEND APPLICATIONS.— In considering applications for grants under this section, the Secretary shall provide applicants with a reasonable opportunity to correct any defects in those applications before making final awards, including by allowing applicants to revise a submitted Cybersecurity Plan.

"(l) APPORTIONMENT.— For fiscal year 2022 and each fiscal year thereafter, the Secretary shall apportion amounts appropriated to carry out this section among eligible entities as follows:

"(1) BASELINE AMOUNT.— The Secretary shall first apportion—

"(A) 0.25 percent of such amounts to each of American Samoa, the Commonwealth of the Northern Mariana Islands, Guam, and the United States Virgin Islands;

"(B) 1 percent of such amounts to each of the remaining States; and

"(C) 3 percent of such amounts to Tribal governments.

"(2) REMAINDER.— The Secretary shall apportion the remainder of such amounts to States as follows:

"(A) 50 percent of such remainder in the ratio that the population of each State, bears to the population of all States; and

"(B) 50 percent of such remainder in the ratio that the population of each State that resides in rural areas, bears to the population of all States that resides in rural areas.

"(3) APPORTIONMENT AMONG TRIBAL GOVERNMENTS.— In determining how to apportion amounts to Tribal governments under paragraph (1)(C), the Secretary shall consult with the

Secretary of the Interior and Tribal governments.

"(4) MULTI-ENTITY GRANTS.— An amount received from a multi-entity grant awarded under subsection (f)(1) by a State or Tribal government that is a member of the multi-entity group shall qualify as an apportionment for the purpose of this subsection.

"(m) FEDERAL SHARE.—

"(1) IN GENERAL.— The Federal share of the cost of an activity carried out using funds made available with a grant under this section may not exceed—

"(A) in the case of a grant to an eligible entity—

"(i) for fiscal year 2022, 90 percent;

"(ii) for fiscal year 2023, 80 percent;

"(iii) for fiscal year 2024, 70 percent; and

"(iv) for fiscal year 2025, 60 percent; and

"(B) in the case of a grant to a multi-entity group—

"(i) for fiscal year 2022, 100 percent;

"(ii) for fiscal year 2023, 90 percent;

"(iii) for fiscal year 2024, 80 percent; and

"(iv) for fiscal year 2025, 70 percent.

"(2) WAIVER.—

"(A) IN GENERAL.— The Secretary may waive or modify the requirements of paragraph (1) if an eligible entity or multi-entity group demonstrates economic hardship.

"(B) GUIDELINES.— The Secretary shall establish and publish guidelines for determining what constitutes economic hardship for the purposes of this subsection.

"(C) CONSIDERATIONS.— In developing guidelines under subparagraph (B), the Secretary shall consider, with respect to the jurisdiction of an eligible entity—

"(i) changes in rates of unemployment in the jurisdiction from previous years;

"(ii) changes in the percentage of individuals who are eligible to receive benefits under the supplemental nutrition assistance program established under the Food and Nutrition Act of 2008 (7 U.S.C. 2011 et seq.)

from previous years; and

"(iii) any other factors the Secretary considers appropriate.

"(3) WAIVER FOR TRIBAL GOVERNMENTS.— Notwithstanding paragraph (2), the Secretary, in consultation with the Secretary of the Interior and Tribal governments, may waive or modify the requirements of paragraph (1) for 1 or more Tribal governments if the Secretary determines that the waiver is in the public interest.

"(n) RESPONSIBILITIES OF GRANTEES.—

"(1) CERTIFICATION.— Each eligible entity or multi-entity group that receives a grant under this section shall certify to the Secretary that the grant will be used—

"(A) for the purpose for which the grant is awarded; and

"(B) in compliance with subsections (d) and (j).

"(2) AVAILABILITY OF FUNDS TO LOCAL GOVERNMENTS AND RURAL AREAS.—

"(A) IN GENERAL.— Subject to subparagraph (C), not later than 45 days after the date on which an eligible entity or multi-entity group receives a grant under this section, the eligible entity or multi-entity group shall, without imposing unreasonable or unduly burdensome requirements as a condition of receipt, obligate or otherwise make available to local governments within the jurisdiction of the eligible entity or the eligible entities that comprise the multi-entity group, consistent with the Cybersecurity Plan of the eligible entity or the Cybersecurity Plans of the eligible entities that comprise the multi-entity group—

"(i) not less than 80 percent of funds available under the grant;

"(ii) with the consent of the local governments, items, services, capabilities, or activities having a value of not less than 80 percent of the amount of the grant; or

"(iii) with the consent of the local governments, grant funds combined with other items, services, capabilities, or activities having the total value of not less than 80 percent of the amount of the grant.

"(B) AVAILABILITY TO RURAL AREAS.— In obligating funds, items, services, capabilities, or activities to local governments under subparagraph (A), the eligible entity or eligible entities that comprise the multi-entity group shall ensure that rural areas within the jurisdiction of the eligible entity or the eligible entities that comprise the multi-entity group receive not less than—

"(i) 25 percent of the amount of the grant awarded to the eligible entity;

"(ii) items, services, capabilities, or activities having a value of not less than 25 percent of the amount of the grant awarded to the eligible entity; or

"(iii) grant funds combined with other items, services, capabilities, or activities having the total value of not less than 25 percent of the grant awarded to the eligible entity.

"(C) EXCEPTIONS.— This paragraph shall not apply to—

"(i) any grant awarded under this section that solely supports activities that are integral to the development or revision of the Cybersecurity Plan of the eligible entity; or

"(ii) the District of Columbia, the Commonwealth of Puerto Rico, American Samoa, the Commonwealth of the Northern Mariana Islands, Guam, the United States Virgin Islands, or a Tribal government.

"(3) CERTIFICATIONS REGARDING DISTRIBUTION OF GRANT FUNDS TO LOCAL GOVERNMENTS.— An eligible entity or multi-entity group shall certify to the Secretary that the eligible entity or multi-entity group has made the distribution to local governments required under paragraph (2).

"(4) EXTENSION OF PERIOD.—

"(A) IN GENERAL.— An eligible entity or multi-entity group may request in writing that the Secretary extend the period of time specified in paragraph (2) for an additional period of time.

"(B) APPROVAL.— The Secretary may approve a request for an extension under subparagraph (A) if the Secretary determines the extension is necessary to ensure that the obligation and expenditure of grant funds align with the purpose of the State and Local Cybersecurity Grant Program.

"(5) DIRECT FUNDING.— If an eligible entity does not make a distribution to a local government required under paragraph (2) in a timely fashion, the local government may petition the Secretary to request the Secretary to provide funds directly to the local government.

"(6) LIMITATION ON CONSTRUCTION.— A grant awarded under this section may not be used to acquire land or to construct, remodel, or perform alterations of buildings or other physical facilities.

"(7) CONSULTATION IN ALLOCATING FUNDS.— An eligible entity applying for a grant under this section shall agree to consult the Chief Information Officer, the Chief Information Security Officer, or an equivalent official of the eligible entity in allocating funds from a grant awarded under this section.

"(8) PENALTIES.— In addition to other remedies available to the Secretary, if an eligible entity violates a requirement of this subsection, the Secretary may—

"(A) terminate or reduce the amount of a grant awarded under this section to the eligible entity; or

"(B) distribute grant funds previously awarded to the eligible entity—

"(i) in the case of an eligible entity that is a State, directly to the appropriate local government as a replacement grant in an amount determined by the Secretary; or

"(ii) in the case of an eligible entity that is a Tribal government, to another Tribal government or Tribal governments as a replacement grant in an amount determined by the Secretary.

"(o) CONSULTATION WITH STATE, LOCAL, AND TRIBAL REPRESENTATIVES.— In carrying out this section, the Secretary shall consult with State, local, and Tribal representatives with professional experience relating to cybersecurity, including representatives of associations representing State, local, and Tribal governments, to inform—

"(1) guidance for applicants for grants under this section, including guidance for Cybersecurity Plans;

"(2) the study of risk-based formulas required under subsection (q)(4);

"(3) the development of guidelines required under subsection (m)(2)(B); and

"(4) any modifications described in subsection (q)(2)(D).

"(p) NOTIFICATION TO CONGRESS.— Not later than 3 business days before the date on which the Department announces the award of a grant to an eligible entity under this section, including an announcement to the eligible entity, the Secretary shall provide to the appropriate committees of Congress notice of the announcement.

"(q) REPORTS, STUDY, AND REVIEW.—

"(1) ANNUAL REPORTS BY GRANT RECIPIENTS.—

"(A) IN GENERAL.— Not later than 1 year after the date on which an eligible entity receives a grant under this section for the purpose of implementing the Cybersecurity Plan of the eligible entity, including an eligible entity that comprises a multi-entity group that receives a grant for that purpose, and annually thereafter until 1 year after the date on which funds from the grant are expended or returned, the eligible entity shall submit to the Secretary a report that, using the metrics described in the Cybersecurity Plan of the eligible entity, describes the progress of the eligible entity in—

"(i) implementing the Cybersecurity Plan of the eligible entity; and

"(ii) reducing cybersecurity risks to, and identifying, responding to, and recovering from cybersecurity threats to, information systems owned or operated by, or on behalf of, the eligible entity or, if the eligible entity is a State, local governments within the jurisdiction of the eligible entity.

"(B) ABSENCE OF PLAN.— Not later than 1 year after the date on which an eligible entity that does not have a

Cybersecurity Plan receives funds under this section, and annually thereafter until 1 year after the date on which funds from the grant are expended or returned, the eligible entity shall submit to the Secretary a report describing how the eligible entity obligated and expended grant funds to—

"(i) develop or revise a Cybersecurity Plan; or

"(ii) assist with the activities described in subsection (d)(4).

"(2) ANNUAL REPORTS TO CONGRESS.— Not less frequently than annually, the Secretary, acting through the Director, shall submit to Congress a report on—

"(A) the use of grants awarded under this section;

"(B) the proportion of grants used to support cybersecurity in rural areas;

"(C) the effectiveness of the State and Local Cybersecurity Grant Program;

"(D) any necessary modifications to the State and Local Cybersecurity Grant Program; and

"(E) any progress made toward—

"(i) developing, implementing, or revising Cybersecurity Plans; and

"(ii) reducing cybersecurity risks to, and identifying, responding to, and recovering from cybersecurity threats to, information systems owned or operated by, or on behalf of, State, local, or Tribal governments as a result of the award of grants under this section.

"(3) PUBLIC AVAILABILITY.—

"(A) IN GENERAL.— The Secretary, acting through the Director, shall make each report submitted under paragraph (2) publicly available, including by making each report available on the website of the Agency.

"(B) REDACTIONS.— In making each report publicly available under subparagraph (A), the Director may make redactions that the Director, in consultation with each eligible entity, determines necessary to protect classified or other information exempt from disclosure under section 552 of title 5, United States Code (commonly referred to as the 'Freedom of Information Act').

"(4) STUDY OF RISK-BASED FORMULAS.—

"(A) IN GENERAL.— Not later than September 30, 2024, the Secretary, acting through the Director, shall submit to the appropriate committees of Congress a study and legislative recommendations on the potential use of a risk-based formula for apportioning funds under this section, including—

"(i) potential components that could be included in a risk-based formula, including the potential impact of those components on support for rural areas under this section;

"(ii) potential sources of data and information necessary for the implementation of a risk-based formula;

"(iii) any obstacles to implementing a risk-based formula, including obstacles that require a legislative solution;

"(iv) if a risk-based formula were to be implemented for fiscal year 2026, a recommended risk-based formula for the State and Local Cybersecurity Grant Program; and

"(v) any other information that the Secretary, acting through the Director, determines necessary to help Congress understand the progress towards, and obstacles to, implementing a risk-based formula.

"(B) INAPPLICABILITY OF PAPERWORK REDUCTION ACT.— The requirements of chapter 35 of title 44, United States Code (commonly referred to as the 'Paperwork Reduction Act'), shall not apply to any action taken to carry out this paragraph.

"(5) TRIBAL CYBERSECURITY NEEDS REPORT.— Not later than 2 years after the date of enactment of this section, the Secretary, acting through the Director, shall submit to Congress a report that—

"(A) describes the cybersecurity needs of Tribal governments, which shall be determined in consultation with the Secretary of the Interior and Tribal governments; and

"(B) includes any recommendations for addressing the cybersecurity needs of Tribal governments, including any necessary modifications to the State and Local Cybersecurity Grant Program to better serve Tribal governments.

"(6) GAO REVIEW.— Not later than 3 years after the date of enactment of this section, the Comptroller General of the United States shall conduct a review of the State and Local Cybersecurity Grant Program, including—

"(A) the grant selection process of the Secretary; and

"(B) a sample of grants awarded under this section.

"(r) AUTHORIZATION OF APPROPRIATIONS.—

"(1) IN GENERAL.— There are authorized to be appropriated for activities under this section—

"(A) for fiscal year 2022, $200,000,000;

"(B) for fiscal year 2023, $400,000,000;

"(C) for fiscal year 2024, $300,000,000; and

"(D) for fiscal year 2025, $100,000,000.

"(2) TRANSFERS AUTHORIZED.—

"(A) IN GENERAL.— During a fiscal year, the Secretary or the head of any component of the Department that administers the State and Local Cybersecurity Grant Program may transfer not more than 5 percent of the amounts appropriated pursuant to paragraph (1) or other amounts appropriated to carry out the State and Local Cybersecurity Grant Program for that fiscal year to an account of the Department for salaries, expenses, and other administrative costs incurred for the management, administration, or evaluation of this section.

"(B) ADDITIONAL APPROPRIATIONS.— Any funds transferred under subparagraph (A) shall be in addition to any funds appropriated to the Department or the components described in subparagraph (A) for salaries, expenses, and other administrative costs.

"(s) TERMINATION.—

"(1) IN GENERAL.— Subject to paragraph (2), the requirements of this section shall terminate on September 30, 2025.

"(2) EXCEPTION.— The reporting requirements under subsection (q) shall terminate on the date that is 1 year after the date on which the final funds from a grant under this section are expended or returned.".

(b) CLERICAL AMENDMENT.— The table of contents in section 1(b) of the Homeland Security Act of 2002 (Public Law 107-296; 116 Stat. 2135), is amended by inserting after the item relating to section 2217 the following:

"Sec. 2218. State and Local Cybersecurity Grant Program.".

Provisions of the National Defense Authorization Act for Fiscal Year 2022

PUBLIC LAW 117-81

Provisions of the National Defense Authorization Act for Fiscal Year 2022

[(Public Law 117–81)]

[As Amended Through P.L. 117–263, Enacted December 23, 2022]

[Currency: This publication is a compilation of Public Law 117-81. It was last amended by the public law listed in the As Amended Through note above and below at the bottom of each page of the pdf version and reflects current law through the date of the enactment of the public law listed at https://www.govinfo.gov/app/collection/comps/]

[Note: While this publication does not represent an official version of any Federal statute, substantial efforts have been made to ensure the accuracy of its contents. The official version of Federal law is found in the United States Statutes at Large and in the United States Code. The legal effect to be given to the Statutes at Large and the United States Code is established by statute (1 U.S.C. 112, 204).]

AN ACT To authorize appropriations for fiscal year 2022 for military activities of the Department of Defense, for military construction, and for defense activities of the Department of Energy, to prescribe military personnel strengths for such fiscal year, and for other purposes.

Be it enacted by the Senate and House of Representatives of the United States of America in Congress assembled,

SECTION 1. SHORT TITLE.

This Act may be cited as the "National Defense Authorization Act for Fiscal Year 2022".

SEC. 2. ORGANIZATION OF ACT INTO DIVISIONS; TABLE OF CONTENTS.

(a) DIVISIONS.—This Act is organized into six divisions as follows:

* * * * * * *

(6) Division F—Other Non-Department of Defense Matters.

(b) TABLE OF CONTENTS.— The table of contents for this Act is as follows:

* * * * * * *

Sec. 1506. Matters concerning cyber personnel requirements.
Sec. 1507. Assignment of certain budget control responsibilities to commander of United States Cyber Command.
Sec. 1508. Coordination between United States Cyber Command and private sector.
Sec. 1509. Assessment of cyber posture and operational assumptions and development of targeting strategies and supporting capabilities.
Sec. 1510. Assessing capabilities to counter adversary use of ransomware, capabilities, and infrastructure.
Sec. 1511. Comparative analysis of cybersecurity capabilities.
Sec. 1512. Eligibility of owners and operators of critical infrastructure to receive certain Department of Defense support and services.
Sec. 1513. Report on potential Department of Defense support and assistance for increasing the awareness of the Cybersecurity and Infrastructure Security Agency of cyber threats and vulnerabilities affecting critical infrastructure.

* * * * * * *

TITLE LVII—OTHER MATTERS

Sec. 5701. Limitation on assistance to countries in default.
Sec. 5702. Sean and David Goldman Child Abduction Prevention and Return Act of 2014 amendment.
Sec. 5703. Chief of mission concurrence.
Sec. 5704. Report on efforts of the Coronavirus Repatriation Task Force.

DIVISION F—OTHER NON-DEPARTMENT OF DEFENSE MATTERS

* * * * * * *

SEC. 3. [10 U.S.C. 101 note] CONGRESSIONAL DEFENSE COMMITTEES.

In this Act, the term "congressional defense committees" has the meaning given that term in section 101(a)(16) of title 10, United States Code.

* * * * * * *

DIVISION A— DEPARTMENT OF DEFENSE

AUTHORIZATIONS

* * * * * * *

TITLE V— MILITARY PERSONNEL POLICY

* * * * * * *

Subtitle B— Reserve Component Management

* * * * * * *

Sec. 516. Enhancement of National Guard Youth Challenge Program.
Sec. 517. Report on methods to enhance support from the reserve components in response to catastrophic incidents.

* * * * * * *

Subtitle B— Reserve Component Management

* * * * * * *

SEC. 516. ENHANCEMENT OF NATIONAL GUARD YOUTH CHALLENGE PROGRAM.

(a) AUTHORITY.— During fiscal years 2022 and 2023, the Secretary of Defense may provide assistance to a National Guard Youth Challenge Program of a State—

(1) in addition to assistance under subsection (d) of section 509 of title 32, United States Code;

(2) that is not subject to the matching requirement under such subsection; and

(3) for—

(A) new program start-up costs; or

(B) a workforce development program.

(b) LIMITATIONS.—

(1) MATCHING.— The Secretary may not provide additional

assistance under this section to a State that does not comply with the fund matching requirement under such subsection regarding assistance under such subsection.

(2) TOTAL ASSISTANCE.— Total assistance under this section to all States may not exceed $5,000,000 of the funds appropriated for the National Guard Youth Challenge Program for fiscal year 2022.

(c) REPORTING.— Any assistance provided under this section shall be included in the annual report under subsection (k) of section 509 of such title.

SEC. 517. REPORT ON METHODS TO ENHANCE SUPPORT FROM THE RESERVE COMPONENTS IN RESPONSE TO CATASTROPHIC INCIDENTS.

(a) IN GENERAL.— Not later than 180 days after the date of the enactment of this Act, the Secretary of Defense, in consultation and coordination with the Federal Emergency Management Agency, the National Security Council, the Council of Governors, and the National Governors Association, shall submit to the appropriate congressional committees a report that includes—

(1) a detailed examination of the policy framework for the reserve components, consistent with existing authorities, to provide support to other Federal agencies in response to catastrophic incidents;

(2) identify major statutory or policy impediments to such support; and

(3) recommendations for legislation as appropriate.

(b) CONTENTS.— The report submitted under this section shall include a description of—

(1) the assessment of the Secretary, informed by consultation with the Federal Emergency Management Agency, the National Security Council, the Council of Governors, and the National Governors Association, regarding—

(A) the sufficiency of current authorities for the reimbursement of reserve component personnel during catastrophic incidents under title 10 and title 32, United States Code; and

(B) specifically whether reimbursement authorities are sufficient to ensure that military training and readiness are not degraded to fund disaster response, or use of such authorities degrades the effectiveness of the Disaster Relief Fund;

(2) the plan of the Secretary to ensure there is parallel and consistent policy in the application of the authorities granted under section 12304a of title 10, United States Code, and section 502(f) of title 32, United States Code, including—

(A) a description of the disparities between benefits and protections under Federal law versus State active duty;

(B) recommended solutions to achieve parity at the Federal level; and

(C) recommended changes at the State level, if appropriate;

(3) the plan of the Secretary to ensure there is parity of benefits and protections for members of the Armed Forces employed as part of the response to catastrophic incidents under title 32 or title 10, United States Code, and recommendations for addressing shortfalls; and

(4) a review, by the Federal Emergency Management Agency, of the current policy for, and an assessment of the sufficiency of, reimbursement authority for the use of the reserve components, both to the Department of Defense and to the States, during catastrophic incidents, including any policy and legal limitations, and cost assessment impact on Federal funding.

(c) DEFINITIONS.— In this section:

(1) The term "appropriate congressional committees" means the following:

(A) The congressional defense committees;

(B) The Committee on Homeland Security of the House of Representatives.

(C) The Committee on Homeland Security and Governmental Affairs of the Senate.

(D) The Committee on Transportation and Infrastructure of the House of Representatives.

(E) The Committee on Commerce, Science, and Transportation of the Senate.

(2) The term "catastrophic incident" has the meaning given that term in section 501 of the Homeland Security Act of 2002 (Public Law 107-296; 6 U.S.C. 311).

* * * * * * *

TITLE X—GENERAL PROVISIONS

* * * * * * *

Subtitle F— Studies and Reports

* * * * * * *

Sec. 1063. Extension of reporting requirement regarding enhancement of information sharing and coordination of military training between Department Of Homeland Security and Department Of Defense.

* * * * * * *

Subtitle F—Studies and Reports

* * * * * * *

SEC. 1063. EXTENSION OF REPORTING REQUIREMENT REGARDING ENHANCEMENT OF INFORMATION SHARING AND COORDINATION OF MILITARY TRAINING BETWEEN DEPARTMENT OF HOMELAND SECURITY AND DEPARTMENT OF DEFENSE.

Section 1014(d)(3) of the National Defense Authorization Act for Fiscal Year 2017 (Public Law 114-328) is amended by striking "December 31, 2022" and inserting "December 31, 2023".

* * * * * * *

TITLE XV— CYBERSPACE-RELATED MATTERS

Subtitle A— Matters Related to Cyber Operations and Cyber Forces

Sec. 1501. Development of taxonomy of cyber capabilities.

Subtitle B— Matters Related to Department of Defense Cybersecurity and Information Technology implementation plans.

Subtitle C— Matters Related to Federal Cybersecurity

Subtitle A— Matters Related to Cyber Operations and Cyber Forces

SEC. 1501. DEVELOPMENT OF TAXONOMY OF CYBER CAPABILITIES.

(a) IN GENERAL.— Not later than 180 days after the date of the enactment of this Act, the Secretary of Defense shall develop a taxonomy of cyber capabilities, including software, hardware, middleware, code, other information technology, and accesses, designed for use in cyber effects operations.

(b) REPORT.—

(1) IN GENERAL.— Not later than 30 days after the development of the taxonomy of cyber capabilities required under subsection (a), the Secretary of Defense shall submit to the congressional defense committees a report regarding such taxonomy.

(2) ELEMENTS.— The report required under paragraph (1) shall include the following:

(A) The definitions associated with each category contained within the taxonomy of cyber capabilities developed pursuant to subsection (a).

(B) Recommendations for improved reporting mechanisms to Congress regarding such taxonomy of cyber capabilities, using amounts from the Cyberspace Activities Budget of the Department of Defense.

(C) Recommendations for modifications to the notification requirement under section 396 of title 10, United States Code, in order that such notifications would include information relating to such taxonomy of cyber capabilities, including with respect to both physical and nonphysical cyber effects.

(D) Any other elements the Secretary determines appropriate.

SEC. 1502. EXTENSION OF SUNSET FOR PILOT PROGRAM ON REGIONAL CYBERSECURITY TRAINING CENTER FOR THE ARMY NATIONAL GUARD.

Section 1651(e) of the John S. McCain National Defense Authorization Act for Fiscal Year 2019 (Public Law 115-232; 32 U.S.C. 501 note) is amended by striking "2022" and inserting "2024".

SEC. 1503. MODIFICATION OF THE PRINCIPAL CYBER ADVISOR.

(a) IN GENERAL.— Paragraph (1) of section 932(c) of the

National Defense Authorization Act for Fiscal Year 2014 (Public Law 113-66; 10 U.S.C. 2224 note) is amended to read as follows:

"(1) DESIGNATION.— (A) The Secretary shall designate, from among the personnel of the Office of the Under Secretary of Defense for Policy, a Principal Cyber Advisor to act as the principal advisor to the Secretary on military cyber forces and activities.

"(B) The Secretary may only designate an official under this paragraph if such official was appointed to the position in which such official serves by and with the advice and consent of the Senate."

(b) DESIGNATION OF DEPUTY PRINCIPAL CYBER ADVISOR.— Section 905(a)(1) of the National Defense Authorization Act for Fiscal Year 2020 (Public Law 116-92; 10 U.S.C. 391 note) is amended by striking "Office of the Secretary of Defense" and inserting "Office of the Under Secretary of Defense for Policy".

(c) BRIEFING.— Not later than 90 days after the date of the enactment of this Act, the Deputy Secretary of Defense shall brief the Committee on Armed Services of the Senate and the Committee on Armed Services of the House of Representatives on such recommendations as the Deputy Secretary may have for alternate reporting structures for the Principal Cyber Advisor and the Deputy Principal Cyber Advisor within the Office of the Under Secretary for Policy.

SEC. 1504. EVALUATION OF DEPARTMENT OF DEFENSE CYBER GOVERNANCE.

(a) IN GENERAL.— Not later than April 1, 2023, the Secretary of Defense shall complete an evaluation and review of the Department of Defense's current cyber governance construct.

(b) SCOPE.— The evaluation and review conducted pursuant to subsection (a) shall—

(1) assess the performance of the Department of Defense in carrying out the pillars of the cyber strategy and lines of efforts established in the most recent cyber posture review, including—

(A) conducting military cyberspace operations of offensive, defensive, and protective natures;

(B) securely operating technologies associated with information networks, industrial control systems, operational technologies, weapon systems, and weapon platforms; and

(C) enabling, encouraging, and supporting the security of international, industrial, and academic partners;

(2) analyze and assess the current institutional constructs across the Office of the Secretary of Defense, Joint Staff, military services, and combatant commands involved with and responsible for the execution of and civilian oversight for the responsibilities specified in paragraph (1);

(3) analyze and assess the delineation of responsibilities within the current institutional construct within the Office of the Secretary of Defense for addressing the objectives of the 2018 Department of Defense Cyber Strategy and any superseding strategies, as well as identifying potential seams in responsibility;

(4) examine the Department's policy, legislative, and regulatory regimes related to cyberspace and cybersecurity matters, including the 2018 Department of Defense Cyber Strategy and any superseding strategies, for sufficiency in carrying out the responsibilities specified in paragraph (1);

(5) examine the Office of the Secretary of Defense's current alignment for the integration and coordination of cyberspace activities with other aspects of information operations, including information warfare and electromagnetic spectrum operations;

(6) examine the current roles and responsibilities of each Principal Staff Assistant to the Secretary of Defense as such relate to the responsibilities specified in paragraph (1), and identify redundancy, duplication, or matters requiring deconfliction or clarification;

(7) evaluate and, as appropriate, implement relevant managerial innovation from the private sector in the management of complex missions, including enhanced cross-functional teaming;

(8) evaluate the state of collaboration among each Principal Staff Assistant in matters related to acquisition of cyber capabilities and other enabling technologies supporting the

responsibilities specified in paragraph (1);

(9) analyze and assess the Department's performance in and posture for building and retaining the requisite workforce necessary to perform the responsibilities specified in paragraph (1);

(10) determine optimal governance structures related to the management and advancement of the Department's cyber workforce, including those structures defined under and evaluated pursuant to section 1649 of the National Defense Authorization Act for Fiscal Year 2020 (Public Law 116-92) and section 1726 of the National Defense Authorization Act for Fiscal Year 2021 (Public Law 116-283);

(11) develop policy and legislative recommendations, as appropriate, to delineate and deconflict the roles and responsibilities of United States Cyber Command in defending and protecting the Department of Defense Information Network (DoDIN), with the responsibility of the Chief Information Officer, the Defense Information Systems Agency, and the military services to securely operate technologies described in paragraph (1)(B);

(12) develop policy and legislative recommendations to enhance the authority of the Chief Information Officers within the military services, specifically as such relates to executive and budgetary control over matters related to such services' information technology security, acquisition, and value;

(13) develop policy and legislative recommendations, as appropriate, for optimizing the institutional constructs across the Office of the Secretary of Defense, Joint Staff, military services, and combatant commands involved with and responsible for the responsibilities specified in paragraph (1);

(14) assess the need to retain or modify the relationships, authorities, roles, and responsibilities of the Principal Cyber Advisor described in section 392a(a) of title 10, United States Code;

(15) assess the organizational construct of the Department of Defense and how authorities, roles, and responsibilities for matters relating to cyber activities are distributed among the Under Secretaries, Assistant Secretaries, and Deputy Assistant Secretaries of Defense and among civilian officials within the

military departments with roles and responsibilities relating to cyber activities;

(16) make recommendations for changes to statutes affecting the organizational construct of the Department of Defense to improve the oversight, management, and coordination of—

(A) policies, programs, and strategies relating to cyber activities;

(B) the execution of the authorities of the United States Cyber Command; and

(C) other matters relating to cyber activities; and

(17) make recommendations for any legislation determined appropriate.

(c) INTERIM BRIEFINGS.— Not later than 90 days after the commencement of the evaluation and review conducted pursuant to subsection (a) and every 30 days thereafter, the Secretary of Defense shall brief the congressional defense committees on interim findings of such evaluation and review.

(d) REPORT.— Not later than 30 days after the completion of the evaluation and review conducted pursuant to subsection (a), the Secretary of Defense shall submit to the congressional defense committees a report on such evaluation and review.

SEC. 1505. [10 U.S.C. 394 note] OPERATIONAL TECHNOLOGY AND MISSION-RELEVANT TERRAIN IN CYBERSPACE.

(a) MISSION-RELEVANT TERRAIN.— Not later than January 1, 2025, the Secretary of Defense shall complete mapping of mission-relevant terrain in cyberspace for Defense Critical Assets and Task Critical Assets at sufficient granularity to enable mission thread analysis and situational awareness, including required—

(1) decomposition of missions reliant on such Assets;

(2) identification of access vectors;

(3) internal and external dependencies;

(4) topology of networks and network segments;

(5) cybersecurity defenses across information and operational technology on such Assets; and

(6) identification of associated or reliant weapon systems.

(b) COMBATANT COMMAND RESPONSIBILITIES.— Not later than January 1, 2024, the Commanders of United States European Command, United States Indo-Pacific Command, United States Northern Command, United States Strategic Command, United States Space Command, United States Transportation Command, and other relevant Commands, in coordination with the Commander of United States Cyber Command, in order to enable effective mission thread analysis, cyber situational awareness, and effective cyber defense of Defense Critical Assets and Task Critical Assets under their control or in their areas of responsibility, shall develop, institute, and make necessary modifications to—

(1) internal combatant command processes, responsibilities, and functions;

(2) coordination with service components under their operational control, United States Cyber Command, Joint Forces Headquarters-Department of Defense Information Network, and the service cyber components;

(3) combatant command headquarters' situational awareness posture to ensure an appropriate level of cyber situational awareness of the forces, facilities, installations, bases, critical infrastructure, and weapon systems under their control or in their areas of responsibility, including, in particular, Defense Critical Assets and Task Critical Assets; and

(4) documentation of their mission-relevant terrain in cyberspace.

(c) DEPARTMENT OF DEFENSE CHIEF INFORMATION OFFICER RESPONSIBILITIES.—

(1) IN GENERAL.— Not later than November 1, 2023, the Chief Information Officer of the Department of Defense shall establish or make necessary changes to policy, control systems standards, risk management framework and authority to operate policies, and cybersecurity reference architectures to provide baseline cybersecurity requirements for operational technology in forces, facilities, installations, bases, critical infrastructure, and weapon systems across the Department of Defense Information Network.

(2) IMPLEMENTATION OF POLICIES.— The Chief Information Officer of the Department of Defense shall leverage acquisition

guidance, concerted assessment of the Department's operational technology enterprise, and coordination with the military department principal cyber advisors and chief information officers to drive necessary change and implementation of relevant policy across the Department's forces, facilities, installations, bases, critical infrastructure, and weapon systems.

(3) ADDITIONAL RESPONSIBILITIES.— The Chief Information Officer of the Department of Defense shall ensure that policies, control systems standards, and cybersecurity reference architectures—

(A) are implementable by components of the Department;

(B) limit adversaries' ability to reach or manipulate control systems through cyberspace;

(C) appropriately balance non-connectivity and monitoring requirements;

(D) include data collection and flow requirements;

(E) interoperate with and are informed by the operational community's workflows for defense of information and operational technology in the forces, facilities, installations, bases, critical infrastructure, and weapon systems across the Department;

(F) integrate and interoperate with Department mission assurance construct; and

(G) are implemented with respect to Defense Critical Assets and Task Critical Assets.

(d) UNITED STATES CYBER COMMAND OPERATIONAL RESPONSIBILITIES.— Not later than January 1, 2025, the Commander of United States Cyber Command shall make necessary modifications to the mission, scope, and posture of Joint Forces Headquarters-Department of Defense Information Network to ensure that Joint Forces Headquarters—

(1) has appropriate visibility of operational technology in the forces, facilities, installations, bases, critical infrastructure, and weapon systems across the Department of Defense Information Network, including, in particular, Defense Critical Assets and Task Critical Assets;

(2) can effectively command and control forces to defend such operational technology; and

(3) has established processes for—

(A) incident and compliance reporting;

(B) ensuring compliance with Department of Defense cybersecurity policy; and

(C) ensuring that cyber vulnerabilities, attack vectors, and security violations, including, in particular, those specific to Defense Critical Assets and Task Critical Assets, are appropriately managed.

(e) UNITED STATES CYBER COMMAND FUNCTIONAL RESPONSIBILITIES.— Not later than January 1, 2025, the Commander of United States Cyber Command shall—

(1) ensure in its role of Joint Forces Trainer for the Cyberspace Operations Forces that operational technology cyber defense is appropriately incorporated into training for the Cyberspace Operations Forces;

(2) delineate the specific force composition requirements within the Cyberspace Operations Forces for specialized cyber defense of operational technology, including the number, size, scale, and responsibilities of defined Cyber Operations Forces elements;

(3) develop and maintain, or support the development and maintenance of, a joint training curriculum for operational technology-focused Cyberspace Operations Forces;

(4) support the Chief Information Officer of the Department of Defense as the Department's senior official for the cybersecurity of operational technology under this section;

(5) develop and institutionalize, or support the development and institutionalization of, tradecraft for defense of operational technology across local defenders, cybersecurity service providers, cyber protection teams, and service-controlled forces;

(6) develop and institutionalize integrated concepts of operation, operational workflows, and cybersecurity architectures for defense of information and operational technology in the forces, facilities, installations, bases, critical infrastructure, and weapon systems across the Department of

Defense Information Network, including, in particular, Defense Critical Assets and Task Critical Assets, including—

(A) deliberate and strategic sensoring of such Network and Assets;

(B) instituting policies governing connections across and between such Network and Assets;

(C) modelling of normal behavior across and between such Network and Assets;

(D) engineering data flows across and between such Network and Assets;

(E) developing local defenders, cybersecurity service providers, cyber protection teams, and service-controlled forces' operational workflows and tactics, techniques, and procedures optimized for the designs, data flows, and policies of such Network and Assets;

(F) instituting of model defensive cyber operations and Department of Defense Information Network operations tradecraft; and

(G) integrating of such operations to ensure interoperability across echelons; and

(7) advance the integration of the Department of Defense's mission assurance, cybersecurity compliance, cybersecurity operations, risk management framework, and authority to operate programs and policies.

(f) SERVICE RESPONSIBILITIES.— Not later than January 1, 2025, the Secretaries of the military departments, through the service principal cyber advisors, chief information officers, the service cyber components, and relevant service commands, shall make necessary investments in operational technology in the forces, facilities, installations, bases, critical infrastructure, and weapon systems across the Department of Defense Information Network and the service-controlled forces responsible for defense of such operational technology to—

(1) ensure that relevant local network and cybersecurity forces are responsible for defending operational technology across the forces, facilities, installations, bases, critical infrastructure, and weapon systems, including, in particular, Defense Critical Assets and Task Critical Assets;

(2) ensure that relevant local operational technology-focused system operators, network and cybersecurity forces, mission defense teams and other service-retained forces, and cyber protection teams are appropriately trained, including through common training and use of cyber ranges, as appropriate, to execute the specific requirements of cybersecurity operations in operational technology;

(3) ensure that all Defense Critical Assets and Task Critical Assets are monitored and defended by Cybersecurity Service Providers;

(4) ensure that operational technology is appropriately sensored and appropriate cybersecurity defenses, including technologies associated with the More Situational Awareness for Industrial Control Systems Joint Capability Technology Demonstration, are employed to enable defense of Defense Critical Assets and Task Critical Assets;

(5) implement Department of Defense Chief Information Officer policy germane to operational technology, including, in particular, with respect to Defense Critical Assets and Task Critical Assets;

(6) plan for, designate, and train dedicated forces to be utilized in operational technology-centric roles across the military services and United States Cyber Command; and

(7) ensure that operational technology, as appropriate, is not easily accessible via the internet and that cybersecurity investments accord with mission risk to and relevant access vectors for Defense Critical Assets and Task Critical Assets.

(g) OFFICE OF THE SECRETARY OF DEFENSE RESPONSIBILITIES.—Not later than January 1, 2023, the Secretary of Defense shall—

(1) assess and finalize Office of the Secretary of Defense components' roles and responsibilities for the cybersecurity of operational technology in the forces, facilities, installations, bases, critical infrastructure, and weapon systems across the Department of Defense Information Network;

(2) assess the need to establish centralized or dedicated funding for remediation of cybersecurity gaps in operational technology across the Department of Defense Information Network;

(3) make relevant modifications to the Department of

Defense's mission assurance construct, Mission Assurance Coordination Board, and other relevant bodies to drive—

(A) prioritization of kinetic and non-kinetic threats to the Department's missions and minimization of mission risk in the Department's war plans;

(B) prioritization of relevant mitigations and investments to harden and assure the Department's missions and minimize mission risk in the Department's war plans; and

(C) completion of mission relevant terrain mapping of Defense Critical Assets and Task Critical Assets and population of associated assessment and mitigation data in authorized repositories;

(4) make relevant modifications to the Strategic Cybersecurity Program; and

(5) drive and provide oversight of the implementation of this section.

(h) BUDGET ROLLOUT BRIEFINGS.—

(1) IN GENERAL.— Beginning not later than 30 days after the date of the enactment of this Act, each of the Secretaries of the military departments, the Commander of United States Cyber Command, and the Chief Information Officer of the Department of Defense shall provide annual updates to the Committee on Armed Services of the Senate and the Committee on Armed Services of the House of Representatives on activities undertaken and progress made to carry out this section.

(2) ANNUAL BRIEFINGS.— Not later than one year after the date of the enactment of this Act and not less frequently than annually thereafter until January 1, 2024, the Under Secretary of Defense for Policy, the Under Secretary of Defense for Acquisition and Sustainment, the Chief Information Officer, and the Joint Staff J6, representing the combatant commands, shall individually or together provide briefings to the Committee on Armed Services of the Senate and the Committee on Armed Services of the House of Representatives on activities undertaken and progress made to carry out this section.

(i) IMPLEMENTATION.—

(1) IN GENERAL.— In implementing this section, the Secretary of Defense shall prioritize the cybersecurity and

EC. 1506. [10 U.S.C. 394 note]

cyber defense of Defense Critical Assets and Task Critical Assets and shape cyber investments, policy, operations, and deployments to ensure cybersecurity and cyber defense.

(2) APPLICATION.— This section shall apply to assets owned and operated by the Department of Defense, as well as to applicable non-Department assets essential to the projection, support, and sustainment of military forces and operations worldwide.

(j) DEFINITION.— In this section:

(1) MISSION-RELEVANT TERRAIN IN CYBERSPACE.— "mission-relevant terrain in cyberspace" has the meaning given such term as specified in Joint Publication 6-0.

(2) OPERATIONAL TECHNOLOGY.— The term "operational technology" means control systems or controllers, communication architectures, and user interfaces that monitor or control infrastructure and equipment operating in various environments, such as weapon systems, utility or energy production and distribution, or medical, logistics, nuclear, biological, chemical, or manufacturing facilities.

SEC. 1506. MATTERS CONCERNING CYBER PERSONNEL REQUIREMENTS.

(a) IN GENERAL.— The Secretary of Defense, acting through the Under Secretary of Defense for Personnel and Readiness and the Chief Information Officer of the Department of Defense, in consultation with Secretaries of the military departments and the head of any other organization or element of the Department the Secretary determines appropriate, shall—

(1) determine the overall workforce requirement of the Department for cyberspace and information warfare military personnel across the active and reserve components of the Armed Forces (other than the Coast Guard) and for civilian personnel, and in doing so shall—

(A) consider personnel in positions securing the Department of Defense Information Network and associated enterprise information technology, defense agencies and field activities, and combatant commands, including current billets primarily associated with the Department of Defense Cyber Workforce Framework;

(B) consider the mix between military and civilian personnel, active and reserve components, and the use of the National Guard;

(C) develop a talent management strategy that covers accessions, training, and education; and

(D) consider such other elements as the Secretary determines appropriate;

(2) assess current and future cyber education curriculum and requirements for military and civilian personnel, including—

(A) acquisition personnel;

(B) accessions and recruits to the military services;

(C) cadets and midshipmen at the military service academies and enrolled in the Senior Reserve Officers' Training Corps;

(D) information environment and cyberspace military and civilian personnel; and

(E) non-information environment cyberspace military and civilian personnel;

(3) identify appropriate locations for information warfare and cyber education for military and civilian personnel, including—

(A) the military service academies;

(B) the senior level service schools and intermediate level service schools specified in section 2151(b) of title 10, United States Code;

(C) the Air Force Institute of Technology;

(D) the National Defense University;

(E) the Joint Special Operations University;

(F) the Command and General Staff Colleges;

(G) the War Colleges;

(H) any military education institution attached to or operating under any institution specified in this paragraph;

(I) any other military educational institution of the Department identified by the Secretary for purposes of this section;

(J) the Cyber Centers of Academic Excellence; and

(K) potential future educational institutions of the Federal Government in accordance with the assessment required under subsection (b); and

(4) determine—

(A) whether the cyberspace domain mission requires a graduate level professional military education college on par with and distinct from the war colleges for the Army, Navy, and Air Force as in existence on the day before the date of the enactment of this Act;

(B) whether such a college should be joint; and

(C) where such a college should be located.

(b) ASSESSMENT.— In identifying appropriate locations for information warfare and cyber education for military and civilian personnel at potential future educational institutions of the Federal Government pursuant to subsection (a)(3)(K), the Secretary of Defense, acting through the Under Secretary of Defense for Personnel and Readiness and the Chief Information Officer of the Department of Defense, in consultation with Secretaries of the military departments, the head of any other organization or element of the Department the Secretary determines appropriate, the Secretary of Homeland Security, and the National Cyber Director, shall assess the feasibility and advisability of establishing a National Cyber Academy or similar institute for the purpose of educating and training civilian and military personnel for service in cyber, information, and related fields throughout the Federal Government.

(c) REPORTS REQUIRED.—

(1) EDUCATION.— Not later than November 1, 2022, the Secretary of Defense shall provide the Committee on Armed Services of the Senate and the Committee on Armed Services of the House of Representatives a briefing and, not later than January 1, 2023, the Secretary shall submit to such committees a report, on—

(A) talent strategy to satisfy future cyber education requirements at appropriate locations referred to in subsection (a)(3); and

(B) the findings of the Secretary in assessing cyber education curricula and identifying such locations.

(2) WORKFORCE.— Not later than November 1, 2024, the Secretary of Defense shall provide the Committee on Armed Services of the Senate and the Committee on Armed Services of the House of Representatives a briefing and, not later than January 1, 2025, the Secretary shall submit to such committees a report, on—

(A) the findings of the Secretary in determining pursuant to subsection (a)(1) the overall workforce requirement of the Department of Defense for cyberspace and information warfare military personnel across the active and reserve components of the Armed Forces (other than the Coast Guard) and for civilian personnel;

(B) such recommendations as the Secretary may have relating to such requirement; and

(C) such legislative or administrative action as the Secretary identifies as necessary to effectively satisfy such requirement.

(d) EDUCATION DESCRIBED.— In this section, the term "education" includes formal education requirements, such as degrees and certification in targeted subject areas, as well as general training, including—

(1) upskilling;

(2) knowledge, skills, and abilities; and

(3) nonacademic professional development.

SEC. 1507. [10 U.S.C. 167b note] ASSIGNMENT OF CERTAIN BUDGET CONTROL RESPONSIBILITIES TO COMMANDER OF UNITED STATES CYBER COMMAND.

(a) ASSIGNMENT OF RESPONSIBILITIES.—

(1) IN GENERAL.— The Commander of United States Cyber Command shall, subject to the authority, direction, and control of the Principal Cyber Advisor of the Department of Defense, be responsible for directly controlling and managing the planning, programming, budgeting, and execution of resources to train, equip, operate, and sustain the Cyber Mission Forces.

(2) EFFECTIVE DATE AND APPLICABILITY.— Paragraph (1) shall take effect on the date of the enactment of this Act and apply—

(A) on January 1, 2022, for controlling and managing budget execution; and

(B) beginning with fiscal year 2024 and each fiscal year thereafter for directly controlling and managing the planning, programming, budgeting, and execution of resources.

(b) ELEMENTS.—

(1) IN GENERAL.— The responsibilities assigned to the Commander of United States Cyber Command pursuant to subsection (a)(1) shall include the following:

(A) Preparation of a program objective memorandum and budget estimate submission for the resources required to train, equip, operate, and sustain the Cyber Mission Forces.

(B) Preparation of budget materials pertaining to United States Cyber Command for inclusion in the budget justification materials that are submitted to Congress in support of the Department of Defense budget for a fiscal year (as submitted with the budget of the President for a fiscal year under section 1105(a) of title 31, United States Code) that is separate from any other military service or component of the Department.

(2) RESPONSIBILITIES NOT DELEGATED.— The responsibilities assigned to the Commander of United States Cyber Command pursuant to subsection (a)(1) shall not include the following:

(A) Military pay and allowances.

(B) Funding for facility support that is provided by the military services.

(c) IMPLEMENTATION PLAN.—

(1) IN GENERAL.— Not later than the date that is 30 days after the date of the enactment of this Act, the Comptroller General of the Department of Defense and the Commander of United States Cyber Command, in coordination with Chief Information Officer of the Department, the Principal Cyber Advisor, the Under Secretary of Defense for Acquisition and Sustainment, Cost Assessment and Program Evaluation, and the Secretaries of the military departments, shall jointly develop an implementation plan for the transition of

responsibilities assigned to the Commander of United States Cyber Command pursuant to subsection (a)(1).

(2) ELEMENTS.— The implementation plan developed under paragraph (1) shall include the following:

(A) A budgetary review to identify appropriate resources for transfer to the Commander of United States Cyber Command for carrying out responsibilities assigned pursuant to subsection (a)(1).

(B) Definitions of appropriate roles and responsibilities.

(C) Specification of all program elements and sub-elements, and the training, equipment, Joint Cyber Warfighting Architecture capabilities, other enabling capabilities and infrastructure, intelligence support, operations, and sustainment investments in each such program element and sub-element for which the Commander of United States Cyber Command is responsible.

(D) Specification of all program elements and sub-elements, and the training, equipment, Joint Cyber Warfighting Architecture capabilities, other enabling capabilities and infrastructure, intelligence support, operations, and sustainment investments in each such program element and sub-element relevant to or that support the Cyber Mission Force for which the Secretaries of the military departments are responsible.

(E) Required levels of civilian and military staffing within United States Cyber Command to carry out subsection (a)(1), and an estimate of when such levels of staffing will be achieved.

(d) BRIEFING.—

(1) IN GENERAL.— Not later than the earlier of the date on which the implementation plan under subsection (c) is developed or the date that is 90 days after the date of the enactment of this Act, the Secretary of Defense shall provide the congressional defense committees a briefing on the implementation plan.

(2) ELEMENTS.— The briefing required by paragraph (1) shall address any recommendations for when and how the

Secretary of Defense should delegate to the Commander of United States Cyber Command budget authority for the Cyber Operations Forces (as such term is defined in the memorandum issued by the Secretary of Defense on December 12, 2019, relating to the definition of "Department of Defense Cyberspace Operations Forces (DoD COF)"), after successful implementation of the responsibilities described in subsection (a) relating to the Cyber Mission Forces.

SEC. 1508. [10 U.S.C. 2224 note] COORDINATION BETWEEN UNITED STATES CYBER COMMAND AND PRIVATE SECTOR.

(a) VOLUNTARY PROCESS.— Not later than January 1, 2023, the Commander of United States Cyber Command shall establish a voluntary process to engage with private sector information technology and cybersecurity entities to explore and develop methods and plans through which the capabilities, knowledge, and actions of—

(1) private sector entities operating inside the United States to defend against foreign malicious cyber actors could assist, or be coordinated with, the actions of United States Cyber Command operating outside the United States against such foreign malicious cyber actors; and

(2) United States Cyber Command operating outside the United States against foreign malicious cyber actors could assist, or be coordinated with, the actions of private sector entities operating inside the United States against such foreign malicious cyber actors.

(b) ANNUAL BRIEFING.—

(1) IN GENERAL.— During the period beginning on March 1, 2022, and ending on March 1, 2026, the Commander of United States Cyber Command shall, not less frequently than once each year, provide to the Committee on Armed Services of the Senate and the Committee on Armed Services of the House of Representatives a briefing on the status of any activities conducted pursuant to subsection (a).

(2) ELEMENTS.— Each briefing provided under paragraph (1) shall include the following:

(A) Such recommendations for legislative or administrative action as the Commander of United States

Cyber Command considers appropriate to improve and facilitate the exploration and development of methods and plans under subsection (a).

(B) Such recommendations as the Commander may have for increasing private sector participation in such exploration and development.

(C) A description of the challenges encountered in carrying out subsection (a), including any concerns expressed to the Commander by private sector partners regarding participation in such exploration and development.

(D) Information relating to how such exploration and development with the private sector could assist military planning by United States Cyber Command.

(E) Such other matters as the Commander considers appropriate.

(c) CONSULTATION.— In developing the process described in subsection (a), the Commander of United States Cyber Command shall consult with the Director of the Cybersecurity and Infrastructure Security Agency of the Department of Homeland Security and the heads of any other Federal agencies the Commander considers appropriate.

(d) INTEGRATION WITH OTHER EFFORTS.— The Commander of United States Cyber Command shall ensure that the process described in subsection (a) makes use of, builds upon, and, as appropriate, integrates with and does not duplicate, other efforts of the Department of Homeland Security and the Department of Defense relating to cybersecurity, including the following:

(1) The Joint Cyber Defense Collaborative of the Cybersecurity and Infrastructure Security Agency.

(2) The Cybersecurity Collaboration Center and Enduring Security Framework of the National Security Agency.

(3) The office for joint cyber planning of the Department of Homeland Security.

(e) PROTECTION OF TRADE SECRETS AND PROPRIETARY INFORMATION.— The Commander of United States Cyber Command shall ensure that any trade secret or proprietary information of a private sector entity engaged with the Department of Defense through the process established under subsection (a) that is made known to the Department pursuant to such process remains private and protected unless otherwise explicitly authorized by such entity.

(f) RULE OF CONSTRUCTION.— Nothing in this section may be construed to authorize United States Cyber Command to conduct operations inside the United States or for private sector entities to conduct offensive cyber activities outside the United States, except to the extent such operations or activities are permitted by a provision of law in effect on the day before the date of the enactment of this Act.

SEC. 1509. ASSESSMENT OF CYBER POSTURE AND OPERATIONAL ASSUMPTIONS AND DEVELOPMENT OF TARGETING STRATEGIES AND SUPPORTING CAPABILITIES.

(a) ASSESSMENT OF CYBER POSTURE OF ADVERSARIES AND OPERATIONAL ASSUMPTIONS OF UNITED STATES GOVERNMENT.—

(1) IN GENERAL.— Not later than one year after the date of the enactment of this Act, the Commander of United States Cyber Command, the Under Secretary of Defense for Policy, and the Under Secretary of Defense for Intelligence and Security, shall jointly sponsor or conduct an assessment, including, if appropriate, a war-game or tabletop exercise, of the current and emerging offensive and defensive cyber posture of adversaries of the United States and the current operational assumptions and plans of the Armed Forces for offensive cyber operations during potential crises or conflict.

(2) ELEMENTS.— The assessment required under paragraph (1) shall include consideration of the following:

(A) Changes to strategies, operational concepts, operational preparation of the environment, and rules of engagement.

(B) Opportunities provided by armed forces in theaters of operations and other innovative alternatives.

(C) Changes in intelligence community (as such term is defined in section 3 of the National Security Act of 1947 (50 U.S.C. 3003)) targeting and operations in support of the Department of Defense.

(D) Adversary capabilities to deny or degrade United States activities in cyberspace.

(E) Adversaries' targeting of United States critical

infrastructure and implications for United States policy.

(F) Potential effect of emerging technologies, such as fifth generation mobile networks, expanded use of cloud information technology services, and artificial intelligence.

(G) Changes in Department of Defense organizational design.

(H) The effect of private sector cybersecurity research.

(F) Adequacy of intelligence support to cyberspace operations by Combat Support Agencies and Service Intelligence Centers.

(b) DEVELOPMENT OF TARGETING STRATEGIES, SUPPORTING CAPABILITIES, AND OPERATIONAL CONCEPTS.—

(1) IN GENERAL.— Not later than one year after the date of the enactment of this Act, the Commander of United States Cyber Command shall—

(A) assess and establish the capabilities, capacities, tools, and tactics required to support targeting strategies for—

(i) day-to-day persistent engagement of adversaries, including support to information operations;

(ii) support to geographic combatant commanders at the onset of hostilities and during sustained conflict; and

(iii) deterrence of attacks on United States critical infrastructure, including the threat of counter value responses;

(B) develop future cyber targeting strategies and capabilities across the categories of cyber missions and targets with respect to which—

(i) time-consuming and human effort-intensive stealthy operations are required to acquire and maintain access to targets, and the mission is so important it is worthwhile to expend such efforts to hold such targets at risk;

(ii) target prosecution requires unique access and exploitation tools and technologies, and the target importance justifies the efforts, time, and expense relating thereto;

(iii) operational circumstances do not allow for and do not require spending the time and human effort required for stealthy, nonattributable, and continuous access to targets;

(iv) capabilities are needed to rapidly prosecute targets that have not been previously planned and that can be accessed and exploited using known, available tools and techniques; and

(v) targets may be prosecuted with the aid of automated techniques to achieve speed, mass, and scale;

(C) develop strategies for appropriate utilization of Cyber Mission Teams in support of combatant command objectives as—

(i) adjuncts to or substitutes for kinetic operations; or

(ii) independent means to achieve novel tactical, operational, and strategic objectives; and

(D) develop collection and analytic support strategies for the service intelligence centers to assist operations by United States Cyber Command and the Service Cyber Components.

(2) BRIEFING REQUIRED.—

(A) IN GENERAL.— Not later than 30 days after the date on which all activities required under paragraph (1) have been completed, the Commander of United States Cyber Command shall provide the congressional defense committees a briefing on such activities.

(B) ELEMENTS.— The briefing provided pursuant to subparagraph (A) shall include the following:

(i) Recommendations for such legislative or administrative action as the Commander of United States Cyber Command considers necessary to address capability shortcomings.

(ii) Plans to address such capability shortcomings.

(c) COUNTRY-SPECIFIC ACCESS STRATEGIES.—

(1) IN GENERAL.— Not later than one year after the date on

which all activities required under subsection (b)(1) have been completed, the Commander of United States Cyber Command shall complete development of country-specific access strategies for the Russian Federation, the People's Republic of China, the Democratic People's Republic of Korea, and the Islamic Republic of Iran.

(2) ELEMENTS.— Each country-specific access strategy developed under paragraph (1) shall include the following:

(A) Specification of desired and required—

(i) outcomes;

(ii) cyber warfighting architecture, including—

(I) tools and redirectors;

(II) access platforms; and

(III) data analytics, modeling, and simulation capacity;

(iii) specific means to achieve and maintain persistent access and conduct command and control and exfiltration against hard targets and in operationally challenging environments across the continuum of conflict;

(iv) intelligence, surveillance, and reconnaissance support;

(v) operational partnerships with allies;

(vi) rules of engagement;

(vii) personnel, training, and equipment; and

(viii) targeting strategies, including strategies that do not demand deliberate targeting and precise access to achieve effects; and

(B) recommendations for such policy or resourcing changes as the Commander of United States Cyber Command considers appropriate to address access shortfalls.

(3) CONSULTATION REQUIRED.— The Commander of United States Cyber Command shall develop the country-specific access strategies under paragraph (1) independently but in consultation with the following:

(A) The Director of the National Security Agency.

(B) The Director of the Central Intelligence Agency.

(C) The Director of the Defense Advanced Research Projects Agency.

(D) The Director of the Strategic Capabilities Office.

(E) The Under Secretary of Defense for Policy.

(F) The Principal Cyber Advisor to the Secretary of Defense.

(G) The Commanders of all other combatant commands.

(4) BRIEFING.— Upon completion of the country-specific access strategies under paragraph (1), the Commander of United States Cyber Command shall provide the Deputy Secretary of Defense, the Vice Chairman of the Joint Chiefs of Staff, the Committee on Armed Services of the Senate, and the Committee on Armed Services of the House of Representatives a briefing on such strategies.

(d) DEFINITION.— In this section, the term "critical infrastructure" has the meaning given such term in section 1016(e) of Public Law 107-56 (42 U.S.C. 5195c(e)).

SEC. 1510. ASSESSING CAPABILITIES TO COUNTER ADVERSARY USE OF RANSOMWARE, CAPABILITIES, AND INFRASTRUCTURE.

(a) COMPREHENSIVE ASSESSMENT AND RECOMMENDATIONS REQUIRED.— Not later than 180 days after the date of enactment of this section, the Secretary of Defense shall—

(1) conduct a comprehensive assessment of the policy, capacity, and capabilities of the Department of Defense to diminish and defend the United States from the threat of ransomware attacks, including—

(A) an assessment of the current and potential threats and risks to national and economic security posed by—

(i) large-scale and sophisticated criminal cyber enterprises that provide large-scale and sophisticated cyber attack capabilities and infrastructure used to conduct ransomware attacks; and

(ii) organizations that conduct or could conduct ransomware attacks or other attacks that use the capabilities and infrastructure described in clause (i) on a large scale against important assets and systems in the United States, including critical infrastructure;

(B) an assessment of—

(i) the threat posed to the Department of Defense Information Network and the United States by the large-scale and sophisticated criminal cyber enterprises, capabilities, and infrastructure described in subparagraph (A); and

(ii) the current and potential role of United States Cyber Command in addressing the threat referred to in clause (i) including—

(I) the threshold at which United States Cyber Command should respond to such a threat; and

(II) the capacity for United States Cyber Command to respond to such a threat without harmful effects on other United States Cyber Command missions;

(C) an identification of the current and potential Department efforts, processes, and capabilities to deter and counter the threat referred to in subparagraph (B)(i), including through offensive cyber effects operations;

(D) an assessment of the application of the defend forward and persistent engagement operational concepts and capabilities of the Department to deter and counter the threat of ransomware attacks against the United States;

(E) a description of the efforts of the Department in interagency processes, and joint collaboration with allies and partners of the United States, to address the growing threat from large-scale and sophisticated criminal cyber enterprises that conduct ransomware attacks and could conduct attacks with other objectives;

(F) a determination of the extent to which the governments of countries in which large-scale and sophisticated criminal cyber enterprises are principally located are tolerating the activities of such enterprises, have interactions with such enterprises, could direct their operations, and could suppress such enterprises;

(G) an assessment as to whether the large-scale and sophisticated criminal cyber enterprises described in subparagraph (F) are perfecting and practicing attack techniques and capabilities at scale that can be co-opted and placed in the service of the country in which such enterprises are principally located; and

(H) identification of such legislative or administrative action as may be necessary to more effectively counter the threat of ransomware attacks; and

(2) develop recommendations for the Department to build capabilities to develop and execute innovative methods to deter and counter the threat of ransomware attacks prior to and in response to the launching of such attacks.

(b) BRIEFING.— Not later than 210 days after the date of the enactment of this Act, the Secretary of Defense shall brief the congressional defense committees on the comprehensive assessment completed under paragraph (1) of subsection (a) and the recommendations developed under paragraph (2) of such subsection.

(c) DEFINITION.— In this section, the term "critical infrastructure" has the meaning given such term in section 1016(e) of Public Law 107-56 (42 U.S.C. 5195c(e)).

SEC. 1511. COMPARATIVE ANALYSIS OF CYBERSECURITY CAPABILITIES.

(a) COMPARATIVE ANALYSIS REQUIRED.— Not later than 180 days after the date of the enactment of this Act, the Chief Information Officer and the Director of Cost Assessment and Program Evaluation (CAPE) of the Department of Defense, in consultation with the Principal Cyber Advisor to the Secretary of Defense and the Chief Information Officers of each of the military departments, shall jointly sponsor a comparative analysis, to be conducted by the Director of the National Security Agency and the Director of the Defense Information Systems Agency, of the following:

(1) The cybersecurity tools, applications, and capabilities offered as options on enterprise software agreements for cloud-based productivity and collaboration suites, such as is offered under the Defense Enterprise Office Solution and Enterprise Software Agreement contracts with Department of Defense components, relative to the cybersecurity tools, applications, and capabilities that are currently deployed in, or required by,

the Department to conduct—

 (A) asset discovery;

 (B) vulnerability scanning;

 (C) conditional access (also known as "comply-to-connect");

 (D) event correlation;

 (E) patch management and remediation;

 (F) endpoint query and control;

 (G) endpoint detection and response;

 (H) data rights management;

 (I) data loss prevention;

 (J) data tagging;

 (K) data encryption;

 (L) security information and event management; and

 (M) security orchestration, automation, and response.

(2) The identity, credential, and access management (ICAM) system, and associated capabilities to enforce the principle of least privilege access, offered as an existing option on an enterprise software agreement described in paragraph (1), relative to—

 (A) the requirements of such system described in the Zero Trust Reference Architecture of the Department; and

 (B) the requirements of such system under development by the Defense Information Systems Agency.

(3) The artificial intelligence and machine-learning capabilities associated with the tools, applications, and capabilities described in paragraphs (1) and (2), and the ability to host Government or third-party artificial intelligence and machine-learning algorithms pursuant to contracts referred to in paragraph (1) for such tools, applications, and capabilities.

(4) The network consolidation and segmentation capabilities offered on the enterprise software agreements described in paragraph (1) relative to capabilities projected in the Zero Trust Reference Architecture.

(5) The automated orchestration and interoperability among the tools, applications, and capabilities described in

paragraphs (1) through (4).

(b) ELEMENTS OF COMPARATIVE ANALYSIS.— The comparative analysis conducted under subsection (a) shall include an assessment of the following:

(1) Costs.

(2) Performance.

(3) Sustainment.

(4) Scalability.

(5) Training requirements.

(6) Maturity.

(7) Human effort requirements.

(8) Speed of integrated operations.

(9) Ability to operate on multiple operating systems and in multiple cloud environments.

(10) Such other matters as the Chief Information Officer and the Director of Cost Assessment and Program Evaluation consider appropriate.

(c) BRIEFING REQUIRED.— Not later than 30 days after the date on which the comparative analysis required under subsection (a) is completed, the Chief Information Officer and the Director of Cost Assessment and Program Evaluation (CAPE) of the Department of Defense shall jointly provide the congressional defense committees with a briefing on the findings of the Chief Information Officer and the Director with respect to such analysis, together with such recommendations for legislative or administrative action as the Chief Information Officer and the Director may have with respect to the matters covered by such analysis.

SEC. 1512. ELIGIBILITY OF OWNERS AND OPERATORS OF CRITICAL INFRASTRUCTURE TO RECEIVE CERTAIN DEPARTMENT OF DEFENSE SUPPORT AND SERVICES.

Section 2012 of title 10, United States Codeis amended—

(1) in subsection (e)—

(A) by redesignating paragraph (3) as paragraph (4); and

(B) by inserting after paragraph (2) the following new paragraph:

"(3) Owners and operators of critical infrastructure (as such term is defined in section 1016(e) of Public Law 107-56 (42 U.S.C. 5195c(e)))."

; and

(2) in subsection (f), by adding at the end the following new paragraph:

"(5) Procedures to ensure that assistance provided to an entity specified in subsection (e)(3) is provided in a manner that is consistent with similar assistance provided under authorities applicable to other Federal departments and agencies, including the authorities of the Cybersecurity and Infrastructure Security Agency of the Department of Homeland Security pursuant to title XXII of the Homeland Security Act of 2002 (6 U.S.C. 651 et seq.)."

SEC. 1513. REPORT ON POTENTIAL DEPARTMENT OF DEFENSE SUPPORT AND ASSISTANCE FOR INCREASING THE AWARENESS OF THE CYBERSECURITY AND INFRASTRUCTURE SECURITY AGENCY OF CYBER THREATS AND VULNERABILITIES AFFECTING CRITICAL INFRASTRUCTURE.

(a) REPORT REQUIRED.— Not later than 270 days after the date of the enactment of this Act, the Secretary of Defense, in consultation with the Secretary of Homeland Security and the National Cyber Director, shall submit to the Committee on Armed Services of the Senate and the Committee on Armed Services of the House of Representatives a report that provides recommendations on how the Department of Defense can improve support and assistance to the Cybersecurity and Infrastructure Security Agency of the Department of Homeland Security to increase awareness of cyber threats and vulnerabilities affecting information technology and networks supporting critical infrastructure within the United States, including critical infrastructure of the Department and critical infrastructure relating to the defense of the United States.

(b) ELEMENTS OF REPORT.— The report required by subsection (a) shall—

(1) assess and identify areas in which the Department of Defense could provide support or assistance, including through information sharing and voluntary network monitoring

programs, to the Cybersecurity and Infrastructure Security Agency to expand or increase technical understanding and awareness of cyber threats and vulnerabilities affecting critical infrastructure;

(2) identify and assess any legal, policy, organizational, or technical barriers to carrying out paragraph (1);

(3) assess and describe any legal or policy changes necessary to enable the Department to carry out paragraph (1) while preserving privacy and civil liberties;

(4) assess and describe the budgetary and other resource effects on the Department of carrying out paragraph (1); and

(5) provide a notional time-phased plan, including milestones, to enable the Department to carry out paragraph (1).

(c) CRITICAL INFRASTRUCTURE DEFINED.— In this section, the term "critical infrastructure" has the meaning given such term in section 1016(e) of Public Law 107-56 (42 U.S.C. 5195c(e)).

Subtitle B— Matters Related to Department of Defense Cybersecurity and Information Technology

SEC. 1521. [10 U.S.C. 2224 note] ENTERPRISE-WIDE PROCUREMENT OF CYBER DATA PRODUCTS AND SERVICES.

(a) PROGRAM.— Not later than one year after the date of the enactment of this Act, the Secretary of Defense shall designate an executive agent for Department of Defense-wide procurement of cyber data products and services. The executive agent shall establish a program management office responsible for such procurement, and the program manager of such program office shall be responsible for the following:

(1) Surveying components of the Department for the cyber data products and services needs of such components.

(2) Conducting market research of cyber data products and services.

(3) Developing or facilitating development of requirements, both independently and through consultation with components, for the acquisition of cyber data products and services.

(4) Developing and instituting model contract language for the acquisition of cyber data products and services, including contract language that facilitates components' requirements for ingesting, sharing, using and reusing, structuring, and analyzing data derived from such products and services.

(5) Conducting procurement of cyber data products and services on behalf of the Department of Defense, including negotiating contracts with a fixed number of licenses based on aggregate component demand and negotiation of extensible contracts.

(6) Carrying out the responsibilities specified in paragraphs (1) through (5) with respect to the cyber data products and services needs of the Cyberspace Operations Forces, such as cyber data products and services germane to cyberspace topology and identification of adversary threat activity and infrastructure, including—

(A) facilitating the development of cyber data products and services requirements for the Cyberspace Operations Forces, conducting market research regarding the future cyber data products and services needs of the Cyberspace Operations Forces, and conducting acquisitions pursuant to such requirements and market research;

(B) coordinating cyber data products and services acquisition and management activities with Joint Cyber Warfighting Architecture acquisition and management activities, including activities germane to data storage, data management, and development of analytics;

(C) implementing relevant Department of Defense and United States Cyber Command policy germane to acquisition of cyber data products and services;

(D) leading or informing the integration of relevant datasets and services, including Government-produced threat data, commercial cyber threat information, collateral telemetry data, topology-relevant data, sensor data, and partner-provided data; and

(E) facilitating the development of tradecraft and operational workflows based on relevant cyber data products and services.

(b) COORDINATION.— In implementing this section, each

component of the Department of Defense shall coordinate its cyber data products and services requirements and potential procurement plans relating to such products and services with the program management office established pursuant to subsection (a) so as to enable such office to determine if satisfying such requirements or procurement of such products and services on an enterprise-wide basis would serve the best interests of the Department.

(c) PROHIBITION.— Beginning not later than 540 days after the date of the enactment of this Act, no component of the Department of Defense may independently procure a cyber data product or service that has been procured by the program management office established pursuant to subsection (a), unless—

(1) such component is able to procure such product or service at a lower per-unit price than that available through such office; or

(2) such office has approved such independent purchase.

(d) EXCEPTION.— United States Cyber Command and the National Security Agency may conduct joint procurements of products and services, including cyber data products and services, except that the requirements of subsections (b) and (c) shall not apply to the National Security Agency.

(e) DEFINITION.— In this section, the term "cyber data products and services" means commercially-available datasets and analytic services germane to offensive cyber, defensive cyber, and DODIN operations, including products and services that provide technical data, indicators, and analytic services relating to the targets, infrastructure, tools, and tactics, techniques, and procedures of cyber threats.

SEC. 1522. [10 U.S.C. 4571 note] LEGACY INFORMATION TECHNOLOGIES AND SYSTEMS ACCOUNTABILITY.

(a) IN GENERAL.— Not later than 270 days after the date of the enactment of this Act, the Secretaries of the Army, Navy, and Air Force shall each initiate efforts to identify legacy applications, software, and information technology within their respective Departments and eliminate any such application, software, or information technology that is no longer required.

(b) SPECIFICATIONS.— To carry out subsection (a), that Secretaries of the Army, Navy, and Air Force shall each document the following:

(1) An identification of the applications, software, and information technologies that are considered active or operational, but which are judged to no longer be required by the respective Department.

(2) Information relating to the sources of funding for the applications, software, and information technologies identified pursuant to paragraph (1).

(3) An identification of the senior official responsible for each such application, software, or information technology.

(4) A plan to discontinue use and funding for each such application, software, or information technology.

(c) EXEMPTION.— Any effort substantially similar to that described in subsections (a) and (b) that is being carried out by the Secretary of the Army, Navy, or Air Force as of the date of the enactment of this Act and completed not later 180 days after such date shall be treated as satisfying the requirements under such subsections.

(d) REPORT.— Not later than 270 days after the date of the enactment of this Act, the Secretaries of the Army, Navy, and Air Force shall each submit to the congressional defense committees the documentation required under subsection (b).

SEC. 1523. UPDATE RELATING TO RESPONSIBILITIES OF CHIEF INFORMATION OFFICER.

Paragraph (1) of section 142(b) of title 10, United States Code, is amended—

(1) in subparagraphs (A), (B), and (C), by striking "(other than with respect to business management)" each place it appears; and

(2) by amending subparagraph (D) to read as follows:

"(D) exercises authority, direction, and control over the Activities of the Cybersecurity Directorate, or any successor organization, of the National Security Agency, funded through the Information Systems Security Program;"

SEC. 1524. [10 U.S.C. 2224 note] PROTECTIVE DOMAIN NAME SYSTEM

WITHIN THE DEPARTMENT OF DEFENSE.

(a) IN GENERAL.— Not later than 120 days after the date of the enactment of this Act, the Secretary of Defense shall ensure each component of the Department of Defense uses a Protective Domain Name System (PDNS) instantiation offered by the Department.

(b) EXEMPTIONS.— The Secretary of Defense may exempt a component of the Department from using a PDNS instantiation for any reason except with respect to cost or technical application.

(c) REPORT TO CONGRESS.— Not later than 150 days after the date of the enactment of this Act, the Secretary of Defense shall submit to the congressional defense committees a report that includes information relating to—

(1) each component of the Department of Defense that uses a PDNS instantiation offered by the Department;

(2) each component exempt from using a PDNS instantiation pursuant to subsection (b); and

(3) efforts to ensure that each PDNS instantiation offered by the Department connects and shares relevant and timely data.

SEC. 1525. CYBERSECURITY OF WEAPON SYSTEMS.

Section 1640 of the National Defense Authorization Act for Fiscal Year 2018 (Public Law 115-91; 10 U.S.C. 2224 note), is amended by adding at the end the following new subsection:

"(f) ANNUAL REPORTS.— Not later than August 30, 2022, and annually thereafter through 2024, the Secretary of Defense shall provide to the congressional defense committees a report on the work of the Program, including information relating to staffing and accomplishments.".

SEC. 1526. ASSESSMENT OF CONTROLLED UNCLASSIFIED INFORMATION PROGRAM.

Section 1648 of the National Defense Authorization Act for Fiscal Year 2020 (Public Law 116-92; 10 U.S.C. 2224 note), is amended—

(1) in subsection (a), by striking "February 1, 2020" and inserting "180 days after the date of the enactment of the National Defense Authorization Act for Fiscal Year 2022"; and

(2) in subsection (b), by amending paragraph (4) to read as

follows:

"(4) Definitions for 'Controlled Unclassified Information' (CUI) and 'For Official Use Only' (FOUO), policies regarding protecting information designated as either of such, and an explanation of the 'DoD CUI Program' and Department of Defense compliance with the responsibilities specified in Department of Defense Instruction (DoDI) 5200.48, 'Controlled Unclassified Information (CUI),' including the following:

"(A) The extent to which the Department of Defense is identifying whether information is CUI via a contracting vehicle and marking documents, material, and media containing such information in a clear and consistent manner.

"(B) Recommended regulatory or policy changes to ensure consistency and clarity in CUI identification and marking requirements.

"(C) Circumstances under which commercial information is considered CUI, and any impacts to the commercial supply chain associated with security and marking requirements pursuant to this paragraph.

"(D) Benefits and drawbacks of requiring all CUI to be marked with a unique CUI legend, versus requiring that all data marked with an appropriate restricted legend be handled as CUI.

"(E) The extent to which the Department of Defense clearly delineates Federal Contract Information (FCI) from CUI.

"(F) Examples or scenarios to illustrate information that is and is not CUI."

.

SEC. 1527. [10 U.S.C. 2224 note] CYBER DATA MANAGEMENT.

(a) IN GENERAL.— The Commander of United States Cyber Command and the Secretaries of the military departments, in coordination with the Principal Cyber Advisor to the Secretary, the Chief Information Officer and the Chief Data Officer of the Department of Defense, and the Chairman of the Joint Chiefs of Staff, shall—

(1) access, acquire, and use mission-relevant data to support offensive cyber, defensive cyber, and DODIN operations from the intelligence community, other elements of the Department of Defense, and the private sector;

(2) develop policy, processes, and operating procedures governing the access, ingest, structure, storage, analysis, and combination of mission-relevant data, including—

(A) intelligence data;

(B) internet traffic, topology, and activity data;

(C) cyber threat information;

(D) Department of Defense Information Network sensor, tool, routing infrastructure, and endpoint data; and

(E) other data management and analytic platforms pertinent to United States Cyber Command missions that align with the principles of Joint All Domain Command and Control;

(3) pilot efforts to develop operational workflows and tactics, techniques, and procedures for the operational use of mission-relevant data by the Cyberspace Operations Forces; and

(4) evaluate data management platforms used to carry out paragraphs (1), (2), and (3) to ensure such platforms operate consistently with the Deputy Secretary of Defense's Data Decrees signed on May 5, 2021.

(b) ROLES AND RESPONSIBILITIES.—

(1) IN GENERAL.— Not later than 270 days after the date of the enactment of this Act, the Commander of United States Cyber Command and the Secretaries of the military departments, in coordination with the Principal Cyber Advisor to the Secretary, the Chief Information Officer and Chief Data Officer of the Department of Defense, and the Chairman of the Joint Chiefs of Staff, shall establish the specific roles and responsibilities of the following in implementing each of the tasks required under subsection (a):

(A) United States Cyber Command.

(B) Program offices responsible for the components of the Joint Cyber Warfighting Architecture.

(C) The military services.

(D) Entities in the Office of the Secretary of Defense.

(E) Any other program office, headquarters element, or operational component newly instantiated or determined relevant by the Secretary.

(2) BRIEFING.— Not later than 300 days after the date of the enactment of this Act, the Secretary of Defense shall provide to the congressional defense committees a briefing on the roles and responsibilities established under paragraph (1).

SEC. 1528. [10 U.S.C. 2224 note] ZERO TRUST STRATEGY, PRINCIPLES, MODEL ARCHITECTURE, AND IMPLEMENTATION PLANS.

(a) IN GENERAL.— Not later than 270 days after the date of the enactment of this Act, the Chief Information Officer of the Department of Defense and the Commander of United States Cyber Command shall jointly develop a zero trust strategy, principles, and a model architecture to be implemented across the Department of Defense Information Network, including classified networks, operational technology, and weapon systems.

(b) STRATEGY, PRINCIPLES, AND MODEL ARCHITECTURE ELEMENTS.— The zero trust strategy, principles, and model architecture required under subsection (a) shall include, at a minimum, the following elements:

(1) Prioritized policies and procedures for establishing implementations of mature zero trust enabling capabilities within on-premises, hybrid, and pure cloud environments, including access control policies that determine which persona or device shall have access to which resources and the following:

(A) Identity, credential, and access management.

(B) Macro and micro network segmentation, whether in virtual, logical, or physical environments.

(C) Traffic inspection.

(D) Application security and containment.

(E) Transmission, ingest, storage, and real-time analysis of cybersecurity metadata endpoints, networks, and storage devices.

(F) Data management, data rights management, and access controls.

(G) End-to-end encryption.

(H) User access and behavioral monitoring, logging, and analysis.

(I) Data loss detection and prevention methodologies.

(J) Least privilege, including system or network administrator privileges.

(K) Endpoint cybersecurity, including secure host, endpoint detection and response, and comply-to-connect requirements.

(L) Automation and orchestration.

(M) Configuration management of virtual machines, devices, servers, routers, and similar to be maintained on a single virtual device approved list (VDL).

(2) Policies specific to operational technology, critical data, infrastructures, weapon systems, and classified networks.

(3) Specification of enterprise-wide acquisitions of capabilities conducted or to be conducted pursuant to the policies referred to in paragraph (2).

(4) Specification of standard zero trust principles supporting reference architectures and metrics-based assessment plan.

(5) Roles, responsibilities, functions, and operational workflows of zero trust cybersecurity architecture and information technology personnel—

(A) at combatant commands, military services, and defense agencies; and

(B) Joint Forces Headquarters-Department of Defense Information Network.

(c) ARCHITECTURE DEVELOPMENT AND IMPLEMENTATION.— In developing and implementing the zero trust strategy, principles, and model architecture required under subsection (a), the Chief Information Officer of the Department of Defense and the Commander of United States Cyber Command shall—

(1) coordinate with—

(A) the Principal Cyber Advisor to the Secretary of Defense;

(B) the Director of the National Security Agency Cybersecurity Directorate;

(C) the Director of the Defense Advanced Research Projects Agency;

(D) the Chief Information Officer of each military service;

(E) the Commanders of the cyber components of the military services;

(F) the Principal Cyber Advisor of each military service;

(G) the Chairman of the Joints Chiefs of Staff; and

(H) any other component of the Department of Defense as determined by the Chief Information Officer and the Commander;

(2) assess the utility of the Joint Regional Security Stacks, automated continuous endpoint monitoring program, assured compliance assessment solution, and each of the defenses at the Internet Access Points for their relevance and applicability to the zero trust architecture and opportunities for integration or divestment;

(3) employ all available resources, including online training, leveraging commercially available zero trust training material, and other Federal agency training, where feasible, to implement cybersecurity training on zero trust at the—

(A) executive level;

(B) cybersecurity professional or implementer level; and

(C) general knowledge levels for Department of Defense users;

(4) facilitate cyber protection team and cybersecurity service provider threat hunting and discovery of novel adversary activity;

(5) assess and implement means to effect Joint Force Headquarters-Department of Defense Information Network's automated command and control of the entire Department of Defense Information Network;

(6) assess the potential of and, as appropriate, encourage, use of third-party cybersecurity-as-a-service models;

(7) engage with and conduct outreach to industry, academia, international partners, and other departments and

agencies of the Federal Government on issues relating to deployment of zero trust architectures;

(8) assess the current Comply-to-Connect Plan; and

(9) review past and conduct additional pilots to guide development, including—

(A) utilization of networks designated for testing and accreditation under section 1658 of the National Defense Authorization Act for Fiscal Year 2020 (Public Law 116-92; 10 U.S.C. 2224 note);

(B) use of automated red team products for assessment of pilot architectures; and

(C) accreditation of piloted cybersecurity products for enterprise use in accordance with the findings on enterprise accreditation standards conducted pursuant to section 1654 of such Act (Public Law 116-92).

(d) IMPLEMENTATION PLANS.—

(1) IN GENERAL.— Not later than one year after the finalization of the zero trust strategy, principles, and model architecture required under subsection (a), the head of each military department and the head of each component of the Department of Defense shall transmit to the Chief Information Officer of the Department and the Commander of Joint Forces Headquarters-Department of Defense Information Network a draft plan to implement such zero trust strategy, principles, and model architecture across the networks of their respective components and military departments.

(2) ELEMENTS.— Each implementation plan transmitted pursuant to paragraph (1) shall include, at a minimum, the following:

(A) Specific acquisitions, implementations, instrumentations, and operational workflows to be implemented across unclassified and classified networks, operational technology, and weapon systems.

(B) A detailed schedule with target milestones and required expenditures.

(C) Interim and final metrics, including a phase migration plan.

(D) Identification of additional funding, authorities,

and policies, as may be required.

(E) Requested waivers, exceptions to Department of Defense policy, and expected delays.

(e) IMPLEMENTATION OVERSIGHT.—

(1) IN GENERAL.— The Chief Information Officer of the Department of Defense shall—

(A) assess the implementation plans transmitted pursuant to subsection (d)(1) for—

(i) adequacy and responsiveness to the zero trust strategy, principles, and model architecture required under subsection (a); and

(ii) appropriate use of enterprise-wide acquisitions;

(B) ensure, at a high level, the interoperability and compatibility of individual components' Solutions Architectures, including the leveraging of enterprise capabilities where appropriate through standards derivation, policy, and reviews;

(C) use the annual investment guidance of the Chief to ensure appropriate implementation of such plans, including appropriate use of enterprise-wide acquisitions;

(D) track use of waivers and exceptions to policy;

(E) use the Cybersecurity Scorecard to track and drive implementation of Department components; and

(F) leverage the authorities of the Commander of Joint Forces Headquarters-Department of Defense Information Network and the Director of the Defense Information Systems Agency to begin implementation of such zero trust strategy, principles, and model architecture.

(2) ASSESSMENTS OF FUNDING.— Not later than March 31, 2024, and annually thereafter, each Principal Cyber Advisor of a military service shall include in the annual budget certification of such military service, as required by section 392a(c)(4) of title 10, United States Code, an assessment of the adequacy of funding requested for each proposed budget for the purposes of carrying out the implementation plan for such military service under subsection (d)(1).

(f) INITIAL BRIEFINGS.—

(1) ON MODEL ARCHITECTURE.— Not later than 90 days after finalizing the zero trust strategy, principles, and model architecture required under subsection (a), the Chief Information Officer of the Department of Defense and the Commander of Joint Forces Headquarters-Department of Defense Information Network shall provide to the congressional defense committees a briefing on such zero trust strategy, principles, and model architecture.

(2) ON IMPLEMENTATION PLANS.— Not later than 90 days after the receipt by the Chief Information Officer of the Department of Defense of an implementation plan transmitted pursuant to subsection (d)(1), the secretary of a military department, in the case of an implementation plan pertaining to a military department or a military service, or the Chief Information Officer of the Department, in the case of an implementation plan pertaining to a remaining component of the Department, as the case may be, shall provide to the congressional defense committees a briefing on such implementation plan.

(g) ANNUAL BRIEFINGS.— Effective February 1, 2022, at each of the annual cybersecurity budget review briefings of the Chief Information Officer of the Department of Defense and the military services for congressional staff, until January 1, 2030, the Chief Information Officer and the head of each of the military services shall provide updates on the implementation in their respective networks of the zero trust strategy, principles, and model architecture.

SEC. 1529. [10 U.S.C. 2224 note] DEMONSTRATION PROGRAM FOR AUTOMATED SECURITY VALIDATION TOOLS.

(a) DEMONSTRATION PROGRAM REQUIRED.— Not later than October 1, 2024, the Chief Information Officer of the Department of Defense, acting through the Director of the Defense Information Systems Agency of the Department, shall complete a demonstration program to demonstrate and assess an automated security validation capability to assist the Department by—

(1) mitigating cyber hygiene challenges;

(2) supporting ongoing efforts of the Department to assess weapon systems resiliency;

(3) quantifying enterprise security effectiveness of

enterprise security controls, to inform future acquisition decisions of the Department;

(4) assisting portfolio managers with balancing capability costs and capability coverage of the threat landscape; and

(5) supporting the Department's Cybersecurity Analysis and Review threat framework.

(b) CONSIDERATIONS.— In developing capabilities for the demonstration program required under subsection (a), the Chief Information Officer shall consider—

(1) integration into automated security validation tools of advanced commercially available threat intelligence;

(2) metrics and scoring of security controls;

(3) cyber analysis, cyber campaign tracking, and cybersecurity information sharing;

(4) integration into cybersecurity enclaves and existing cybersecurity controls of security instrumentation and testing capability;

(5) endpoint sandboxing; and

(6) use of actual adversary attack methodologies.

(c) COORDINATION WITH MILITARY SERVICES.— In carrying out the demonstration program required under subsection (a), the Chief Information Officer, acting through the Director of the Defense Information Systems Agency, shall coordinate demonstration program activities with complementary efforts on-going within the military services, defense agencies, and field agencies.

(d) INDEPENDENT CAPABILITY ASSESSMENT.— In carrying out the demonstration program required under subsection (a), the Chief Information Officer, acting through the Director of the Defense Information Systems Agency and in coordination with the Director, Operational Test and Evaluation, shall perform operational testing to evaluate the operational effectiveness, suitability, and cybersecurity of the capabilities developed under the demonstration program.

(e) BRIEFING.—

(1) INITIAL BRIEFING.— Not later than April 1, 2022, the Chief Information Officer shall brief the Committee on Armed Services of the Senate and the Committee on Armed Services of the House of Representatives on the plans and status of the

Chief Information Officer with respect to the demonstration program required under subsection (a).

(2) FINAL BRIEFING.— Not later than October 31, 2024, the Chief Information Officer shall brief the Committee on Armed Services of the Senate and the Committee on Armed Services of the House of Representatives on the results and findings of the Chief Information Officer with respect to the demonstration program required under subsection (a).

SEC. 1530. IMPROVEMENTS TO CONSORTIUM OF UNIVERSITIES TO ADVISE SECRETARY OF DEFENSE ON CYBERSECURITY MATTERS.

Section 1659 of the National Defense Authorization Act for Fiscal Year 2020 (Public Law 116-92; 10 U.S.C. 391 note) is amended—

(1) in subsection (a)—

(A) in the matter preceding paragraph (1), by striking "one or more consortia" and inserting "a consortium"; and

(B) in paragraph (1), by striking "or consortia";

(2) in subsection (b), by striking "or consortia";

(3) in subsection (c)—

(A) by amending paragraph (1) to read as follows:

"(1) DESIGNATION OF ADMINISTRATIVE CHAIR.— The Secretary of Defense shall designate the National Defense University College of Information and Cyberspace to function as the administrative chair of the consortium established pursuant to subsection (a)."

;

(B) by striking paragraph (2);

(C) by redesignating paragraphs (3) and (4) as paragraphs (2) and (3), respectively;

(D) in paragraph (2), as so redesignated—

(i) in the matter preceding subparagraph (A)—

(I) by striking "Each administrative" and inserting "The administrative"; and

(II) by striking "a consortium" and inserting "the consortium"; and

(ii) in subparagraph (A), by striking "for the term

specified by the Secretary under paragraph (1)"; and

(E) by amending paragraph (3), as so redesignated, to read as follows:

"(3) EXECUTIVE COMMITTEE.— The Secretary, in consultation with the administrative chair, may form an executive committee for the consortium that is comprised of representatives of the Federal Government to assist the chair with the management and functions of the consortium."

; and

(4) by amending subsection (d) to read as follows:

"(d) CONSULTATION.— The Secretary shall meet with such members of the consortium as the Secretary considers appropriate, not less frequently than twice each year or at such periodicity as is agreed to by the Secretary and the consortium."

.

SEC. 1531. DIGITAL DEVELOPMENT INFRASTRUCTURE PLAN AND WORKING GROUP.

(a) PLAN REQUIRED.— Not later than one year after the date of the enactment of this Act, the Secretary of Defense, acting through the working group established under subsection (d)(1), shall develop a plan for the establishment of a modern information technology infrastructure that supports state of the art tools and modern processes to enable effective and efficient development, testing, fielding, and continuous updating of artificial intelligence-capabilities.

(b) CONTENTS OF PLAN.— The plan developed pursuant to subsection (a) shall include at a minimum the following:

(1) A technical plan and guidance for necessary technical investments in the infrastructure described in subsection (a) that address critical technical issues, including issues relating to common interfaces, authentication, applications, platforms, software, hardware, and data infrastructure.

(2) A governance structure, together with associated policies and guidance, to support the implementation throughout the Department of such plan.

(3) Identification and minimum viable instantiations of

prototypical development and platform environments with such infrastructure, including enterprise data sets assembled under subsection (e).

(c) HARMONIZATION WITH DEPARTMENTAL EFFORTS.— The plan developed pursuant to subsection (a) shall include a description of the aggregated and consolidated financial and personnel requirements necessary to implement each of the following Department of Defense documents:

(1) The Department of Defense Digital Modernization Strategy.

(2) The Department of Defense Data Strategy.

(3) The Department of Defense Cloud Strategy.

(4) The Department of Defense Software Modernization Strategy.

(5) The Department-wide software science and technology strategy required under section 255 of the National Defense Authorization Act for Fiscal Year 2020 (10 U.S.C. 2223a note).

(6) The Department of Defense Artificial Intelligence Data Initiative.

(7) The Joint All-Domain Command and Control Strategy.

(8) Such other documents as the Secretary determines appropriate.

(d) WORKING GROUP.—

(1) ESTABLISHMENT.— Not later than 60 days after the date of the enactment of this Act, the Secretary of Defense shall establish a working group on digital development infrastructure implementation to develop the plan required under subsection (a).

(2) MEMBERSHIP.— The working group established under paragraph (1) shall be composed of individuals selected by the Secretary of Defense to represent each of the following:

(A) The Office of Chief Data Officer (CDO).

(B) The Component Offices of Chief Information Officer and Chief Digital Officer.

(C) The office of the official designated under subsection (b) of section 238 of the John S. McCain National Defense Authorization Act for Fiscal Year 2019

(Public Law 115–232; 10 U.S.C. note prec. 4061).

(D) The Office of the Under Secretary of Defense for Research & Engineering (OUSD (R&E)).

(E) The Office of the Under Secretary of Defense for Acquisition & Sustainment (OUSD (A&S)).

(F) The Office of the Under Secretary of Defense for Intelligence & Security (OUSD (I&S)).

(G) Service Acquisition Executives.

(H) The Office of the Director of Operational Test and Evaluation (DOT&E).

(I) The office of the Director of the Defense Advanced Research Projects Agency (DARPA).

(J) Digital development infrastructure programs, including the appropriate activities of the military services and defense agencies.

(K) Such other officials of the Department of Defense as the Secretary determines appropriate.

(3) CHAIRPERSON.— The chairperson of the working group established under paragraph (1) shall be the Chief Information Officer of the Department of Defense, or such other official as the Secretary of Defense considers appropriate.

(4) CONSULTATION.— The working group shall consult with such experts outside of the Department of Defense as the working group considers necessary to develop the plan required under subsection (a).

(e) STRATEGIC DATA NODE.— To enable efficient access to enterprise data sets referred to in subsection (b)(3) for users with authorized access, the Secretary of Defense shall assemble such enterprise data sets in the following areas:

(1) Human resources.

(2) Budget and finance.

(3) Acquisition.

(4) Logistics.

(5) Real estate.

(6) Health care.

(7) Such other areas as the Secretary considers appropriate.

(f) REPORT.— Not later than 180 days after the date of the enactment of this Act, the Secretary of Defense shall submit to the congressional defense committees a report on the status of the development of the plan required under subsection (a).

SEC. 1532. [10 U.S.C. 2191 note] STUDY REGARDING ESTABLISHMENT WITHIN THE DEPARTMENT OF DEFENSE OF A DESIGNATED CENTRAL PROGRAM OFFICE TO OVERSEE ACADEMIC ENGAGEMENT PROGRAMS RELATING TO ESTABLISHING CYBER TALENT ACROSS THE DEPARTMENT.

(a) IN GENERAL.— Not later than 270 days after the date of the enactment of this Act, the Secretary of Defense shall submit to the congressional defense committees a study regarding the need, feasibility, and advisability of establishing within the Department of Defense a designated central program office responsible for overseeing covered academic engagement programs across the Department. Such study shall examine the following:

(1) Whether the Department's cyber-focused academic engagement needs more coherence, additional coordination, or improved management, and whether a designated central program office would provide such benefits.

(2) How such a designated central program office would coordinate and harmonize Department programs relating to covered academic engagement programs.

(3) Metrics such office would use to measure the effectiveness of covered academic engagement programs.

(4) Whether such an office is necessary to serve as an identifiable entry point to the Department by the academic community.

(5) Whether the cyber discipline with respect to academic engagement should be treated separately from other STEM fields.

(6) How such an office would interact with the consortium universities (established pursuant to section 1659 of the National Defense Authorization Act for Fiscal Year 2020 (10 U.S.C. 391 note)) to assist the Secretary on cybersecurity matters.

(7) Whether the establishment of such an office would have an estimated net savings for the Department.

(b) CONSULTATION.— In conducting the study required under subsection (a), the Secretary of Defense shall consult with and solicit recommendations from academic institutions and stakeholders, including primary, secondary, and post-secondary educational institutions.

(c) DETERMINATION.—

(1) IN GENERAL.— Upon completion of the study required under subsection (a), the Secretary of Defense shall make a determination regarding the establishment within the Department of Defense of a designated central program office responsible for overseeing covered academic engagement programs across the Department.

(2) IMPLEMENTATION.— If the Secretary of Defense makes an affirmative determination in accordance with paragraph (1), the Secretary shall establish within the Department of Defense a designated central program office responsible for overseeing covered academic programs across the Department. Not later than 180 days after such a determination, the Secretary shall promulgate such rules and regulations as are necessary to so establish such an office.

(3) NEGATIVE DETERMINATION.— If the Secretary of Defense makes a negative determination in accordance with paragraph (1), the Secretary shall submit to the congressional defense committees notice of such determination, together with a justification for such determination. Such justification shall include—

(A) how the Secretary intends to coordinate and harmonize covered academic engagement programs; and

(B) measures to determine effectiveness of covered academic engagement programs absent a designated central program office responsible for overseeing covered academic programs across the Department.

(d) REPORT.— Not later than 270 days after the date of the enactment of this Act, the Secretary of Defense shall submit to the congressional defense committees a report that updates the matters required for inclusion in the reports required pursuant to section 1649 of the National Defense Authorization Act for Fiscal Year 2020 (Public Law 116-92) and section 1726(c) of the William M. (Mac) Thornberry National Defense Authorization Act for Fiscal

Year 2021 (Public Law 116-283).

(e) DEFINITION.— In this section, the term "covered academic engagement program" means each of the following:

(1) Primary, secondary, or post-secondary education programs with a cyber focus.

(2) Recruitment or retention programs for Department of Defense cyberspace personnel, including scholarship programs.

(3) Academic partnerships focused on establishing cyber talent.

(4) Cyber enrichment programs.

SEC. 1533. REPORT ON THE CYBERSECURITY MATURITY MODEL CERTIFICATION PROGRAM.

(a) REPORT REQUIRED.— Not later than 90 days after the date of the enactment of this Act, the Secretary of Defense shall submit to the Committee on Armed Services of the Senate and the Committee on Armed Services of the House of Representatives a report on the plans and recommendations of the Secretary for the Cyber Maturity Model Certification program.

(b) CONTENTS.— The report submitted under subsection (a) shall include the following:

(1) The programmatic changes required in the Cyber Maturity Model Certification program to address the plans and recommendations of the Secretary of Defense referred to in such subsection.

(2) The strategy of the Secretary for rulemaking for such program and the process for the Cybersecurity Maturity Model Certification rule.

(3) The budget and resources required to support such program.

(4) A plan for communication and coordination with the defense industrial base regarding such program.

(5) The coordination needed within the Department of Defense and between Federal agencies for such program.

(6) The applicability of such program requirements to universities and academic partners of the Department.

(7) A plan for communication and coordination with such universities and academic partners regarding such program.

(8) Plans and explicit public announcement of processes for reimbursement of cybersecurity compliance expenses for small and non-traditional businesses in the defense industrial base.

(9) Plans for ensuring that persons seeking a Department contract for the first time are not required to expend funds to acquire cybersecurity capabilities and a certification required to perform under a contract as a precondition for bidding on such a contract without reimbursement in the event that such persons do not receive a contract award.

(10) Clarification of roles and responsibilities of prime contractors for assisting and managing cybersecurity performance of subcontractors.

(11) Such additional matters as the Secretary considers appropriate.

SEC. 1534. DEADLINE FOR REPORTS ON ASSESSMENT OF CYBER RESILIENCY OF NUCLEAR COMMAND AND CONTROL SYSTEM.

Subsection (c) of section 499 of title 10, United States Code, is amended—

(1) in the heading, by striking "Report" and inserting "Reports";

(2) in paragraph (1), in the matter preceding subparagraph (A)—

(A) by striking "The Commanders" and inserting "For each assessment conducted under subsection (a), the Commanders"; and

(B) by striking "the assessment required by subsection (a)" and inserting "the assessment";

(3) in paragraph (2), by striking "the report" and inserting "each report"; and

(4) in paragraph (3)—

(A) by striking "The Secretary" and inserting "Not later than 90 days after the date of the submission of a report under paragraph (1), the Secretary"; and

(B) by striking "required by paragraph (1)".

Subtitle C—Matters Related to Federal Cybersecurity

SEC. 1541. CAPABILITIES OF THE CYBERSECURITY AND INFRASTRUCTURE SECURITY AGENCY TO IDENTIFY THREATS TO INDUSTRIAL CONTROL SYSTEMS.

(a) IN GENERAL.— Section 2209 of the Homeland Security Act of 2002 (6 U.S.C. 659) is amended—

(1) in subsection (e)(1)—

(A) in subparagraph (G), by striking "and;" after the semicolon;

(B) in subparagraph (H), by inserting "and" after the semicolon; and

(C) by adding at the end the following new subparagraph:

"(I) activities of the Center address the security of both information technology and operational technology, including industrial control systems;"; and

(2) by adding at the end the following new subsection:

"(q) INDUSTRIAL CONTROL SYSTEMS.— The Director shall maintain capabilities to identify and address threats and vulnerabilities to products and technologies intended for use in the automated control of critical infrastructure processes. In carrying out this subsection, the Director shall—

"(1) lead Federal Government efforts, in consultation with Sector Risk Management Agencies, as appropriate, to identify and mitigate cybersecurity threats to industrial control systems, including supervisory control and data acquisition systems;

"(2) maintain threat hunting and incident response capabilities to respond to industrial control system cybersecurity risks and incidents;

"(3) provide cybersecurity technical assistance to industry end-users, product manufacturers, Sector Risk Management Agencies, other Federal agencies, and other industrial control system stakeholders to identify, evaluate, assess, and mitigate vulnerabilities;

"(4) collect, coordinate, and provide vulnerability information to the industrial control systems community by, as appropriate, working closely with security researchers, industry end-users, product manufacturers,

Sector Risk Management Agencies, other Federal agencies, and other industrial control systems stakeholders; and

"(5) conduct such other efforts and assistance as the Secretary determines appropriate.".

(b) REPORT TO CONGRESS.— Not later than 180 days after the date of the enactment of this Act and every six months thereafter during the subsequent 4-year period, the Director of the Cybersecurity and Infrastructure Security Agency of the Department of Homeland Security shall provide to the Committee on Homeland Security of the House of Representatives and the Committee on Homeland Security and Governmental Affairs of the Senate a briefing on the industrial control systems capabilities of the Agency under section 2209 of the Homeland Security Act of 2002 (6 U.S.C. 659), as amended by subsection (a).

(c) GAO REVIEW.— Not later than two years after the date of the enactment of this Act, the Comptroller General of the United States shall review implementation of the requirements of subsections (e)(1)(I) and (p) of section 2209 of the Homeland Security Act of 2002 (6 U.S.C. 659), as amended by subsection (a), and submit to the Committee on Homeland Security of the House of Representatives and the Committee on Homeland Security and Governmental Affairs of the Senate a report that includes findings and recommendations relating to such implementation. Such report shall include information on the following:

(1) Any interagency coordination challenges to the ability of the Director of the Cybersecurity and Infrastructure Security Agency of the Department of Homeland Security to lead Federal efforts to identify and mitigate cybersecurity threats to industrial control systems pursuant to subsection (p)(1) of such section.

(2) The degree to which the Agency has adequate capacity, expertise, and resources to carry out threat hunting and incident response capabilities to mitigate cybersecurity threats to industrial control systems pursuant to subsection (p)(2) of such section, as well as additional resources that would be needed to close any operational gaps in such capabilities.

(3) The extent to which industrial control system stakeholders sought cybersecurity technical assistance from the Agency pursuant to subsection (p)(3) of such section, and the utility and effectiveness of such technical assistance.

(4) The degree to which the Agency works with security researchers and other industrial control systems stakeholders, pursuant to subsection (p)(4) of such section, to provide vulnerability information to the industrial control systems community.

SEC. 1542. CYBERSECURITY VULNERABILITIES.

Section 2209 of the Homeland Security Act of 2002 (6 U.S.C. 659) is amended—

(1) in subsection (a)—

(A) by redesignating paragraphs (4) through (8) as paragraphs (5) through (9), respectively; and

(B) by inserting after paragraph (3) the following new paragraph:

"(4) the term 'cybersecurity vulnerability' has the meaning given the term 'security vulnerability' in section 102 of the Cybersecurity Information Sharing Act of 2015 (6 U.S.C. 1501);."

(2) in subsection (c)—

(A) in paragraph (5)—

(i) in subparagraph (A), by striking "and" after the semicolon at the end;

(ii) by redesignating subparagraph (B) as subparagraph (C);

(iii) by inserting after subparagraph (A) the following new subparagraph:

"(B) sharing mitigation protocols to counter cybersecurity vulnerabilities pursuant to subsection (n), as appropriate; and"; and

(iv) in subparagraph (C), as so redesignated, by inserting "and mitigation protocols to counter cybersecurity vulnerabilities in accordance with subparagraph (B), as appropriate," before "with Federal";

(B) in paragraph (7)(C), by striking "sharing" and inserting "share"; and

(C) in paragraph (9), by inserting "mitigation protocols to counter cybersecurity vulnerabilities, as appropriate," after "measures,";

(3) by redesignating subsection (o) as subsection (p); and

(4) by inserting after subsection (n) following new subsection:

"(o) PROTOCOLS TO COUNTER CERTAIN CYBERSECURITY VULNERABILITIES.— The Director may, as appropriate, identify, develop, and disseminate actionable protocols to mitigate cybersecurity vulnerabilities to information systems and industrial control systems, including in circumstances in which such vulnerabilities exist because software or hardware is no longer supported by a vendor.".

SEC. 1543. REPORT ON CYBERSECURITY VULNERABILITIES.

(a) REPORT.— Not later than one year after the date of the enactment of this Act, the Director of the Cybersecurity and Infrastructure Security Agency of the Department of Homeland Security shall submit to the Committee on Homeland Security of the House of Representatives and the Committee on Homeland Security and Governmental Affairs of the Senate a report on how the Agency carries out subsection (n) of section 2209 of the Homeland Security Act of 2002 to coordinate vulnerability disclosures, including disclosures of cybersecurity vulnerabilities (as such term is defined in such section), and subsection (o) of such section to disseminate actionable protocols to mitigate cybersecurity vulnerabilities to information systems and industrial control systems, that include the following:

(1) A description of the policies and procedures relating to the coordination of vulnerability disclosures.

(2) A description of the levels of activity in furtherance of such subsections (n) and (o) of such section 2209.

(3) Any plans to make further improvements to how information provided pursuant to such subsections can be shared (as such term is defined in such section 2209) between the Department and industry and other stakeholders.

(4) Any available information on the degree to which such information was acted upon by industry and other stakeholders.

(5) A description of how privacy and civil liberties are preserved in the collection, retention, use, and sharing of

vulnerability disclosures.

(b) FORM.— The report required under subsection (b) shall be submitted in unclassified form but may contain a classified annex.

SEC. 1544. [6 U.S.C. 663 note] COMPETITION RELATING TO CYBERSECURITY VULNERABILITIES.

The Under Secretary for Science and Technology of the Department of Homeland Security, in consultation with the Director of the Cybersecurity and Infrastructure Security Agency of the Department, may establish an incentive-based program that allows industry, individuals, academia, and others to compete in identifying remediation solutions for cybersecurity vulnerabilities (as such term is defined in section 2209 of the Homeland Security Act of 2002) to information systems (as such term is defined in such section 2209) and industrial control systems, including supervisory control and data acquisition systems.

SEC. 1545. STRATEGY.

Section 2210 of the Homeland Security Act of 2002 (6 U.S.C. 660) is amended by adding at the end the following new subsection:

"(e) HOMELAND SECURITY STRATEGY TO IMPROVE THE CYBERSECURITY OF STATE, LOCAL, TRIBAL, AND TERRITORIAL GOVERNMENTS.—

"(1) IN GENERAL.—

"(A) REQUIREMENT.— Not later than one year after the date of the enactment of this subsection, the Secretary, acting through the Director, shall, in coordination with the heads of appropriate Federal agencies, State, local, Tribal, and territorial governments, and other stakeholders, as appropriate, develop and make publicly available a Homeland Security Strategy to Improve the Cybersecurity of State, Local, Tribal, and Territorial Governments.

"(B) RECOMMENDATIONS AND REQUIREMENTS.— The strategy required under subparagraph (A) shall provide recommendations relating to the ways in which the Federal Government should support and promote the ability of State, local, Tribal, and territorial governments to identify, mitigate against, protect against, detect, respond to, and recover from cybersecurity risks (as such term is defined in section 2209), cybersecurity threats, and incidents (as such term is defined in section 2209).

"(2) CONTENTS.— The strategy required under paragraph (1) shall—

"(A) identify capability gaps in the ability of State, local, Tribal, and territorial governments to identify, protect against, detect, respond to, and recover from cybersecurity risks, cybersecurity threats, incidents, and ransomware incidents;

"(B) identify Federal resources and capabilities that are available or could be made available to State, local, Tribal, and territorial governments to help those governments identify, protect against, detect, respond to, and recover from cybersecurity risks, cybersecurity threats, incidents, and ransomware incidents;

"(C) identify and assess the limitations of Federal resources and capabilities available to State, local, Tribal, and territorial governments to help those governments identify, protect against, detect, respond to, and recover from cybersecurity risks, cybersecurity threats, incidents, and ransomware incidents and make recommendations to address such limitations;

"(D) identify opportunities to improve the coordination of the Agency with Federal and non-Federal entities, such as the Multi-State Information Sharing and Analysis Center, to improve—

"(i) incident exercises, information sharing and incident notification procedures;

"(ii) the ability for State, local, Tribal, and territorial governments to voluntarily adapt and implement guidance in Federal binding operational directives; and

"(iii) opportunities to leverage Federal schedules for cybersecurity investments under section 502 of title 40, United States Code;

"(E) recommend new initiatives the Federal Government should undertake to improve the ability of State, local, Tribal, and territorial governments to identify, protect against, detect, respond to, and recover from cybersecurity risks, cybersecurity threats, incidents, and ransomware incidents;

"(F) set short-term and long-term goals that will improve the ability of State, local, Tribal, and territorial governments to identify, protect against, detect, respond to, and recover from cybersecurity risks, cybersecurity threats, incidents, and ransomware incidents; and

"(G) set dates, including interim benchmarks, as appropriate for State, local, Tribal, and territorial governments to establish baseline capabilities to identify, protect against, detect, respond to, and recover from cybersecurity risks, cybersecurity threats, incidents, and ransomware incidents.

"(3) CONSIDERATIONS.— In developing the strategy required under paragraph (1), the Director, in coordination with the heads of appropriate Federal agencies, State, local, Tribal, and territorial governments, and other stakeholders, as appropriate, shall consider—

"(A) lessons learned from incidents that have affected State, local, Tribal, and territorial governments, and exercises with Federal and non-Federal entities;

"(B) the impact of incidents that have affected State, local, Tribal, and territorial governments, including the resulting costs to such governments;

"(C) the information related to the interest and ability of state and non-state threat actors to compromise information systems (as such term is defined in section 102 of the Cybersecurity Act of 2015 (6 U.S.C. 1501)) owned or operated by State, local, Tribal, and territorial governments; and

"(D) emerging cybersecurity risks and cybersecurity threats to State, local, Tribal, and territorial governments resulting from the deployment of new technologies.

"(4) EXEMPTION.— Chapter 35 of title 44, United States Code (commonly known as the 'Paperwork Reduction Act'), shall not apply to any action to implement this subsection.".

SEC. 1546. CYBER INCIDENT RESPONSE PLAN.

Subsection (c) of section 2210 of the Homeland Security Act of 2002 (6 U.S.C. 660) is amended—

(1) by striking "regularly update" and inserting "update not less often than biennially"; and

(2) by adding at the end the following new sentence: "The Director, in consultation with relevant Sector Risk Management Agencies and the National Cyber Director, shall develop mechanisms to engage with stakeholders to educate such stakeholders regarding Federal Government cybersecurity roles and responsibilities for cyber incident response.".

SEC. 1547. [6 U.S.C. 665h] NATIONAL CYBER EXERCISE PROGRAM.

(a) IN GENERAL.— Subtitle A of title XXII of the Homeland Security Act of 2002 (6 U.S.C. 651 et seq.) is amended by adding at the end the following new section:

"SEC. 2220B. NATIONAL CYBER EXERCISE PROGRAM

"(a) ESTABLISHMENT OF PROGRAM.—

"(1) IN GENERAL.— There is established in the Agency the National Cyber Exercise Program (referred to in this section as the 'Exercise Program') to evaluate the National Cyber Incident Response Plan, and other related plans and strategies.

"(2) REQUIREMENTS.—

"(A) IN GENERAL.— The Exercise Program shall be—

"(i) based on current risk assessments, including credible threats, vulnerabilities, and consequences;

"(ii) designed, to the extent practicable, to simulate the partial or complete incapacitation of a government or critical infrastructure network resulting from a cyber incident;

"(iii) designed to provide for the systematic evaluation of cyber readiness and enhance operational understanding of the cyber incident response system and relevant information sharing agreements; and

"(iv) designed to promptly develop after-action reports and plans that can quickly incorporate lessons learned into future operations.

"(B) MODEL EXERCISE SELECTION.— The Exercise Program shall—

"(i) include a selection of model exercises that government and private entities can readily adapt for use; and

"(ii) aid such governments and private entities with the design, implementation, and evaluation of exercises that—

"(I) conform to the requirements described in subparagraph (A);

"(II) are consistent with any applicable national, State, local, or Tribal strategy or plan; and

"(III) provide for systematic evaluation of readiness.

"(3) CONSULTATION.— In carrying out the Exercise Program, the Director may consult with appropriate representatives from Sector Risk Management Agencies, the Office of the National Cyber Director, cybersecurity research stakeholders, and Sector Coordinating Councils.

"(b) DEFINITIONS.— In this section:

"(1) STATE.— The term 'State' means any State of the United States, the District of Columbia, the Commonwealth of Puerto Rico, the Northern Mariana Islands, the United States Virgin Islands, Guam, American Samoa, and any other territory or possession of the United States.

"(2) PRIVATE ENTITY.— The term 'private entity' has the meaning given such term in section 102 of the Cybersecurity Information Sharing Act of 2015 (6 U.S.C. 1501).

"(c) RULE OF CONSTRUCTION.— Nothing in this section shall be construed to affect the authorities or responsibilities of the Administrator of the Federal Emergency Management Agency pursuant to section 648 of the Post-Katrina Emergency Management Reform Act of 2006 (6 U.S.C. 748)."

(b) TITLE XXII TECHNICAL AND CLERICAL AMENDMENTS.—

(1) TECHNICAL AMENDMENTS.—

(A) HOMELAND SECURITY ACT OF 2002.— Subtitle A of title XXII of the Homeland Security Act of 2002 (6 U.S.C. 651 et seq.) is amended—

(i) in section 2202(c) (6 U.S.C. 652(c))—

(I) in paragraph (11), by striking "and" after the semicolon;

(II) in the first paragraph (12) (relating to appointment of a Cybersecurity State Coordinator) by striking "as described in section 2215; and" and inserting "as described in section 2217;";

(III) by redesignating the second paragraph (12) (relating to the .gov internet domain) as paragraph (13); and

(IV) by redesignating the third paragraph (12) (relating to carrying out such other duties and responsibilities) as paragraph (14);

(ii) in the first section 2215 (6 U.S.C. 665; relating to the duties and authorities relating to .gov internet domain), by amending the section enumerator and heading to read as follows:

"SEC. 2215. DUTIES AND AUTHORITIES RELATING TO .GOV INTERNET DOMAIN";

(iii) in the second section 2215 (6 U.S.C. 665b; relating to the joint cyber planning office), by amending the section enumerator and heading to read as follows:

"SEC. 2216. JOINT CYBER PLANNING OFFICE"

;

(iv) in the third section 2215 (6 U.S.C. 665c; relating to the Cybersecurity State Coordinator), by amending the section enumerator and heading to read as follows:

"SEC. 2217. CYBERSECURITY STATE COORDINATOR"

;

(v) in the fourth section 2215 (6 U.S.C. 665d; relating to Sector Risk Management Agencies), by amending the section enumerator and heading to read as follows:

"SEC. 2218. SECTOR RISK MANAGEMENT AGENCIES"

;

(vi) in section 2216 (6 U.S.C. 665e; relating to the Cybersecurity Advisory Committee), by amending the section enumerator and heading to read as follows:

"SEC.   2219.   CYBERSECURITY   ADVISORY COMMITTEE"

;

(vii) in section 2217 (6 U.S.C. 665f; relating to Cybersecurity Education and Training Programs), by amending the section enumerator and heading to read as follows:

"SEC. 2220. CYBERSECURITY EDUCATION AND TRAINING PROGRAMS"

; and

(viii) in section 2218 (6 U.S.C. 665g; relating to the State and Local Cybersecurity Grant Program), by amending the section enumerator and heading to read as follows:

"SEC. 2220A. STATE AND LOCAL CYBERSECURITY GRANT PROGRAM"

.

(B) CONSOLIDATED APPROPRIATIONS ACT, 2021.— Paragraph (1) of section 904(b) of division U of the Consolidated Appropriations Act, 2021 (Public Law 116-260) is amended, in the matter preceding subparagraph (A), by inserting "of 2002" after "Homeland Security Act".

(2) CLERICAL AMENDMENT.— The table of contents in section 1(b) of the Homeland Security Act of 2002 is further amended by striking the items relating to sections 2214 through 2218 and inserting the following new items:

"Sec. 2214. National Asset Database.
"Sec. 2215. Duties and authorities relating to .gov internet domain.
"Sec. 2216. Joint cyber planning office.
"Sec. 2217. Cybersecurity State Coordinator.
"Sec. 2218. Sector Risk Management Agencies.
"Sec. 2219. Cybersecurity Advisory Committee.
"Sec. 2220. Cybersecurity Education and Training Programs.

"Sec. 2220A. State and Local Cybersecurity Grant Program.
"Sec. 2220B. National cyber exercise program."

.

SEC. 1548. CYBERSENTRY PROGRAM OF THE CYBERSECURITY AND INFRASTRUCTURE SECURITY AGENCY.

(a) IN GENERAL.— Title XXII of the Homeland Security Act of 2002 (6 U.S.C. 651 et seq.) is further amended by adding at the end the following new section:

"SEC. 2220C. [6 U.S.C. 665i] CYBERSENTRY PROGRAM

"(a) ESTABLISHMENT.— There is established in the Agency a program, to be known as 'CyberSentry', to provide continuous monitoring and detection of cybersecurity risks to critical infrastructure entities that own or operate industrial control systems that support national critical functions, upon request and subject to the consent of such owner or operator.

"(b) ACTIVITIES.— The Director, through CyberSentry, shall—

"(1) enter into strategic partnerships with critical infrastructure owners and operators that, in the determination of the Director and subject to the availability of resources, own or operate regionally or nationally significant industrial control systems that support national critical functions, in order to provide technical assistance in the form of continuous monitoring of industrial control systems and the information systems that support such systems and detection of cybersecurity risks to such industrial control systems and other cybersecurity services, as appropriate, based on and subject to the agreement and consent of such owner or operator;

"(2) leverage sensitive or classified intelligence about cybersecurity risks regarding particular sectors, particular adversaries, and trends in tactics, techniques, and procedures to advise critical infrastructure owners and operators regarding mitigation measures and share information as appropriate;

"(3) identify cybersecurity risks in the information technology and information systems that support industrial control systems which could be exploited by adversaries attempting to gain access to such industrial control systems, and work with owners and operators to remediate such vulnerabilities;

"(4) produce aggregated, anonymized analytic products, based on threat hunting and continuous monitoring and detection activities and partnerships, with findings and recommendations that can be disseminated to critical infrastructure owners and operators; and

"(5) support activities authorized in accordance with section 1501 of the National Defense Authorization Act for Fiscal Year 2022.

"(c) PRIVACY REVIEW.— Not later than 180 days after the date of enactment of this section, the Privacy Officer of the Agency under section 2202(h) shall—

"(1) review the policies, guidelines, and activities of CyberSentry for compliance with all applicable privacy laws, including such laws governing the acquisition, interception, retention, use, and disclosure of communities; and

"(2) submit to the Committee on Homeland Security of the House of Representatives and the Committee on Homeland Security and Governmental Affairs of the Senate a report certifying compliance with all applicable privacy laws as referred to in paragraph (1), or identifying any instances of noncompliance with such privacy laws.

"(d) REPORT TO CONGRESS.— Not later than one year after the date of the enactment of this section, the Director shall provide to the Committee on Homeland Security of the House of Representatives and the Committee on Homeland Security and Governmental Affairs of the Senate a briefing and written report on implementation of this section.

"(e) SAVINGS.— Nothing in this section may be construed to permit the Federal Government to gain access to information of a remote computing service provider to the public or an electronic service provider to the public, the disclosure of which is not permitted under section 2702 of title 18, United States Code.

"(f) DEFINITIONS.— In this section:

"(1) CYBERSECURITY RISK.— The term 'cybersecurity risk' has the meaning given such term in section 2209(a).

"(2) INDUSTRIAL CONTROL SYSTEM.— The term 'industrial control system' means an information system used to monitor and/or control industrial processes such as manufacturing, product handling, production, and distribution, including supervisory control and data acquisition (SCADA) systems used to monitor and/or control geographically dispersed assets, distributed control systems (DCSs), Human-Machine Interfaces (HMIs), and programmable logic controllers that control localized processes.

"(3) INFORMATION SYSTEM.— The term 'information system' has the meaning given such term in section 102 of the Cybersecurity Act of 2015 (enacted as division N of the Consolidated Appropriations Act, 2016 (Public Law 114-113; 6 U.S.C. 1501(9)).

"(g) TERMINATION.— The authority to carry out a program under this section shall terminate on the date that is seven years after the date of the enactment of this section."

.

(b) CLERICAL AMENDMENT.— The table of contents in section 1(b) of the Homeland Security Act of 2002 is further amended by adding after the item relating to section 2220B the following new item:

"Sec. 2220C. CyberSentry program."

.

(c) CONTINUOUS MONITORING AND DETECTION.— Section 2209(c)(6) of the Homeland Security Act of 2002 (6 U.S.C. 659) is amended by inserting ", which may take the form of continuous monitoring and detection of cybersecurity risks to critical infrastructure entities that own or operate industrial control systems that support national critical functions" after "mitigation, and remediation".

SEC. 1549. STRATEGIC ASSESSMENT RELATING TO INNOVATION OF INFORMATION SYSTEMS AND CYBERSECURITY THREATS.

(a) RESPONSIBILITIES OF DIRECTOR.— Section 2202(c)(3) of the Homeland Security Act of 2002 (6 U.S.C. 652) is amended by striking the semicolon at the end and adding the following: ", including by carrying out a periodic strategic assessment of the related programs and activities of the Agency to ensure such programs and activities contemplate the innovation of information systems and changes in cybersecurity risks and cybersecurity threats;"

(b) REPORT.—

(1) IN GENERAL.— Not later than 240 days after the date of the enactment of this Act and not fewer than once every three years thereafter, the Director of the Cybersecurity and Infrastructure Security Agency shall submit to the Committee on Homeland Security of the House of Representatives and the Committee on Homeland Security and Governmental Affairs of the Senate a strategic assessment for the purposes described in paragraph (2).

(2) PURPOSES.— The purposes described in this paragraph are the following:

(A) A description of the existing programs and activities administered in furtherance of section 2202(c)(3) of the Homeland Security Act of 2002 (6 U.S.C. 652).

(B) An assessment of the capability of existing programs and activities administered by the Agency in furtherance of such section to monitor for, manage, mitigate, and defend against cybersecurity risks and cybersecurity threats.

(C) An assessment of past or anticipated technological trends or innovation of information systems or information technology that have the potential to affect the efficacy of the programs and activities administered by the Agency in furtherance of such section.

(D) A description of any changes in the practices of the Federal workforce, such as increased telework, affect the efficacy of the programs and activities administered by the Agency in furtherance of section 2202(c)(3).

(E) A plan to integrate innovative security tools, technologies, protocols, activities, or programs to improve the programs and activities administered by the Agency in furtherance of such section.

(F) A description of any research and development activities necessary to enhance the programs and activities administered by the Agency in furtherance of such section.

(G) A description of proposed changes to existing programs and activities administered by the Agency in furtherance of such section, including corresponding milestones for implementation.

(H) Information relating to any new resources or authorities necessary to improve the programs and activities administered by the Agency in furtherance of such section.

(c) DEFINITIONS.— In this section:

(1) The term "Agency" means the Cybersecurity and Infrastructure Security Agency.

(2) The term "cybersecurity purpose" has the meaning given such term in section 102(4) of the Cybersecurity Information Sharing Act of 2015 (6 U.S.C. 1501(4)).

(3) The term "cybersecurity risk" has the meaning given such term in section 2209(a)(2) of the Homeland Security Act of 2002 (U.S.C. 659(a)(2)).

(4) The term "information system" has the meaning given such term in section 3502(8) of title 44, United States Code.

(5) The term "information technology" has the meaning given such term in 3502(9) of title 44, United States Code.

(6) The term "telework" has the meaning given the term in section 6501(3) of title 5, United States Code.

SEC. 1550. [6 U.S.C. 652 note] PILOT PROGRAM ON PUBLIC-PRIVATE PARTNERSHIPS WITH INTERNET ECOSYSTEM COMPANIES TO DETECT AND DISRUPT ADVERSARY CYBER OPERATIONS.

(a) PILOT REQUIRED.— Not later than one year after the date of the enactment of this Act, the Secretary, acting through the Director of the Cybersecurity and Infrastructure Security Agency of the Department of Homeland Security and in coordination with the Secretary of Defense and the National Cyber Director, shall commence a pilot program to assess the feasibility and advisability of entering into public-private partnerships with internet ecosystem companies to facilitate, within the bounds of applicable provisions of law and such companies' terms of service, policies, procedures, contracts, and other agreements, actions by such companies to discover and disrupt use by malicious cyber actors of the platforms, systems, services, and infrastructure of such companies.

(b) PUBLIC-PRIVATE PARTNERSHIPS.—

(1) IN GENERAL.— In carrying out the pilot program under subsection (a), the Secretary shall seek to enter into one or more public-private partnerships with internet ecosystem companies.

(2) VOLUNTARY PARTICIPATION.—

(A) IN GENERAL.— Participation by an internet ecosystem company in a public-private partnership under the pilot program, including in any activity described in subsection (c), shall be voluntary.

(B) PROHIBITION.— No funds appropriated by any Act may be used to direct, pressure, coerce, or otherwise require that any internet ecosystem company take any action on their platforms, systems, services, or infrastructure as part of the pilot program.

(c) AUTHORIZED ACTIVITIES.— In carrying out the pilot program under subsection (a), the Secretary may—

(1) provide assistance to a participating internet ecosystem company to develop effective know-your-customer processes and requirements;

(2) provide information, analytics, and technical assistance to improve the ability of participating companies to detect and prevent illicit or suspicious procurement, payment, and account creation on their own platforms, systems, services, or infrastructure;

(3) develop and socialize best practices for the collection, retention, and sharing of data by participating internet ecosystem companies to support discovery of malicious cyber activity, investigations, and attribution on the platforms, systems, services, or infrastructure of such companies;

(4) provide to participating internet ecosystem companies actionable, timely, and relevant information, such as information about ongoing operations and infrastructure, threats, tactics, and procedures, and indicators of compromise, to enable such companies to detect and disrupt the use by malicious cyber actors of the platforms, systems, services, or infrastructure of such companies;

(5) provide recommendations for (but not design, develop, install, operate, or maintain) operational workflows, assessment and compliance practices, and training that participating internet ecosystem companies can implement to reliably detect and disrupt the use by malicious cyber actors of the platforms, systems, services, or infrastructure of such companies;

(6) provide recommendations for accelerating, to the greatest extent practicable, the automation of existing or implemented operational workflows to operate at line-rate in order to enable real-time mitigation without the need for manual review or action;

(7) provide recommendations for (but not design, develop, install, operate, or maintain) technical capabilities to enable participating internet ecosystem companies to collect and analyze data on malicious activities occurring on the platforms, systems, services, or infrastructure of such companies to detect and disrupt operations of malicious cyber actors; and

(8) provide recommendations regarding relevant mitigations for suspected or discovered malicious cyber activity and thresholds for action.

(d) COMPETITION CONCERNS.— Consistent with section 1905 of title 18, United States Code, the Secretary shall ensure that any trade secret or proprietary information of a participating internet ecosystem company made known to the Federal Government pursuant to a public-private partnership under the pilot program remains private and protected unless explicitly authorized by such company.

(e) IMPARTIALITY.— In carrying out the pilot program under subsection (a), the Secretary may not take any action that is intended primarily to advance the particular business interests of an internet ecosystem company but is authorized to take actions that advance the interests of the United States, notwithstanding differential impact or benefit to a given company's or given companies' business interests.

(f) RESPONSIBILITIES.—

(1) SECRETARY OF HOMELAND SECURITY.— The Secretary shall exercise primary responsibility for the pilot program under subsection (a), including organizing and directing authorized activities with participating Federal Government organizations and internet ecosystem companies to achieve the objectives of the pilot program.

(2) NATIONAL CYBER DIRECTOR.— The National Cyber Director shall support prioritization and cross-agency coordination for the pilot program, including ensuring appropriate participation by participating agencies and the

identification and prioritization of key private sector entities and initiatives for the pilot program.

(3) SECRETARY OF DEFENSE.— The Secretary of Defense shall provide support and resources to the pilot program, including the provision of technical and operational expertise drawn from appropriate and relevant officials and components of the Department of Defense, including the National Security Agency, United States Cyber Command, the Chief Information Officer, the Office of the Secretary of Defense, military department Principal Cyber Advisors, and the Defense Advanced Research Projects Agency.

(g) PARTICIPATION OF OTHER FEDERAL GOVERNMENT COMPONENTS.— The Secretary may invite to participate in the pilot program required under subsection (a) the heads of such departments or agencies as the Secretary considers appropriate.

(h) INTEGRATION WITH OTHER EFFORTS.— The Secretary shall ensure that the pilot program required under subsection (a) makes use of, builds upon, and, as appropriate, integrates with and does not duplicate other efforts of the Department of Homeland Security and the Department of Defense relating to cybersecurity, including the following:

(1) The Joint Cyber Defense Collaborative of the Cybersecurity and Infrastructure Security Agency of the Department of Homeland Security.

(2) The Cybersecurity Collaboration Center and Enduring Security Framework of the National Security Agency.

(i) RULES OF CONSTRUCTION.—

(1) LIMITATION ON GOVERNMENT ACCESS TO DATA.— Nothing in this section authorizes sharing of information, including information relating to customers of internet ecosystem companies or private individuals, from an internet ecosystem company to an agency, officer, or employee of the Federal Government unless otherwise authorized by another provision of law.

(2) STORED COMMUNICATIONS ACT.— Nothing in this section may be construed to permit or require disclosure by a provider of a remote computing service or a provider of an electronic communication service to the public of information not otherwise permitted or required to be disclosed under chapter

121 of title 18, United States Code (commonly known as the "Stored Communications Act").

(3) THIRD PARTY CUSTOMERS.— Nothing in this section may be construed to require a third party, such as a customer or managed service provider of an internet ecosystem company, to participate in the pilot program under subsection (a).

(j) BRIEFINGS.—

(1) INITIAL.—

(A) IN GENERAL.— Not later than one year after the date of the enactment of this Act, the Secretary, in coordination with the Secretary of Defense and the National Cyber Director, shall brief the appropriate committees of Congress on the pilot program required under subsection (a).

(B) ELEMENTS.— The briefing required under subparagraph (A) shall include the following:

(i) The plans of the Secretary for the implementation of the pilot program.

(ii) Identification of key priorities for the pilot program.

(iii) Identification of any potential challenges in standing up the pilot program or impediments, such as a lack of liability protection, to private sector participation in the pilot program.

(iv) A description of the roles and responsibilities in the pilot program of each participating Federal entity.

(2) ANNUAL.—

(A) IN GENERAL.— Not later than two years after the date of the enactment of this Act and annually thereafter for three years, the Secretary, in coordination with the Secretary of Defense and the National Cyber Director, shall brief the appropriate committees of Congress on the progress of the pilot program required under subsection (a).

(B) ELEMENTS.— Each briefing required under subparagraph (A) shall include the following:

(i) Recommendations for addressing relevant policy, budgetary, and legislative gaps to increase the effectiveness of the pilot program.

(ii) Recommendations, such as providing liability protection, for increasing private sector participation in the pilot program.

(iii) A description of the challenges encountered in carrying out the pilot program, including any concerns expressed by internet ecosystem companies regarding participation in the pilot program.

(iv) The findings of the Secretary with respect to the feasibility and advisability of extending or expanding the pilot program.

(v) Such other matters as the Secretary considers appropriate.

(k) TERMINATION.— The pilot program required under subsection (a) shall terminate on the date that is five years after the date of the enactment of this Act.

(l) DEFINITIONS.— In this section:

(1) APPROPRIATE COMMITTEES OF CONGRESS.— The term "appropriate committees of Congress" means—

(A) the Committee on Homeland Security and Governmental Affairs and the Committee on Armed Services of the Senate; and

(B) the Committee on Homeland Security and the Committee on Armed Services of the House of Representatives.

(2) INTERNET ECOSYSTEM COMPANY.— The term "internet ecosystem company" means a business incorporated in the United States that provides cybersecurity services, internet service, content delivery services, Domain Name Service, cloud services, mobile telecommunications services, email and messaging services, internet browser services, or such other services as the Secretary determines appropriate for the purposes of the pilot program under subsection (a).

(3) SECRETARY.— The term "Secretary" means the Secretary of Homeland Security.

SEC. 1551. [22 U.S.C. 8606 note] UNITED STATES-ISRAEL CYBERSECURITY COOPERATION.

(a) GRANT PROGRAM.—

(1) ESTABLISHMENT.— The Secretary, in accordance with the agreement entitled the "Agreement between the Government of the United States of America and the Government of the State of Israel on Cooperation in Science and Technology for Homeland Security Matters", dated May 29, 2008 (or successor agreement), and the requirements specified in paragraph (2), shall establish a grant program at the Department to support—

(A) cybersecurity research and development; and

(B) demonstration and commercialization of cybersecurity technology.

(2) REQUIREMENTS.—

(A) APPLICABILITY.— Notwithstanding section 317 of the Homeland Security Act of 2002 (6 U.S.C. 195c), in carrying out a research, development, demonstration, or commercial application program or activity that is authorized under this section, the Secretary shall require cost sharing in accordance with this paragraph.

(B) RESEARCH AND DEVELOPMENT.—

(i) IN GENERAL.— Except as provided in clause (ii), the Secretary shall require not less than 50 percent of the cost of a research, development, demonstration, or commercial application program or activity described in subparagraph (A) to be provided by a non-Federal source.

(ii) REDUCTION.— The Secretary may reduce or eliminate, on a case-by-case basis, the percentage requirement specified in clause (i) if the Secretary determines that such reduction or elimination is necessary and appropriate.

(C) MERIT REVIEW.— In carrying out a research, development, demonstration, or commercial application program or activity that is authorized under this section, awards shall be made only after an impartial review of the scientific and technical merit of the proposals for such awards has been carried out by or for the Department.

(D) REVIEW PROCESSES.— In carrying out a review under subparagraph (C), the Secretary may use merit review processes developed under section 302(14) of the Homeland Security Act of 2002 (6 U.S.C. 182(14)).

(3) ELIGIBLE APPLICANTS.— An applicant is eligible to receive a grant under this subsection if—

(A) the project of such applicant—

(i) addresses a requirement in the area of cybersecurity research or cybersecurity technology, as determined by the Secretary; and

(ii) is a joint venture between—

(I) (aa) a for-profit business entity, academic institution, National Laboratory, or nonprofit entity in the United States; and

(bb) a for-profit business entity, academic institution, or nonprofit entity in Israel; or

(II) (aa) the Federal Government; and

(bb) the Government of Israel; and

(B) neither such applicant nor the project of such applicant pose a counterintelligence threat, as determined by the Director of National Intelligence.

(4) APPLICATIONS.— To be eligible to receive a grant under this subsection, an applicant shall submit to the Secretary an application for such grant in accordance with procedures established by the Secretary, in consultation with the advisory board established under paragraph (5).

(5) ADVISORY BOARD.—

(A) ESTABLISHMENT.— The Secretary shall establish an advisory board to—

(i) monitor the method by which grants are awarded under this subsection; and

(ii) provide to the Secretary periodic performance reviews of actions taken to carry out this subsection.

(B) COMPOSITION.— The advisory board established under subparagraph (A) shall be composed of three members, to be appointed by the Secretary, of whom—

(i) one shall be a representative of the Federal Government;

(ii) one shall be selected from a list of nominees

provided by the United States-Israel Binational Science Foundation; and

(iii) one shall be selected from a list of nominees provided by the United States-Israel Binational Industrial Research and Development Foundation.

(6) CONTRIBUTED FUNDS.— Notwithstanding section 3302 of title 31, United States Code, the Secretary may, only to the extent provided in advance in appropriations Acts, accept or retain funds contributed by any person, government entity, or organization for purposes of carrying out this subsection. Such funds shall be available, subject to appropriation, without fiscal year limitation.

(7) REPORTS.—

(A) GRANT RECIPIENTS.— Not later than 180 days after the date of completion of a project for which a grant is provided under this subsection, the grant recipient shall submit to the Secretary a report that contains—

(i) a description of how the grant funds were used by the recipient; and

(ii) an evaluation of the level of success of each project funded by the grant.

(B) SECRETARY.— Not later than one year after the date of the enactment of this Act and annually thereafter until the grant program established under this subsection terminates, the Secretary shall submit to the Committees on Homeland Security and Governmental Affairs and Foreign Relations of the Senate and the Committees on Homeland Security and Foreign Affairs of the House of Representatives a report on grants awarded and projects completed under such program.

(8) CLASSIFICATION.— Grants shall be awarded under this subsection only for projects that are considered to be unclassified by both the United States and Israel.

(b) AUTHORIZATION OF APPROPRIATIONS.— There is authorized to be appropriated to carry out this section not less than $6,000,000 for each of fiscal years 2022 through 2026.

(c) DEFINITIONS.— In this section—

(1) the term "cybersecurity research" means research,

including social science research, into ways to identify, protect against, detect, respond to, and recover from cybersecurity threats;

(2) the term "cybersecurity technology" means technology intended to identify, protect against, detect, respond to, and recover from cybersecurity threats;

(3) the term "cybersecurity threat" has the meaning given such term in section 102 of the Cybersecurity Information Sharing Act of 2015 (6 U.S.C. 1501; enacted as title I of the Cybersecurity Act of 2015 (division N of the Consolidated Appropriations Act, 2016 (Public Law 114-113)));

(4) the term "Department" means the Department of Homeland Security;

(5) the term "National Laboratory" has the meaning given such term in section 2 of the Energy Policy Act of 2005 (42 U.S.C. 15801); and

(6) the term "Secretary" means the Secretary of Homeland Security.

SEC. 1552. AUTHORITY FOR NATIONAL CYBER DIRECTOR TO ACCEPT DETAILS ON NONREIMBURSABLE BASIS.

Section 1752(e) of the William M. (Mac) Thornberry National Defense Authorization Act for Fiscal Year 2021 (Public Law 116-283) is amended—

(1) by redesignating paragraphs (1) through (8) as subparagraphs (A) through (H), respectively, and indenting such subparagraphs two ems to the right;

(2) in the matter preceding subparagraph (A), as redesignated by paragraph (1), by striking "The Director may" and inserting the following:

"(1) IN GENERAL.— The Director may"

;

(3) in paragraph (1)—

(A) as redesignated by paragraph (2), by redesignating subparagraphs (C) through (H) as subparagraphs (D) through (I), respectively; and

(B) by inserting after subparagraph (B) the following new subparagraph:

"(C) accept officers or employees of the United States or members of the Armed Forces on a detail from an element of the intelligence community (as such term is defined in section 3(4) of the National Security Act of 1947 (50 U.S.C. 3003(4))) or from another element of the Federal Government on a nonreimbursable basis, as jointly agreed to by the heads of the receiving and detailing elements, for a period not to exceed three years;"

; and

(4) by adding at the end the following new paragraph:

"(2) RULES OF CONSTRUCTION REGARDING DETAILS.— Nothing in paragraph (1)(C) may be construed as imposing any limitation on any other authority for reimbursable or nonreimbursable details. A nonreimbursable detail made pursuant to such paragraph shall not be considered an augmentation of the appropriations of the receiving element of the Office of the National Cyber Director."

* * * * * * *

DIVISION B— MILITARY CONSTRUCTION AUTHORIZATIONS

Sec. 2001. Short title.
Sec. 2002. Expiration of authorizations and amounts required to be specified by law.
Sec. 2003. Effective date and automatic execution of conforming changes to tables of sections, tables of contents, and similar tabular entries.

TITLE XXI— ARMY MILITARY CONSTRUCTION

Sec. 2101. Authorized Army construction and land acquisition projects.
Sec. 2102. Family housing.
Sec. 2103. Authorization of appropriations, Army.
Sec. 2104. Extension of authority to carry out certain fiscal year 2017 project.
Sec. 2105. Additional authority to carry out fiscal year 2018 project

at Fort Bliss, Texas.

Sec. 2106. Modification of authority to carry out certain fiscal year 2021 project.

Sec. 2107. Additional authorized funding source for certain fiscal year 2022 project.

SEC. 2001. SHORT TITLE.

This division and title XLVI of division D may be cited as the "Military Construction Authorization Act for Fiscal Year 2022".

SEC. 2002. EXPIRATION OF AUTHORIZATIONS AND AMOUNTS REQUIRED TO BE SPECIFIED BY LAW.

(a) EXPIRATION OF AUTHORIZATIONS AFTER THREE YEARS.— Except as provided in subsection (b), all authorizations contained in titles XXI through XXVII for military construction projects, land acquisition, family housing projects and facilities, and contributions to the North Atlantic Treaty Organization Security Investment Program (and authorizations of appropriations therefor) shall expire on the later of—

(1) October 1, 2024; or

(2) the date of the enactment of an Act authorizing funds for military construction for fiscal year 2025.

(b) EXCEPTION.— Subsection (a) shall not apply to authorizations for military construction projects, land acquisition, family housing projects and facilities, and contributions to the North Atlantic Treaty Organization Security Investment Program (and authorizations of appropriations therefor), for which appropriated funds have been obligated before the later of—

(1) October 1, 2024; or

(2) the date of the enactment of an Act authorizing funds for fiscal year 2025 for military construction projects, land acquisition, family housing projects and facilities, or contributions to the North Atlantic Treaty Organization Security Investment Program.

SEC. 2003. EFFECTIVE DATE AND AUTOMATIC EXECUTION OF CONFORMING CHANGES TO TABLES OF SECTIONS, TABLES OF CONTENTS, AND SIMILAR TABULAR ENTRIES.

(a) EFFECTIVE DATE.— Titles XXI through XXVII shall take effect on the later of—

(1) October 1, 2021; or

(2) the date of the enactment of this Act.

(b) **[10 U.S.C. 101 note]** ELIMINATION OF NEED FOR CERTAIN SEPARATE CONFORMING AMENDMENTS.—

(1) AUTOMATIC EXECUTION OF CONFORMING CHANGES.— When an amendment made by a provision of this division to a covered defense law adds a section or larger organizational unit to the covered defense law, repeals or transfers a section or larger organizational unit in the covered defense law, or amends the designation or heading of a section or larger organizational unit in the covered defense law, that amendment also shall have the effect of amending any table of sections, table of contents, or similar table of tabular entries in the covered defense law to alter the table to conform to the changes made by the amendment.

(2) EXCEPTIONS.— Paragraph (1) shall not apply to an amendment described in such paragraph when—

(A) the amendment, or a separate clerical amendment enacted at the same time as the amendment, expressly amends a table of sections, table of contents, or similar table of tabular entries in the covered defense law to alter the table to conform to the changes made by the amendment; or

(B) the amendment otherwise expressly exempts itself from the operation of this section.

(3) COVERED DEFENSE LAW.— In this subsection, the term "covered defense law" means—

(A) titles 10, 32, and 37 of the United States Code;

(B) any national defense authorization Act or military construction authorization Act that authorizes funds to be appropriated for a fiscal year to the Department of Defense; and

(C) any other law designated in the text thereof as a covered defense law for purposes of application of this section.

* * * * * * *

DIVISION F— OTHER NON-DEPARTMENT OF DEFENSE

MATTERS

* * * * * * *

TITLE LXIV— DEPARTMENT OF HOMELAND SECURITY MEASURES

Subtitle A— DHS Headquarters, Research and Development, and Related Matters

Subtitle A— DHS Headquarters, Research and Development, and Related Matters

SEC. 6401. EMPLOYEE ENGAGEMENT STEERING COMMITTEE AND ACTION PLAN.

(a) IN GENERAL.— Title VII of the Homeland Security Act of 2002 (6 U.S.C. 341 et seq.) is amended by adding at the end the following new section:

"SEC. 711. [6 U.S.C. 351.Estab] EMPLOYEE ENGAGEMENT

"(a) STEERING COMMITTEE.— Not later than 120 days after the date of the enactment of this section, the Secretary shall establish an employee engagement steering committee, including representatives from operational components, headquarters, and field personnel, including supervisory and nonsupervisory personnel, and employee labor organizations that represent Department employees, and chaired by the Under Secretary for Management, to carry out the following activities:

"(1) Identify factors that have a negative impact on employee engagement, morale, and communications within the Department, such as perceptions about limitations on career progression, mobility, or development opportunities, collected through employee feedback platforms, including through annual employee surveys, questionnaires, and other communications, as appropriate.

"(2) Identify, develop, and distribute initiatives and best practices to improve employee engagement, morale, and communications within the Department, including through annual employee surveys, questionnaires, and other communications, as appropriate.

"(3) Monitor efforts of each component to address employee

engagement, morale, and communications based on employee feedback provided through annual employee surveys, questionnaires, and other communications, as appropriate.

"(4) Advise the Secretary on efforts to improve employee engagement, morale, and communications within specific components and across the Department.

"(5) Conduct regular meetings and report, not less than once per quarter, to the Under Secretary for Management, the head of each component, and the Secretary on Departmentwide efforts to improve employee engagement, morale, and communications.

"(b) ACTION PLAN; REPORTING.— The Secretary, acting through the Chief Human Capital Officer, shall—

"(1) not later than 120 days after the date of the establishment of the employee engagement steering committee under subsection (a), issue a Departmentwide employee engagement action plan, reflecting input from the steering committee and employee feedback provided through annual employee surveys, questionnaires, and other communications in accordance with paragraph (1) of such subsection, to execute strategies to improve employee engagement, morale, and communications within the Department; and

"(2) require the head of each component to—

"(A) develop and implement a component-specific employee engagement plan to advance the action plan required under paragraph (1) that includes performance measures and objectives, is informed by employee feedback provided through annual employee surveys, questionnaires, and other communications, as appropriate, and sets forth how employees and, where applicable, their labor representatives are to be integrated in developing programs and initiatives;

"(B) monitor progress on implementation of such action plan; and

"(C) provide to the Chief Human Capital Officer and the steering committee quarterly reports on actions planned and progress made under this paragraph.

"(c) TERMINATION.— This section shall terminate on the date that is five years after the date of the enactment of this section."

(b) CLERICAL AMENDMENT.— The table of contents in section 1(b) of the Homeland Security Act of 2002 is amended by inserting after the item relating to section 710 the following new item:

"Sec. 711. Employee engagement."

(c) [6 U.S.C. 351 note] SUBMISSIONS TO CONGRESS.—

(1) DEPARTMENT-WIDE EMPLOYEE ENGAGEMENT ACTION PLAN.— The Secretary of Homeland Security, acting through the Chief Human Capital Officer of the Department of Homeland Security, shall submit to the Committee on Homeland Security of the House of Representatives and the Committee on Homeland Security and Governmental Affairs of the Senate the Department-wide employee engagement action plan required under subsection (b)(1) of section 711 of the Homeland Security Act of 2002 (as added by subsection (a) of this section) not later than 30 days after the issuance of such plan under such subsection (b)(1).

(2) COMPONENT-SPECIFIC EMPLOYEE ENGAGEMENT PLANS.— Each head of a component of the Department of Homeland Security shall submit to the Committee on Homeland Security of the House of Representatives and the Committee on Homeland Security and Governmental Affairs of the Senate the component-specific employee engagement plan of each such component required under subsection (b)(2) of section 711 of the Homeland Security Act of 2002 not later than 30 days after the issuance of each such plan under such subsection (b)(2).

SEC. 6402. ANNUAL EMPLOYEE AWARD PROGRAM.

(a) IN GENERAL.— Title VII of the Homeland Security Act of 2002 (6 U.S.C. 341 et seq.), as amended by section 6401 of this Act, is further amended by adding at the end the following new section:

"SEC. 712. [6 U.S.C. 352] ANNUAL EMPLOYEE AWARD PROGRAM

"(a) IN GENERAL.— The Secretary may establish an annual employee award program to recognize Department employees or groups of employees for significant contributions to the achievement of the Department's goals and missions. If such a program is established, the Secretary shall—

"(1) establish within such program categories of awards, each with specific criteria, that emphasize honoring employees who are at the nonsupervisory level;

"(2) publicize within the Department how any employee or group of employees may be nominated for an award;

"(3) establish an internal review board comprised of representatives from Department components, headquarters, and field personnel to submit to the Secretary award recommendations regarding specific employees or groups of employees;

"(4) select recipients from the pool of nominees submitted by the internal review board under paragraph (3) and convene a ceremony at which employees or groups of employees receive such awards from the Secretary; and

"(5) publicize such program within the Department.

"(b) INTERNAL REVIEW BOARD.— The internal review board described in subsection (a)(3) shall, when carrying out its function under such subsection, consult with representatives from operational components and headquarters, including supervisory and nonsupervisory personnel, and employee labor organizations that represent Department employees.

"(c) RULE OF CONSTRUCTION.— Nothing in this section may be construed to authorize additional funds to carry out the requirements of this section or to require the Secretary to provide monetary bonuses to recipients of an award under this section."

.

(b) CLERICAL AMENDMENT.— The table of contents in section 1(b) of the Homeland Security Act of 2002, as amended by section 6401 of this Act, is further amended by inserting after the item relating to section 711 the following new item:

"Sec. 712. Annual employee award program."

.

SEC. 6403. CHIEF HUMAN CAPITAL OFFICER RESPONSIBILITIES.

Section 704 of the Homeland Security Act of 2002 (6 U.S.C. 344) is amended—

(1) in subsection (b)—

(A) in paragraph (1)—

(i) by inserting ", including with respect to leader development and employee engagement," after "policies";

(ii) by striking "and in line" and inserting ", in line"; and

(iii) by inserting "and informed by best practices within the Federal Government and the private sector," after "priorities,";

(B) in paragraph (2), by striking "develop performance measures to provide a basis for monitoring and evaluating" and inserting "use performance measures to evaluate, on an ongoing basis,";

(C) in paragraph (3), by inserting "that, to the extent practicable, are informed by employee feedback" after "policies";

(D) in paragraph (4), by inserting "including leader development and employee engagement programs," before "in coordination";

(E) in paragraph (5), by inserting before the semicolon at the end the following: "that is informed by an assessment, carried out by the Chief Human Capital Officer, of the learning and developmental needs of employees in supervisory and nonsupervisory roles across the Department and appropriate workforce planning initiatives";

(F) by redesignating paragraphs (9) and (10) as paragraphs (13) and (14), respectively; and

(G) by inserting after paragraph (8) the following new paragraphs:

"(9) maintain a catalogue of available employee development opportunities, including the Homeland Security Rotation Program pursuant to section 844, departmental leadership development programs, interagency development programs, and other rotational programs;

"(10) ensure that employee discipline and adverse action programs comply with the requirements of all pertinent laws, rules, regulations, and Federal guidance, and ensure due process for employees;

"(11) analyze each Department or Government-wide Federal workforce satisfaction or morale survey not later than 90 days after the date of the publication of each such survey and submit to the Secretary such analysis, including, as appropriate, recommendations to improve workforce satisfaction or morale within the Department;

"(12) review and approve all component employee engagement action plans to ensure such plans include initiatives responsive to the root cause of employee engagement challenges, as well as outcome-based performance measures and targets to track the progress of such initiatives;"

;

(2) by redesignating subsections (d) and (e) as subsections (e) and (f), respectively;

(3) by inserting after subsection (c) the following new subsection:

"(d) CHIEF LEARNING AND ENGAGEMENT OFFICER.— The Chief Human Capital Officer may designate an employee of the Department to serve as a Chief Learning and Engagement Officer to assist the Chief Human Capital Officer in carrying out this section."

; and

(4) in subsection (e), as so redesignated—

(A) by redesignating paragraphs (2), (3), and (4) as paragraphs (5), (6), and (7), respectively; and

(B) by inserting after paragraph (1) the following new paragraphs:

"(2) information on employee development opportunities catalogued pursuant to paragraph (9) of subsection (b) and any available data on participation rates, attrition rates, and impacts on retention and employee satisfaction;

"(3) information on the progress of Departmentwide strategic workforce planning efforts as determined under paragraph (2) of subsection (b);

"(4) information on the activities of the steering committee established pursuant to section 711(a), including the number of meetings, types of materials developed and distributed, and recommendations made to the Secretary;"

SEC. 6404. [6 U.S.C. 411 note] INDEPENDENT INVESTIGATION AND IMPLEMENTATION PLAN.

(a) IN GENERAL.— Not later than 120 days after the date of the enactment of this Act, the Comptroller General of the United States shall investigate whether the application in the Department of Homeland Security of discipline and adverse actions for managers and non-managers are administered in an equitable and consistent manner that results in the same or substantially similar disciplinary outcomes across the Department that are appropriately calibrated to address the identified misconduct, taking into account relevant aggravating and mitigating factors.

(b) CONSULTATION.— In carrying out the investigation described in subsection (a), the Comptroller General of the United States shall consult with the Under Secretary for Management of the Department of Homeland Security and the employee engagement steering committee established pursuant to subsection (b)(1) of section 711 of the Homeland Security Act of 2002 (as added by section 6401(a) of this Act).

(c) ACTION BY UNDER SECRETARY FOR MANAGEMENT.— Upon completion of the investigation described in subsection (a), the Under Secretary for Management of the Department of Homeland Security shall review the findings and recommendations of such investigation and implement a plan, in consultation with the employee engagement steering committee established pursuant to subsection (b)(1) of section 711 of the Homeland Security Act of 2002, to correct any relevant deficiencies identified by the Comptroller General of the United States in such investigation. The Under Secretary for Management shall direct the employee engagement steering committee to review such plan to inform committee activities and action plans authorized under such section 711.

SEC. 6405. AUTHORIZATION OF THE ACQUISITION PROFESSIONAL CAREER PROGRAM.

(a) IN GENERAL.— Title VII of the Homeland Security Act of 2002 (6 U.S.C. 341 et seq.), as amended by sections 6401 and 6402 of this Act, is further amended by adding at the end the following new section:

"SEC. 713. [6 U.S.C. 353] ACQUISITION PROFESSIONAL CAREER PROGRAM

"(a) ESTABLISHMENT.— There is established in the Department an acquisition professional career program to develop a cadre of acquisition professionals within the Department.

"(b) ADMINISTRATION.— The Under Secretary for Management shall administer the acquisition professional career program established pursuant to subsection (a).

"(c) PROGRAM REQUIREMENTS.— The Under Secretary for Management shall carry out the following with respect to the acquisition professional career program.

"(1) Designate the occupational series, grades, and number of acquisition positions throughout the Department to be included in the program and manage centrally such positions.

"(2) Establish and publish on the Department's website eligibility criteria for candidates to participate in the program.

"(3) Carry out recruitment efforts to attract candidates—

"(A) from institutions of higher education, including such institutions with established acquisition specialties and courses of study, historically Black colleges and universities, and Hispanic-serving institutions;

"(B) with diverse work experience outside of the Federal Government; or

"(C) with military service.

"(4) Hire eligible candidates for designated positions under the program.

"(5) Develop a structured program comprised of acquisition training, on-the-job experience, Department-wide rotations, mentorship, shadowing, and other career development opportunities for program participants.

"(6) Provide, beyond required training established for program participants, additional specialized acquisition training, including small business contracting and innovative acquisition techniques training.

"(d) REPORTS.— Not later than one year after the date of the enactment of this section, and annually thereafter through 2027, the Secretary shall submit to the Committee on Homeland Security of the House of Representatives and the Committee on Homeland Security and Governmental Affairs of the Senate a report on the acquisition professional career program. Each such report shall include the following information:

"(1) The number of candidates approved for the program.

"(2) The number of candidates who commenced participation in the program, including generalized information on such candidates' backgrounds with respect to education and prior work experience, but not including personally identifiable information.

"(3) A breakdown of the number of participants hired under the program by type of acquisition position.

"(4) A list of Department components and offices that participated in the program and information regarding length of time of each program participant in each rotation at such components or offices.

"(5) Program attrition rates and post-program graduation retention data, including information on how such data compare to the prior year's data, as available.

"(6) The Department's recruiting efforts for the program.

"(7) The Department's efforts to promote retention of program participants.

"(e) DEFINITIONS.— In this section:

"(1) HISPANIC-SERVING INSTITUTION.— The term 'Hispanic-serving institution' has the meaning given such term in section 502 of the Higher Education Act of 1965 (20 U.S.C. 1101a).

"(2) HISTORICALLY BLACK COLLEGES AND UNIVERSITIES.— The term 'historically Black colleges and universities' has the meaning given the term 'part B institution' in section 322(2) of Higher Education Act of 1965 (20 U.S.C. 1061(2)).

"(3) INSTITUTION OF HIGHER EDUCATION.— The term 'institution of higher education' has the meaning given such term in section 101 of the Higher Education Act of 1965 (20

U.S.C. 1001).”

.

(b) CLERICAL AMENDMENT.— The table of contents in section 1(b) of the Homeland Security Act of 2002, as amended by sections 6401 and 6402 of this Act, is further amended by inserting after the item relating to section 712 the following new item:

“Sec. 713. Acquisition professional career program.”

.

SEC. 6406. NATIONAL URBAN SECURITY TECHNOLOGY LABORATORY.

(a) IN GENERAL.— Title III of the Homeland Security Act of 2002 (6 U.S.C. 181 et seq.) is amended by adding at the end the following new section:

“SEC. 322. [6 U.S.C. 195h] NATIONAL URBAN SECURITY TECHNOLOGY LABORATORY

“(a) IN GENERAL.— The Secretary, acting through the Under Secretary for Science and Technology, shall designate the laboratory described in subsection (b) as an additional laboratory pursuant to the authority under section 308(c)(2) of this Act. Such laboratory shall be used to test and evaluate emerging technologies and conduct research and development to assist emergency response providers in preparing for, and protecting against, threats of terrorism.

“(b) LABORATORY DESCRIBED.— The laboratory described in this subsection is the laboratory—

“(1) known, as of the date of the enactment of this section, as the National Urban Security Technology Laboratory; and

“(2) transferred to the Department pursuant to section 303(1)(E) of this Act.

“(c) LABORATORY ACTIVITIES.— The National Urban Security Technology Laboratory shall—

“(1) conduct tests, evaluations, and assessments of current and emerging technologies, including, as appropriate, the cybersecurity of such technologies that can connect to the internet, for emergency response providers;

“(2) act as a technical advisor to emergency response providers; and

"(3) carry out other such activities as the Secretary determines appropriate.

"(d) RULE OF CONSTRUCTION.— Nothing in this section may be construed as affecting in any manner the authorities or responsibilities of the Countering Weapons of Mass Destruction Office of the Department."

.

(b) CLERICAL AMENDMENT.— The table of contents in section 1(b) of the Homeland Security Act of 2002 is further amended by inserting after the item relating to section 321 the following new item:

"Sec. 322. National Urban Security Technology Laboratory."

.

SEC. 6407. DEPARTMENT OF HOMELAND SECURITY BLUE CAMPAIGN ENHANCEMENT.

Section 434 of the Homeland Security Act of 2002 (6 U.S.C. 242) is amended—

(1) in subsection (e)(6), by striking "utilizing resources," and inserting "developing and utilizing, in consultation with the Blue Campaign Advisory Board established pursuant to subsection (g), resources"; and

(2) by adding at the end the following new subsections:

"(f) WEB-BASED TRAINING PROGRAMS.— To enhance training opportunities, the Director of the Blue Campaign shall develop web-based interactive training videos that utilize a learning management system to provide online training opportunities. During the 10-year period beginning on the date that is 90 days after the date of the enactment of this subsection such training opportunities shall be made available to the following individuals:

"(1) Federal, State, local, Tribal, and territorial law enforcement officers.

"(2) Non-Federal correction system personnel.

"(3) Such other individuals as the Director determines appropriate.

"(g) BLUE CAMPAIGN ADVISORY BOARD.—

"(1) IN GENERAL.— There is established in the Department a Blue Campaign Advisory Board, which shall be comprised of representatives assigned by the Secretary from—

"(A) the Office for Civil Rights and Civil Liberties of the Department;

"(B) the Privacy Office of the Department; and

"(C) not fewer than four other separate components or offices of the Department.

"(2) CHARTER.— The Secretary is authorized to issue a charter for the Blue Campaign Advisory Board, and such charter shall specify the following:

"(A) The Board's mission, goals, and scope of its activities.

"(B) The duties of the Board's representatives.

"(C) The frequency of the Board's meetings.

"(3) CONSULTATION.— The Director shall consult the Blue Campaign Advisory Board and, as appropriate, experts from other components and offices of the Center for Countering Human Trafficking of the Department regarding the following:

"(A) Recruitment tactics used by human traffickers to inform the development of training and materials by the Blue Campaign.

"(B) The development of effective awareness tools for distribution to Federal and non-Federal officials to identify and prevent instances of human trafficking.

"(C) Identification of additional persons or entities that may be uniquely positioned to recognize signs of human trafficking and the development of materials for such persons.

"(h) CONSULTATION.— With regard to the development of programs under the Blue Campaign and the implementation of such programs, the Director is authorized to consult with State, local, Tribal, and territorial agencies, non-governmental organizations, private sector organizations, and experts."

.

SEC. 6408. MEDICAL COUNTERMEASURES PROGRAM.

(a) IN GENERAL.— Subtitle C of title XIX of the Homeland Security Act of 2002 (6 U.S.C. 597) is amended by adding at the end the following new section:

"SEC. 1932. [6 U.S.C. 597a] MEDICAL COUNTERMEASURES

"(a) IN GENERAL.— Subject to the availability of appropriations, the Secretary shall, as appropriate, establish a medical countermeasures program within the components of the Department to—

"(1) facilitate personnel readiness and protection for the employees and working animals of the Department in the event of a chemical, biological, radiological, nuclear, or explosives attack, naturally occurring disease outbreak, other event impacting health, or pandemic; and

"(2) support the mission continuity of the Department.

"(b) OVERSIGHT.— The Secretary, acting through the Chief Medical Officer of the Department, shall—

"(1) provide programmatic oversight of the medical countermeasures program established under subsection (a); and

"(2) develop standards for—

"(A) medical countermeasure storage, security, dispensing, and documentation;

"(B) maintaining a stockpile of medical countermeasures, including antibiotics, antivirals, antidotes, therapeutics, and radiological countermeasures, as appropriate;

"(C) ensuring adequate partnerships with manufacturers and executive agencies that enable advance prepositioning by vendors of inventories of appropriate medical countermeasures in strategic locations nationwide, based on risk and employee density, in accordance with applicable Federal statutes and regulations;

"(D) providing oversight and guidance regarding the dispensing of stockpiled medical countermeasures;

"(E) ensuring rapid deployment and dispensing of medical countermeasures in a chemical, biological, radiological, nuclear, or explosives attack, naturally occurring disease outbreak, other event impacting health, or pandemic;

"(F) providing training to employees of the Department on medical countermeasures; and

"(G) supporting dispensing exercises.

"(c) MEDICAL COUNTERMEASURES WORKING GROUP.— The Secretary, acting through the Chief Medical Officer of the Department, shall establish a medical countermeasures working group comprised of representatives from appropriate components and offices of the Department to ensure that medical countermeasures standards are maintained and guidance is consistent.

"(d) MEDICAL COUNTERMEASURES MANAGEMENT.— Not later than 120 days after the date on which appropriations are made available to carry out subsection (a), the Chief Medical Officer shall develop and submit to the Secretary an integrated logistics support plan for medical countermeasures, including—

"(1) a methodology for determining the ideal types and quantities of medical countermeasures to stockpile and how frequently such methodology shall be reevaluated;

"(2) a replenishment plan; and

"(3) inventory tracking, reporting, and reconciliation procedures for existing stockpiles and new medical countermeasure purchases.

"(e) TRANSFER.— Not later than 120 days after the date of enactment of this section, the Secretary shall transfer all medical countermeasures-related programmatic and personnel resources from the Under Secretary for Management to the Chief Medical Officer.

"(f) STOCKPILE ELEMENTS.— In determining the types and quantities of medical countermeasures to stockpile under subsection (d), the Secretary, acting through the Chief Medical Officer of the Department—

"(1) shall use a risk-based methodology for evaluating types and quantities of medical countermeasures required; and

"(2) may use, if available—

"(A) chemical, biological, radiological, and nuclear risk assessments of the Department; and

"(B) guidance on medical countermeasures of the Office of the Assistant Secretary for Preparedness and Response and the Centers for Disease Control and Prevention.

"(g) BRIEFING.— Not later than 180 days after the date of enactment of this section, the Secretary shall provide a briefing to the Committee on Homeland Security and Governmental Affairs of the Senate and the Committee on Homeland Security of the House of Representatives regarding—

"(1) the plan developed under subsection (d); and

"(2) implementation of the requirements of this section.

"(h) DEFINITION.— In this section, the term 'medical countermeasures' means antibiotics, antivirals, antidotes, therapeutics, radiological countermeasures, and other countermeasures that may be deployed to protect the employees and working animals of the Department in the event of a chemical, biological, radiological, nuclear, or explosives attack, naturally occurring disease outbreak, other event impacting health, or pandemic."

.

(b) CLERICAL AMENDMENT.— The table of contents in section 1(b) of the Homeland Security Act of 2002 is further amended by inserting after the item relating to section 1931 the following new item:

"Sec. 1932. Medical countermeasures."

.

SEC. 6409. CRITICAL DOMAIN RESEARCH AND DEVELOPMENT.

(a) IN GENERAL.— Subtitle H of title VIII of the Homeland Security Act of 2002 (6 U.S.C. 451 et seq.) is amended by adding at the end the following new section:

"SEC. 890B. [6 U.S.C. 474] HOMELAND SECURITY CRITICAL DOMAIN RESEARCH AND DEVELOPMENT

"(a) IN GENERAL.—

"(1) RESEARCH AND DEVELOPMENT.— The Secretary is authorized to conduct research and development to—

"(A) identify United States critical domains for economic security and homeland security; and

"(B) evaluate the extent to which disruption, corruption, exploitation, or dysfunction of any of such domain poses a substantial threat to homeland security.

"(2) REQUIREMENTS.—

"(A) RISK ANALYSIS OF CRITICAL DOMAINS.— The research under paragraph (1) shall include a risk analysis of each identified United States critical domain for economic security to determine the degree to which there exists a present or future threat to homeland security in the event of disruption, corruption, exploitation, or dysfunction to such domain. Such research shall consider, to the extent possible, the following:

"(i) The vulnerability and resilience of relevant supply chains.

"(ii) Foreign production, processing, and manufacturing methods.

"(iii) Influence of malign economic actors.

"(iv) Asset ownership.

"(v) Relationships within the supply chains of such domains.

"(vi) The degree to which the conditions referred to in clauses (i) through (v) would place such a domain at risk of disruption, corruption, exploitation, or dysfunction.

"(B) ADDITIONAL RESEARCH INTO HIGH-RISK CRITICAL DOMAINS.— Based on the identification and risk analysis of United States critical domains for economic security pursuant to paragraph (1) and subparagraph (A) of this paragraph, respectively, the Secretary may conduct additional research into those critical domains, or specific elements thereof, with respect to which there exists the highest degree of a present or future threat to homeland security in the event of disruption, corruption, exploitation, or dysfunction to such a domain. For each such high-risk domain, or element thereof, such research shall—

"(i) describe the underlying infrastructure and processes;

"(ii) analyze present and projected performance of

industries that comprise or support such domain;

"(iii) examine the extent to which the supply chain of a product or service necessary to such domain is concentrated, either through a small number of sources, or if multiple sources are concentrated in one geographic area;

"(iv) examine the extent to which the demand for supplies of goods and services of such industries can be fulfilled by present and projected performance of other industries, identify strategies, plans, and potential barriers to expand the supplier industrial base, and identify the barriers to the participation of such other industries;

"(v) consider each such domain's performance capacities in stable economic environments, adversarial supply conditions, and under crisis economic constraints;

"(vi) identify and define needs and requirements to establish supply resiliency within each such domain; and

"(vii) consider the effects of sector consolidation, including foreign consolidation, either through mergers or acquisitions, or due to recent geographic realignment, on such industries' performances.

"(3) CONSULTATION.— In conducting the research under paragraph (1) and subparagraph (B) of paragraph (2), the Secretary may consult with appropriate Federal agencies, State agencies, and private sector stakeholders.

"(4) PUBLICATION.— Beginning one year after the date of the enactment of this section, the Secretary shall publish a report containing information relating to the research under paragraph (1) and subparagraph (B) of paragraph (2), including findings, evidence, analysis, and recommendations. Such report shall be updated annually through 2026.

"(b) SUBMISSION TO CONGRESS.— Not later than 90 days after the publication of each report required under paragraph (4) of subsection (a), the Secretary shall transmit to the Committee on Homeland Security of the House of Representatives and the Committee on Homeland Security and Governmental Affairs of the

Senate each such report, together with a description of actions the Secretary, in consultation with appropriate Federal agencies, will undertake or has undertaken in response to each such report.

"(c) DEFINITIONS.— In this section:

"(1) UNITED STATES CRITICAL DOMAINS FOR ECONOMIC SECURITY.— The term 'United States critical domains for economic security' means the critical infrastructure and other associated industries, technologies, and intellectual property, or any combination thereof, that are essential to the economic security of the United States.

"(2) ECONOMIC SECURITY.— The term 'economic security' means the condition of having secure and resilient domestic production capacity, combined with reliable access to the global resources necessary to maintain an acceptable standard of living and to protect core national values.

"(d) AUTHORIZATION OF APPROPRIATIONS.— There is authorized to be appropriated $1,000,000 for each of fiscal years 2022 through 2026 to carry out this section."

.

(b) CLERICAL AMENDMENT.— The table of contents in section 1(b) of the Homeland Security Act of 2002 is further amended by inserting after the item relating to section 890A the following new item:

"Sec. 890B. Homeland security critical domain research and development."

.

SEC. 6410. CBP DONATIONS ACCEPTANCE PROGRAM REAUTHORIZATION.

Section 482 of the Homeland Security Act of 2002 (6 U.S.C. 301a) is amended—

(1) in subsection (a)—

(A) in paragraph (1)—

(i) in subparagraph (B), by inserting "or -leased" before "land"; and

(ii) in subparagraph (C)—

(I) in the matter preceding clause (i), by

inserting "or -leased" before "land";

(II) in clause (i), by striking "$50,000,000" and inserting "$75,000,000"; and

(III) by amending clause (ii) to read as follows:

"(ii) the fair market value of donations with respect to the land port of entry total $75,000,000 or less over the preceding five years."

; and

(B) in paragraph (3), in the matter preceding subparagraph (A), by inserting "or -leased" before "land";

(2) in subsection (b)—

(A) in the matter preceding paragraph (1), by striking "Administrator of the General Services Administration" and inserting "Administrator of General Services";

(B) in paragraph (1)(C)—

(i) in clause (i), by striking "$50,000,000" and inserting "$75,000,000"; and

(ii) by amending clause (ii) to read as follows:

"(ii) the fair market value of donations with respect to the land port of entry total $75,000,000 or less over the preceding five years."

; and

(C) in paragraph (4)—

(i) in subparagraph (A), by striking "terminate" and all that follows through the period at the end and inserting "terminate on December 31, 2026."; and

(ii) in subparagraph (B), by striking "carrying out the terms of an agreement under this subsection if such agreement is entered into before such termination date" and inserting "a proposal accepted for consideration by U.S. Customs and Border Protection or the General Services Administration pursuant to this section or a prior pilot program prior to such termination date";

(3) in subsection (c)(6)(B), by striking "the donation will not be used for the construction of a detention facility or a border

fence or wall." and inserting the following:

"(i) the donation will not be used for the construction of a detention facility or a border fence or wall; and

"(ii) the donor will be notified in the Donations Acceptance Agreement that the donor shall be financially responsible for all costs and operating expenses related to the operation, maintenance, and repair of the donated real property until such time as U.S. Customs and Border Protection provides the donor written notice otherwise."

;

(4) in subsection (d), in the matter preceding paragraph (1), by striking "annual" and inserting "biennial"; and

(5) in subsection (e), by striking "Administrator of the General Services Administration" and inserting "Administrator of General Services".

Subtitle B— Transportation Security

SEC. 6411. SURVEY OF THE TRANSPORTATION SECURITY ADMINISTRATION WORKFORCE REGARDING COVID-19 RESPONSE.

(a) SURVEY.— Not later than one year after the date of the enactment of this Act, the Administrator of the Transportation Security Administration (referred to in this section as the "Administrator"), in consultation with the labor organization certified as the exclusive representative of full- and part-time nonsupervisory Administration personnel carrying out screening functions under section 44901 of title 49, United States Code, shall conduct a survey of the Transportation Security Administration (referred to in this section as the "Administration") workforce regarding the Administration's response to the COVID-19 pandemic. Such survey shall be conducted in a manner that allows for the greatest practicable level of workforce participation.

(b) CONTENTS.— In conducting the survey required under subsection (a), the Administrator shall solicit feedback on the following:

(1) The Administration's communication and collaboration with the Administration's workforce regarding the Administration's response to the COVID-19 pandemic and efforts to mitigate and monitor transmission of COVID-19

among its workforce, including through—

(A) providing employees with personal protective equipment and mandating its use;

(B) modifying screening procedures and Administration operations to reduce transmission among officers and passengers and ensuring compliance with such changes;

(C) adjusting policies regarding scheduling, leave, and telework;

(D) outreach as a part of contact tracing when an employee has tested positive for COVID-19; and

(E) encouraging COVID-19 vaccinations and efforts to assist employees that seek to be vaccinated such as communicating the availability of duty time for travel to vaccination sites and recovery from vaccine side effects.

(2) Any other topic determined appropriate by the Administrator.

(c) REPORT.— Not later than 30 days after completing the survey required under subsection (a), the Administration shall provide a report summarizing the results of the survey to the Committee on Homeland Security of the House of Representatives and the Committee on Commerce, Science, and Transportation of the Senate.

SEC. 6412. TRANSPORTATION SECURITY PREPAREDNESS PLAN.

(a) PLAN REQUIRED.— Section 114 of title 49, United States Code, is amended by adding at the end the following new subsection:

"(x) TRANSPORTATION SECURITY PREPAREDNESS PLAN.—

"(1) IN GENERAL.— Not later than two years after the date of the enactment of this subsection, the Secretary of Homeland Security, acting through the Administrator, in coordination with the Chief Medical Officer of the Department of Homeland Security, and in consultation with the partners identified under paragraphs (3)(A)(i) through (3)(A)(iv), shall develop a transportation security preparedness plan to address the event of a communicable disease outbreak. The Secretary, acting through the Administrator, shall ensure such plan aligns with relevant Federal plans and strategies for communicable disease outbreaks.

"(2) CONSIDERATIONS.— In developing the plan required under paragraph (1), the Secretary, acting through the Administrator, shall consider each of the following:

"(A) The findings of the survey required under section 6411 of the National Defense Authorization Act for Fiscal Year 2022.

"(B) The findings of the analysis required under section 6414 of the National Defense Authorization Act for Fiscal Year 2022.

"(C) The plan required under section 6415 of the National Defense Authorization Act for Fiscal Year 2022.

"(D) All relevant reports and recommendations regarding the Administration's response to the COVID-19 pandemic, including any reports and recommendations issued by the Comptroller General and the Inspector General of the Department of Homeland Security.

"(E) Lessons learned from Federal interagency efforts during the COVID-19 pandemic.

"(3) CONTENTS OF PLAN.— The plan developed under paragraph (1) shall include each of the following:

"(A) Plans for communicating and collaborating in the event of a communicable disease outbreak with the following partners:

"(i) Appropriate Federal departments and agencies, including the Department of Health and Human Services, the Centers for Disease Control and Prevention, the Department of Transportation, the Department of Labor, and appropriate interagency task forces.

"(ii) The workforce of the Administration, including through the labor organization certified as the exclusive representative of full- and part-time non-supervisory Administration personnel carrying out screening functions under section 44901 of this title.

"(iii) International partners, including the International Civil Aviation Organization and foreign governments, airports, and air carriers.

"(iv) Public and private stakeholders, as such term is defined under subsection (t)(1)(C).

"(v) The traveling public.

"(B) Plans for protecting the safety of the Transportation Security Administration workforce, including—

"(i) reducing the risk of communicable disease transmission at screening checkpoints and within the Administration's workforce related to the Administration's transportation security operations and mission;

"(ii) ensuring the safety and hygiene of screening checkpoints and other workstations;

"(iii) supporting equitable and appropriate access to relevant vaccines, prescriptions, and other medical care; and

"(iv) tracking rates of employee illness, recovery, and death.

"(C) Criteria for determining the conditions that may warrant the integration of additional actions in the aviation screening system in response to the communicable disease outbreak and a range of potential roles and responsibilities that align with such conditions.

"(D) Contingency plans for temporarily adjusting checkpoint operations to provide for passenger and employee safety while maintaining security during the communicable disease outbreak.

"(E) Provisions setting forth criteria for establishing an interagency task force or other standing engagement platform with other appropriate Federal departments and agencies, including the Department of Health and Human Services and the Department of Transportation, to address such communicable disease outbreak.

"(F) A description of scenarios in which the Administrator should consider exercising authorities provided under subsection (g) and for what purposes.

"(G) Considerations for assessing the appropriateness of issuing security directives and emergency amendments to regulated parties in various modes of transportation, including surface transportation, and plans for ensuring compliance with such measures.

"(H) A description of any potential obstacles, including funding constraints and limitations to authorities, that could restrict the ability of the Administration to respond appropriately to a communicable disease outbreak.

"(4) DISSEMINATION.— Upon development of the plan required under paragraph (1), the Administrator shall disseminate the plan to the partners identified under paragraph (3)(A) and to the Committee on Homeland Security of the House of Representatives and the Committee on Homeland Security and Governmental Affairs and the Committee on Commerce, Science, and Transportation of the Senate.

"(5) REVIEW OF PLAN.— Not later than two years after the date on which the plan is disseminated under paragraph (4), and biennially thereafter, the Secretary, acting through the Administrator and in coordination with the Chief Medical Officer of the Department of Homeland Security, shall review the plan and, after consultation with the partners identified under paragraphs (3)(A)(i) through (3)(A)(iv), update the plan as appropriate."

.

(b) COMPTROLLER GENERAL REPORT.— Not later than one year after the date on which the transportation security preparedness plan required under subsection (x) of section 114 of title 49, United States Code, as added by subsection (a), is disseminated under paragraph (4) of such subsection (x), the Comptroller General of the United States shall submit to the Committee on Homeland Security of the House of Representatives and the Committee on Commerce, Science, and Transportation of the Senate a report containing the results of a study assessing the transportation security preparedness plan, including an analysis of—

(1) whether such plan aligns with relevant Federal plans and strategies for communicable disease outbreaks; and

(2) the extent to which the Transportation Security Administration is prepared to implement the plan.

SEC. 6413. [49 U.S.C. 114 note] AUTHORIZATION OF TRANSPORTATION SECURITY ADMINISTRATION PERSONNEL DETAILS.

(a) COORDINATION.— Pursuant to sections 106(m) and 114(m) of title 49, United States Code, the Administrator of the Transportation Security Administration may provide Transportation Security Administration personnel, who are not engaged in front line transportation security efforts, to other components of the Department and other Federal agencies to improve coordination with such components and agencies to prepare for, protect against, and respond to public health threats to the transportation security system of the United States.

(b) BRIEFING.— Not later than 180 days after the date of the enactment of this Act, the Administrator shall brief the appropriate congressional committees regarding efforts to improve coordination with other components of the Department of Homeland Security and other Federal agencies to prepare for, protect against, and respond to public health threats to the transportation security system of the United States.

SEC. 6414. TRANSPORTATION SECURITY ADMINISTRATION PREPAREDNESS.

(a) ANALYSIS.—

(1) IN GENERAL.— The Administrator of the Transportation Security Administration shall conduct an analysis of preparedness of the transportation security system of the United States for public health threats. Such analysis shall assess, at a minimum, the following:

(A) The risks of public health threats to the transportation security system of the United States, including to transportation hubs, transportation security stakeholders, Transportation Security Administration (TSA) personnel, and passengers.

(B) Information sharing challenges among relevant components of the Department of Homeland Security, other Federal agencies, international entities, and transportation security stakeholders.

(C) Impacts to TSA policies and procedures for securing the transportation security system.

(2) COORDINATION.— The analysis conducted of the risks

described in paragraph (1)(A) shall be conducted in coordination with the Chief Medical Officer of the Department of Homeland Security, the Secretary of Health and Human Services, and transportation security stakeholders.

(b) BRIEFING.— Not later than 180 days after the date of the enactment of this Act, the Administrator shall brief the appropriate congressional committees on the following:

(1) The analysis required under subsection (a).

(2) Technologies necessary to combat public health threats at security screening checkpoints, such as testing and screening technologies, including temperature screenings, to better protect from future public health threats TSA personnel, passengers, aviation workers, and other personnel authorized to access the sterile area of an airport through such checkpoints, and the estimated cost of technology investments needed to fully implement across the aviation system solutions to such threats.

(3) Policies and procedures implemented by TSA and transportation security stakeholders to protect from public health threats TSA personnel, passengers, aviation workers, and other personnel authorized to access the sterile area through the security screening checkpoints, as well as future plans for additional measures relating to such protection.

(4) The role of TSA in establishing priorities, developing solutions, and coordinating and sharing information with relevant domestic and international entities during a public health threat to the transportation security system, and how TSA can improve its leadership role in such areas.

(c) DEFINITIONS.— In this section:

(1) The term "appropriate congressional committees" means—

(A) the Committee on Homeland Security of the House of Representatives; and

(B) the Committee on Homeland Security and Governmental Affairs and the Committee on Commerce, Science, and Transportation of the Senate.

(2) The term "sterile area" has the meaning given such term in section 1540.5 of title 49, Code of Federal Regulations.

(3) The term "TSA" means the Transportation Security Administration.

SEC. 6415. [49 U.S.C. 44901 note] PLAN TO REDUCE THE SPREAD OF CORONAVIRUS AT PASSENGER SCREENING CHECKPOINTS.

(a) IN GENERAL.— Not later than 90 days after the date of the enactment of this Act, the Administrator, in coordination with the Chief Medical Officer of the Department of Homeland Security, and in consultation with the Secretary of Health and Human Services and the Director of the Centers for Disease Control and Prevention, shall issue and commence implementing a plan to enhance, as appropriate, security operations at airports during the COVID-19 national emergency in order to reduce risk of the spread of the coronavirus at passenger screening checkpoints and among the TSA workforce.

(b) CONTENTS.— The plan required under subsection (a) shall include the following:

(1) An identification of best practices developed and screening technologies deployed in response to the coronavirus among foreign governments, airports, and air carriers conducting aviation security screening operations, as well as among Federal agencies conducting similar security screening operations outside of airports, including in locations where the spread of the coronavirus has been successfully contained, that could be further integrated into the United States aviation security system.

(2) Specific operational changes to aviation security screening operations informed by the identification of best practices and screening technologies under paragraph (1) that could be implemented without degrading aviation security and a corresponding timeline and costs for implementing such changes.

(c) CONSIDERATIONS.— In carrying out the identification of best practices under subsection (b), the Administrator shall take into consideration the following:

(1) Aviation security screening procedures and practices in place at security screening locations, including procedures and practices implemented in response to the coronavirus.

(2) Volume and average wait times at each such security

screening location.

(3) Public health measures already in place at each such security screening location.

(4) The feasibility and effectiveness of implementing similar procedures and practices in locations where such are not already in place.

(5) The feasibility and potential benefits to security, public health, and travel facilitation of continuing any procedures and practices implemented in response to the COVID-19 national emergency beyond the end of such emergency.

(d) CONSULTATION.— In developing the plan required under subsection (a), the Administrator may consult with public and private stakeholders and the TSA workforce, including through the labor organization certified as the exclusive representative of full- and part-time nonsupervisory TSA personnel carrying out screening functions under section 44901 of title 49, United States Code.

(e) SUBMISSION.— Upon issuance of the plan required under subsection (a), the Administrator shall submit the plan to the Committee on Homeland Security of the House of Representatives and the Committee on Commerce, Science, and Transportation of the Senate.

(f) ISSUANCE AND IMPLEMENTATION.— The Administrator shall not be required to issue or implement, as the case may be, the plan required under subsection (a) upon the termination of the COVID-19 national emergency except to the extent the Administrator determines such issuance or implementation, as the case may be, to be feasible and beneficial to security screening operations.

(g) GAO REVIEW.— Not later than one year after the issuance of the plan required under subsection (a) (if such plan is issued in accordance with subsection (f)), the Comptroller General of the United States shall submit to the Committee on Homeland Security of the House of Representatives and the Committee on Commerce, Science, and Transportation of the Senate a review, if appropriate, of such plan and any efforts to implement such plan.

(h) DEFINITIONS.— In this section:

(1) The term "Administrator" means the Administrator of the Transportation Security Administration.

(2) The term "coronavirus" has the meaning given such

term in section 506 of the Coronavirus Preparedness and Response Supplemental Appropriations Act, 2020 (Public Law 116-123).

(3) The term "COVID-19 national emergency" means the national emergency declared by the President under the National Emergencies Act (50 U.S.C. 1601 et seq.) on March 13, 2020, with respect to the coronavirus.

(4) The term "public and private stakeholders" has the meaning given such term in section 114(t)(1)(C) of title 49, United States Code.

(5) The term "TSA" means the Transportation Security Administration.

SEC. 6416. COMPTROLLER GENERAL REVIEW OF DEPARTMENT OF HOMELAND SECURITY TRUSTED TRAVELER PROGRAMS.

Not later than one year after the date of the enactment of this Act, the Comptroller General of the United States shall conduct a review of Department of Homeland Security trusted traveler programs. Such review shall examine the following:

(1) The extent to which the Department of Homeland Security tracks data and monitors trends related to trusted traveler programs, including root causes for identity-matching errors resulting in an individual's enrollment in a trusted traveler program being reinstated.

(2) Whether the Department coordinates with the heads of other relevant Federal, State, local, Tribal, or territorial entities regarding redress procedures for disqualifying offenses not covered by the Department's own redress processes but which offenses impact an individual's enrollment in a trusted traveler program.

(3) How the Department may improve individuals' access to reconsideration procedures regarding a disqualifying offense for enrollment in a trusted traveler program that requires the involvement of any other Federal, State, local, Tribal, or territorial entity.

(4) The extent to which travelers are informed about reconsideration procedures regarding enrollment in a trusted traveler program.

SEC. 6417. [49 U.S.C. 44919 note] ENROLLMENT REDRESS WITH

RESPECT TO DEPARTMENT OF HOMELAND SECURITY TRUSTED TRAVELER PROGRAMS.

Notwithstanding any other provision of law, the Secretary of Homeland Security shall, with respect to an individual whose enrollment in a trusted traveler program was revoked in error extend by an amount of time equal to the period of revocation the period of active enrollment in such a program upon reenrollment in such a program by such an individual.

SEC. 6418. [6 U.S.C. 124h-1] THREAT INFORMATION SHARING.

(a) PRIORITIZATION.— The Secretary of Homeland Security shall prioritize the assignment of officers and intelligence analysts under section 210A of the Homeland Security Act of 2002 (6 U.S.C. 124h) from the Transportation Security Administration and, as appropriate, from the Office of Intelligence and Analysis of the Department of Homeland Security, to locations with participating State, local, and regional fusion centers in jurisdictions with a high-risk surface transportation asset in order to enhance the security of such assets, including by improving timely sharing, in a manner consistent with the protection of privacy rights, civil rights, and civil liberties, of information regarding threats of terrorism and other threats, including targeted violence.

(b) INTELLIGENCE PRODUCTS.— Officers and intelligence analysts assigned to locations with participating State, local, and regional fusion centers under this section shall participate in the generation and dissemination of transportation security intelligence products, with an emphasis on such products that relate to threats of terrorism and other threats, including targeted violence, to surface transportation assets that—

(1) assist State, local, and Tribal law enforcement agencies in deploying their resources, including personnel, most efficiently to help detect, prevent, investigate, apprehend, and respond to such threats;

(2) promote more consistent and timely sharing with and among jurisdictions of threat information; and

(3) enhance the Department of Homeland Security's situational awareness of such threats.

(c) CLEARANCES.— The Secretary of Homeland Security shall make available to appropriate owners and operators of surface transportation assets, and to any other person that the Secretary determines appropriate to foster greater sharing of classified information relating to threats of terrorism and other threats, including targeted violence, to surface transportation assets, the process of application for security clearances under Executive Order No. 13549 (75 Fed. Reg. 162; relating to a classified national security information program) or any successor Executive order.

(d) REPORT TO CONGRESS.— Not later than one year after the date of the enactment of this Act, the Secretary of Homeland Security shall submit to the Committee on Homeland Security of the House of Representatives and the Committee on Homeland Security and Governmental Affairs of the Senate a report that includes a detailed description of the measures used to ensure privacy rights, civil rights, and civil liberties protections in carrying out this section.

(e) GAO REPORT.— Not later than two years after the date of the enactment of this Act, the Comptroller General of the United States shall submit to the Committee on Homeland Security of the House of Representatives and the Committee on Homeland Security and Governmental Affairs of the Senate a review of the implementation of this section, including an assessment of the measures used to ensure privacy rights, civil rights, and civil liberties protections, and any recommendations to improve this implementation, together with any recommendations to improve information sharing with State, local, Tribal, territorial, and private sector entities to prevent, identify, and respond to threats of terrorism and other threats, including targeted violence, to surface transportation assets.

(f) DEFINITIONS.— In this section:

(1) The term "surface transportation asset" includes facilities, equipment, or systems used to provide transportation services by—

(A) a public transportation agency (as such term is defined in section 1402(5) of the Implementing Recommendations of the 9/11 Commission Act of 2007 (Public Law 110-53; 6 U.S.C. 1131(5)));

(B) a railroad carrier (as such term is defined in section 20102(3) of title 49, United States Code);

(C) an owner or operator of—

(i) an entity offering scheduled, fixed-route

transportation services by over-the-road bus (as such term is defined in section 1501(4) of the Implementing Recommendations of the 9/11 Commission Act of 2007 (Public Law 110-53; 6 U.S.C. 1151(4))); or

(ii) a bus terminal; or

(D) other transportation facilities, equipment, or systems, as determined by the Secretary.

(2) The term "targeted violence" means an incident of violence in which an attacker selected a particular target in order to inflict mass injury or death with no discernable political or ideological motivation beyond mass injury or death.

(3) The term "terrorism" means the terms—

(A) domestic terrorism (as such term is defined in section 2331(5) of title 18, United States Code); and

(B) international terrorism (as such term is defined in section 2331(1) of title 18, United States Code).

SEC. 6419. [6 U.S.C. 1137a] LOCAL LAW ENFORCEMENT SECURITY TRAINING.

(a) IN GENERAL.— The Secretary of Homeland Security, in consultation with public and private sector stakeholders, may in a manner consistent with the protection of privacy rights, civil rights, and civil liberties, develop, through the Federal Law Enforcement Training Centers, a training program to enhance the protection, preparedness, and response capabilities of law enforcement agencies with respect to threats of terrorism and other threats, including targeted violence, at a surface transportation asset.

(b) REQUIREMENTS.— If the Secretary of Homeland Security develops the training program described in subsection (a), such training program shall—

(1) be informed by current information regarding tactics used by terrorists and others engaging in targeted violence;

(2) include tactical instruction tailored to the diverse nature of the surface transportation asset operational environment; and

(3) prioritize training officers from law enforcement agencies that are eligible for or receive grants under sections 2003 or 2004 of the Homeland Security Act of 2002 (6 U.S.C.

604 and 605) and officers employed by railroad carriers that operate passenger service, including interstate passenger service.

(c) REPORT.— If the Secretary of Homeland Security develops the training program described in subsection (a), not later than one year after the date on which the Secretary first implements the program, and annually thereafter during each year the Secretary carries out the program, the Secretary shall submit to the Committee on Homeland Security of the House of Representatives and the Committee on Homeland Security and Governmental Affairs of the Senate a report on the program. Each such report shall include, for the year covered by the report—

(1) a description of the curriculum for the training and any changes to such curriculum;

(2) an identification of any contracts entered into for the development or provision of training under the program;

(3) information on the law enforcement agencies the personnel of which received the training, and for each such agency, the number of participants; and

(4) a description of the measures used to ensure the program was carried out to provide for protections of privacy rights, civil rights, and civil liberties.

(d) DEFINITIONS.— In this section:

(1) The term "public and private sector stakeholders" has the meaning given such term in section 114(t)(1)(c) of title 49, United States Code.

(2) The term "surface transportation asset" includes facilities, equipment, or systems used to provide transportation services by—

(A) a public transportation agency (as such term is defined in section 1402(5) of the Implementing Recommendations of the 9/11 Commission Act of 2007 (Public Law 110-53; 6 U.S.C. 1131(5)));

(B) a railroad carrier (as such term is defined in section 20102(3) of title 49, United States Code);

(C) an owner or operator of—

(i) an entity offering scheduled, fixed-route transportation services by over-the-road bus (as such term is defined in section 1501(4) of the Implementing Recommendations of the 9/11 Commission Act of 2007 (Public Law 110-53; 6 U.S.C. 1151(4))); or

(ii) a bus terminal; or

(D) other transportation facilities, equipment, or systems, as determined by the Secretary.

(3) The term "targeted violence" means an incident of violence in which an attacker selected a particular target in order to inflict mass injury or death with no discernable political or ideological motivation beyond mass injury or death.

(4) The term "terrorism" means the terms—

(A) domestic terrorism (as such term is defined in section 2331(5) of title 18, United States Code); and

(B) international terrorism (as such term is defined in section 2331(1) of title 18, United States Code).

SEC. 6420. ALLOWABLE USES OF FUNDS FOR PUBLIC TRANSPORTATION SECURITY ASSISTANCE GRANTS.

Subparagraph (A) of section 1406(b)(2) of the Implementing Recommendations of the 9/11 Commission Act of 2007 (6 U.S.C. 1135(b)(2); Public Law 110-53) is amended by inserting "and associated backfill" after "security training".

SEC. 6421. PERIODS OF PERFORMANCE FOR PUBLIC TRANSPORTATION SECURITY ASSISTANCE GRANTS.

Section 1406 of the Implementing Recommendations of the 9/11 Commission Act of 2007 (6 U.S.C. 1135; Public Law 110-53) is amended—

(1) by redesignating subsection (m) as subsection (n); and

(2) by inserting after subsection (l) the following new subsection:

"(m) PERIODS OF PERFORMANCE.—

"(1) IN GENERAL.— Except as provided in paragraph (2), funds provided pursuant to a grant awarded under this section for a use specified in subsection (b) shall remain available for use by a grant recipient for a period of not fewer than 36 months.

"(2) EXCEPTION.— Funds provided pursuant to a grant awarded under this section for a use specified in subparagraph (M) or (N) of subsection (b)(1) shall remain available for use by a grant recipient for a period of not fewer than 48 months."

.

SEC. 6422. GAO REVIEW OF PUBLIC TRANSPORTATION SECURITY ASSISTANCE GRANT PROGRAM.

(a) IN GENERAL.— The Comptroller General of the United States shall conduct a review of the public transportation security assistance grant program under section 1406 of the Implementing Recommendations of the 9/11 Commission Act of 2007 (6 U.S.C. 1135; Public Law 110-53).

(b) SCOPE.— The review required under paragraph (1) shall include the following:

(1) An assessment of the type of projects funded under the public transportation security grant program referred to in such paragraph.

(2) An assessment of the manner in which such projects address threats to public transportation infrastructure.

(3) An assessment of the impact, if any, of sections 5342 through 5345 (including the amendments made by this Act) on types of projects funded under the public transportation security assistance grant program.

(4) An assessment of the management and administration of public transportation security assistance grant program funds by grantees.

(5) Recommendations to improve the manner in which public transportation security assistance grant program funds address vulnerabilities in public transportation infrastructure.

(6) Recommendations to improve the management and administration of the public transportation security assistance grant program.

(c) REPORT.— Not later than one year after the date of the enactment of this Act and again not later than five years after such date of enactment, the Comptroller General of the United States shall submit to the Committee on Homeland Security of the House of Representatives and the Committee on Homeland Security and Governmental Affairs of the Senate a report on the review required under this section.

SEC. 6423. [6 U.S.C. 114 note] SENSITIVE SECURITY INFORMATION; AVIATION SECURITY.

(a) SENSITIVE SECURITY INFORMATION.—

(1) IN GENERAL.— Not later than 90 days after the date of the enactment of this Act, the Administrator of the Transportation Security Administration (TSA) shall—

(A) ensure clear and consistent designation of "Sensitive Security Information", including reasonable security justifications for such designation;

(B) develop and implement a schedule to regularly review and update, as necessary, TSA Sensitive Security Information identification guidelines;

(C) develop a tracking mechanism for all Sensitive Security Information redaction and designation challenges;

(D) document justifications for changes in position regarding Sensitive Security Information redactions and designations, and make such changes accessible to TSA personnel for use with relevant stakeholders, including air carriers, airport operators, surface transportation operators, and State and local law enforcement, as necessary; and

(E) ensure that TSA personnel are adequately trained on appropriate designation policies.

(2) STAKEHOLDER OUTREACH.— Not later than 180 days after the date of the enactment of this Act, the Administrator of the Transportation Security Administration (TSA) shall conduct outreach to relevant stakeholders described in paragraph (1)(D) that regularly are granted access to Sensitive Security Information to raise awareness of the TSA's policies and guidelines governing the designation and use of Sensitive Security Information.

(b) [49 U.S.C. 114 note] AVIATION SECURITY.—

(1) IN GENERAL.— Not later than 60 days after the date of the enactment of this Act, the Administrator of the Transportation Security Administration shall develop and implement guidelines with respect to domestic and last point of departure airports to—

(A) ensure the inclusion, as appropriate, of air carriers,

domestic airport operators, and other transportation security stakeholders in the development and implementation of security directives and emergency amendments;

(B) document input provided by air carriers, domestic airport operators, and other transportation security stakeholders during the security directive and emergency amendment, development, and implementation processes;

(C) define a process, including timeframes, and with the inclusion of feedback from air carriers, domestic airport operators, and other transportation security stakeholders, for cancelling or incorporating security directives and emergency amendments into security programs;

(D) conduct engagement with foreign partners on the implementation of security directives and emergency amendments, as appropriate, including recognition if existing security measures at a last point of departure airport are found to provide commensurate security as intended by potential new security directives and emergency amendments; and

(E) ensure that new security directives and emergency amendments are focused on defined security outcomes.

(2) BRIEFING TO CONGRESS.— Not later than 90 days after the date of the enactment of this Act, the Administrator of the Transportation Security Administration shall brief the Committee on Homeland Security of the House of Representatives and the Committee on Commerce, Science, and Transportation of the Senate on the guidelines described in paragraph (1).

(3) DECISIONS NOT SUBJECT TO JUDICIAL REVIEW.— Notwithstanding any other provision of law, any action of the Administrator of the Transportation Security Administration under paragraph (1) is not subject to judicial review.

TITLE LXV— OTHER MATTERS RELATING TO FOREIGN AFFAIRS

Sec. 6501. Authorization for United States Participation in the Coalition for Epidemic Preparedness Innovations.

SEC. 6501. [22 U.S.C. 276c-5] AUTHORIZATION FOR UNITED STATES PARTICIPATION IN THE COALITION FOR EPIDEMIC PREPAREDNESS INNOVATIONS.

(a) IN GENERAL.— The United States is authorized to participate in the Coalition for Epidemic Preparedness Innovations (referred to in this section as "CEPI").

(b) INVESTORS COUNCIL AND BOARD OF DIRECTORS.—

(1) INITIAL DESIGNATION.— The President shall designate an employee of the United States Agency for International Development to serve on the Investors Council and, if nominated, on the Board of Directors of CEPI, as a representative of the United States during the period beginning on the date of such designation and ending on September 30, 2022.

(2) ONGOING DESIGNATIONS.— The President may designate an employee of the relevant Federal department or agency with fiduciary responsibility for United States contributions to CEPI to serve on the Investors Council and, if nominated, on the Board of Directors of CEPI, as a representative of the United States.

(3) QUALIFICATIONS.— Any employee designated pursuant

to paragraph (1) or (2) shall have demonstrated knowledge and experience in the field of development and, if designated from a Federal department or agency with primary fiduciary responsibility for United States contributions pursuant to paragraph (2), in the field of public health, epidemiology, or medicine.

(4) COORDINATION.— In carrying out the responsibilities under this section, any employee designated pursuant to paragraph (1) or (2) shall coordinate with the Secretary of Health and Human Services to promote alignment, as appropriate, between CEPI and the strategic objectives and activities of the Secretary of Health and Human Services with respect to the research, development, and procurement of medical countermeasures, consistent with titles III and XXVIII of the Public Health Service Act (42 U.S.C. 241 et seq. and 300hh et seq.).

(c) CONSULTATION.— Not later than 60 days after the date of the enactment of this Act, the employee designated pursuant to subsection (b)(1) shall consult with the Committee on Foreign Relations, the Committee on Appropriations, and the Committee on Health, Education, Labor, and Pensions of the Senate and the Committee on Foreign Affairs, the Committee on Appropriations, and the Committee on Energy and Commerce of the House of Representatives regarding—

(1) the manner and extent to which the United States plans to participate in CEPI, including through the governance of CEPI;

(2) any planned financial contributions from the United States to CEPI; and

(3) how participation in CEPI is expected to support—

(A) the applicable revision of the National Biodefense Strategy required under section 1086 of the National Defense Authorization Act for Fiscal Year 2017 (6 U.S.C. 104); and

(B) any other relevant programs relating to global health security and biodefense.

* * * * * * *

SEC. 6506. UPDATES TO THE NATIONAL STRATEGY FOR COMBATING

TERRORIST AND OTHER ILLICIT FINANCING.

The Countering Russian Influence in Europe and Eurasia Act of 2017 (22 U.S.C. 9501 et seq.) is amended—

(1) in section 261(b)(2)—

(A) by striking "2020" and inserting "2024"; and

(B) by striking "2022" and inserting "2026";

(2) in section 262—

(A) in paragraph (1)—

(i) by striking " in the documents entitled '2015 National Money Laundering Risk Assessment' and '2015 National Terrorist Financing Risk Assessment', " and inserting " in the documents entitled '2020 National Strategy for Combating Terrorist and Other Illicit Financing' and '2022 National Strategy for Combating Terrorist and Other Illicit Financing' "; and

(ii) by striking "the broader counter terrorism strategy of the United States" and inserting "the broader counter terrorism and national security strategies of the United States";

(B) in paragraph (6)—

(i) by striking "Prevention of illicit finance" and inserting "prevention, detection, and disruption of illicit finance";

(ii) by striking "private financial sector" and inserting "private sector, including financial and other relevant industries,"; and

(iii) by striking "with regard to the prevention and detection of illicit finance" and inserting "with regard to the prevention, detection, and disruption of illicit finance"; and

(C) in paragraph (8), by striking "such as so-called cryptocurrencies, other methods that are computer, telecommunications, or Internet-based, cyber crime,".

* * * * * * *

National Cybersecurity Preparedness Consortium Act of 2021

PUBLIC LAW 117-122

National Cybersecurity Preparedness Consortium Act of 2021

[(Public Law 117–122)]

[This law has not been amended]

[Currency: This publication is a compilation of the text of Public Law 117-122. It was last amended by the public law listed in the As Amended Through note above and below at the bottom of each page of the pdf version and reflects current law through the date of the enactment of the public law listed at https://www.govinfo.gov/app/collection/comps/]

[Note: While this publication does not represent an official version of any Federal statute, substantial efforts have been made to ensure the accuracy of its contents. The official version of Federal law is found in the United States Statutes at Large and in the United States Code. The legal effect to be given to the Statutes at Large and the United States Code is established by statute (1 U.S.C. 112, 204).]

AN ACT To authorize the Secretary of Homeland Security to work with cybersecurity consortia for training, and for other purposes.

Be it enacted by the Senate and House of Representatives of the United States of America in Congress assembled,

SECTION 1. [6 U.S.C. 652 note] SHORT TITLE.

This Act may be cited as the "National Cybersecurity Preparedness Consortium Act of 2021".

SEC. 2. NATIONAL CYBERSECURITY PREPAREDNESS CONSORTIUM.

(a) IN GENERAL.—The Secretary may work with one or more consortia to support efforts to address cybersecurity risks and incidents.

(b) ASSISTANCE TO DHS.—The Secretary may work with one or more consortia to carry out the Secretary's responsibility pursuant to section 2202(e)(1)(P) of the Homeland Security Act of 2002 (6 U.S.C. 652(e)(1)(P)) to—

(1) provide training and education to State, Tribal, and

local first responders and officials specifically for preparing for and responding to cybersecurity risks and incidents, in accordance with applicable law;

(2) develop and update a curriculum utilizing existing training and educational programs and models in accordance with section 2209 of the Homeland Security Act of 2002 (6 U.S.C. 659), for State, Tribal, and local first responders and officials, related to cybersecurity risks and incidents;

(3) provide technical assistance services, training, and educational programs to build and sustain capabilities in support of preparedness for and response to cybersecurity risks and incidents, including threats of acts of terrorism, in accordance with such section 2209;

(4) conduct cross-sector cybersecurity training, education, and simulation exercises for entities, including State and local governments and Tribal organizations, critical infrastructure owners and operators, and private industry, to encourage community-wide coordination in defending against and responding to cybersecurity risks and incidents, in accordance with section 2210(c) of the Homeland Security Act of 2002 (6 U.S.C. 660(c));

(5) help States, Tribal organizations, and communities develop cybersecurity information sharing programs, in accordance with section 2209 of the Homeland Security Act of 2002 (6 U.S.C. 659), for the dissemination of homeland security information related to cybersecurity risks and incidents;

(6) help incorporate cybersecurity risk and incident prevention and response into existing State, Tribal, and local emergency plans, including continuity of operations plans; and

(7) assist State governments and Tribal organizations in developing cybersecurity plans.

(c) CONSIDERATIONS REGARDING SELECTION OF A CONSORTIUM.—In selecting a consortium with which to work under this Act, the Secretary shall take into consideration the following:

(1) Prior experience conducting cybersecurity training, education, and exercises for State and local entities.

(2) Geographic diversity of the members of any such consortium so as to maximize coverage of the different regions of the United States.

(3) The participation in such consortium of one or more historically Black colleges and universities, Hispanic-serving institutions, Tribal Colleges and Universities, other minority-serving institutions, and community colleges that participate in the National Centers of Excellence in Cybersecurity program, as carried out by the Department of Homeland Security.

(d) METRICS.—If the Secretary works with a consortium under subsection (a), the Secretary shall measure the effectiveness of the activities undertaken by the consortium under this Act.

(e) OUTREACH.—The Secretary shall conduct outreach to universities and colleges, including, in particular, outreach to historically Black colleges and universities, Hispanic-serving institutions, Tribal Colleges and Universities, other minority-serving institutions, and community colleges, regarding opportunities to support efforts to address cybersecurity risks and incidents, by working with the Secretary under subsection (a).

(f) RULE OF CONSTRUCTION.—Nothing in this section may be construed to authorize a consortium to control or direct any law enforcement agency in the exercise of the duties of the law enforcement agency.

(g) DEFINITIONS.—In this section—

(1) the term "community college" has the meaning given the term "junior or community college" in section 312 of the Higher Education Act of 1965 (20 U.S.C. 1058);

(2) the term "consortium" means a group primarily composed of nonprofit entities, including academic institutions, that develop, update, and deliver cybersecurity training and education in support of homeland security;

(3) the terms "cybersecurity risk" and "incident" have the meanings given those terms in section 2209(a) of the Homeland Security Act of 2002 (6 U.S.C. 659(a));

(4) the term "Department" means the Department of Homeland Security;

(5) the term "Hispanic-serving institution" has the meaning given the term in section 502 of the Higher Education Act of 1965 (20 U.S.C. 1101a);

(6) the term "historically Black college and university" has the meaning given the term "part B institution" in section 322 of the Higher Education Act of 1965 (20 U.S.C. 1061);

(7) the term "minority-serving institution" means an institution of higher education described in section 371(a) of the Higher Education Act of 1965 (20 U.S.C. 1067q(a));

(8) the term "Secretary" means the Secretary of Homeland Security;

(9) The term "State" means any State of the United States, the District of Columbia, the Commonwealth of Puerto Rico, the United States Virgin Islands, Guam, American Samoa, the Commonwealth of the Northern Mariana Islands, and any possession of the United States;

(10) the term "Tribal Colleges and Universities" has the meaning given the term in section 316 of the Higher Education Act of 1965 (20 U.S.C. 1059c); and

(11) the term "Tribal organization" has the meaning given the term in section 4(e) of the Indian Self-Determination and Education Assistance Act (25 U.S.C. 5304(e)).

State and Local Government Cybersecurity Act of 2021

PUBLIC LAW 117-150

State and Local Government Cybersecurity Act of 2021

[(Public Law 117–150)]

[This law has not been amended]

[Currency: This publication is a compilation of Public Law 117-150. It was last amended by the public law listed in the As Amended Through note above and below at the bottom of each page of the pdf version and reflects current law through the date of the enactment of the public law listed at https://www.govinfo.gov/app/collection/comps/]

[Note: While this publication does not represent an official version of any Federal statute, substantial efforts have been made to ensure the accuracy of its contents. The official version of Federal law is found in the United States Statutes at Large and in the United States Code. The legal effect to be given to the Statutes at Large and the United States Code is established by statute (1 U.S.C. 112, 204).]

AN ACT To amend the Homeland Security Act of 2002 to provide for engagements with State, local, Tribal, and territorial governments, and for other purposes.

Be it enacted by the Senate and House of Representatives of the United States of America in Congress assembled,

SECTION 1. [6 U.S.C. 101 note] SHORT TITLE.

This Act may be cited as the "State and Local Government Cybersecurity Act of 2021".

SEC. 2. AMENDMENTS TO THE HOMELAND SECURITY ACT OF 2002.

Subtitle A of title XXII of the Homeland Security Act of 2002 (6 U.S.C. 651 et seq.) is amended—

(1) in section 2201 (6 U.S.C. 651), by adding at the end the following:

"(7) SLTT ENTITY.—The term 'SLTT entity' means a domestic government entity that is a State government, local government, Tribal government, territorial government, or any subdivision thereof."

; and

(2) in section 2209 (6 U.S.C. 659)—

(A) in subsection (c)(6), by inserting "operational and" before "timely";

(B) in subsection (d)(1)(E), by inserting ", including an entity that collaborates with election officials," after "governments"; and

(C) by adding at the end the following:

"(p) COORDINATION ON CYBERSECURITY FOR SLTT ENTITIES.—

"(1) COORDINATION.—The Center shall, upon request and to the extent practicable, and in coordination as appropriate with Federal and non-Federal entities, such as the Multi-State Information Sharing and Analysis Center—

"(A) conduct exercises with SLTT entities;

"(B) provide operational and technical cybersecurity training to SLTT entities to address cybersecurity risks or incidents, with or without reimbursement, related to—

"(i) cyber threat indicators;

"(ii) defensive measures;

"(iii) cybersecurity risks;

"(iv) vulnerabilities; and

"(v) incident response and management;

"(C) in order to increase situational awareness and help prevent incidents, assist SLTT entities in sharing, in real time, with the Federal Government as well as among SLTT entities, actionable—

"(i) cyber threat indicators;

"(ii) defensive measures;

"(iii) information about cybersecurity risks; and

"(iv) information about incidents;

"(D) provide SLTT entities notifications

containing specific incident and malware information that may affect them or their residents;

"(E) provide to, and periodically update, SLTT entities via an easily accessible platform and other means—

"(i) information about tools;

"(ii) information about products;

"(iii) resources;

"(iv) policies;

"(v) guidelines;

"(vi) controls; and

"(vii) other cybersecurity standards and best practices and procedures related to information security, including, as appropriate, information produced by other Federal agencies;

"(F) work with senior SLTT entity officials, including chief information officers and senior election officials and through national associations, to coordinate the effective implementation by SLTT entities of tools, products, resources, policies, guidelines, controls, and procedures related to information security to secure the information systems, including election systems, of SLTT entities;

"(G) provide operational and technical assistance to SLTT entities to implement tools, products, resources, policies, guidelines, controls, and procedures on information security;

"(H) assist SLTT entities in developing policies and procedures for coordinating vulnerability disclosures consistent with international and national standards in the information technology industry; and

"(I) promote cybersecurity education and awareness through engagements with Federal agencies and non-Federal entities.

"(q) REPORT.—Not later than 1 year after the date of enactment of this subsection, and every 2 years thereafter, the Secretary shall submit to the Committee on Homeland Security and Governmental Affairs of the Senate and the Committee on Homeland

Security of the House of Representatives a report on the services and capabilities that the Agency directly and indirectly provides to SLTT entities." "

.

Consolidated Appropriations Act, 202

PUBLIC LAW 116-260, AMENDED

Consolidated Appropriations Act, 2021

[(Public Law 116–260)]

[As Amended Through P.L. 117–328, Enacted December 29, 2022]

[Currency: This publication is a compilation of the text of Public Law 116–260. It was last amended by the public law listed in the As Amended Through note above and below at the bottom of each page of the pdf version and reflects current law through the date of the enactment of the public law listed at https://www.govinfo.gov/app/collection/comps/]

AN ACT Making consolidated appropriations for the fiscal year ending September 30, 2021, providing coronavirus emergency response and relief, and for other purposes.

Be it enacted by the Senate and House of Representatives of the United States of America in Congress assembled,

SECTION 1. SHORT TITLE.

This Act may be cited as the "Consolidated Appropriations Act, 2021".

SEC. 2. TABLE OF CONTENTS.

* * * * * * *

DIVISION U—HOMELAND SECURITY AND GOVERNMENTAL AFFAIRS PROVISIONS

* * * * * * *

DIVISION W— INTELLIGENCE AUTHORIZATION ACT FOR
FISCAL YEAR 2021

* * * * * * *

DIVISION FF— OTHER MATTER

* * * * * * *

* * * * * * *

DIVISION U—HOMELAND SECURITY AND GOVERNMENTAL AFFAIRS PROVISIONS

* * * * * * *

TITLE II— DHS OVERSEAS PERSONNEL ENHANCEMENT ACT OF 2019

SEC. 201. SHORT TITLE.

This title may be cited as the "DHS Overseas Personnel Enhancement Act of 2019".

SEC. 202. OVERSEAS PERSONNEL BRIEFING.

(a) IN GENERAL.— Not later than 90 days after submission of the comprehensive 3-year strategy required under section 1910 of the National Defense Authorization Act for Fiscal Year 2017 (Public Law 114-328) and annually thereafter, the Secretary shall brief the Committee on Homeland Security of the House of Representatives and the Committee on Homeland Security and Governmental Affairs of the Senate regarding Department personnel with primary duties that take place outside of the United States.

(b) REQUIREMENTS.— The briefings required under subsection (a) shall include the following:

(1) A detailed summary of, and deployment schedule for, each type of personnel position with primary duties that take place outside of the United States and how each such position contributes to the Department's mission.

(2) Information related to how the geographic and regional placement of such positions contributes to the Department's mission.

(3) Information related to any risk mitigation plans for each geographic and regional placement, including to address counter-intelligence risks.

(4) Information regarding the costs of deploying or maintaining personnel at each geographic and regional placement, including information on any cost-sharing agreement with foreign partners to cover a portion or all the costs relating to such deployment or maintenance.

(5) Information on guidance and practices to guard against counter-espionage and counter-intelligence threats, including cyber threats, associated with Department personnel.

(6) Information regarding trends in foreign efforts to influence such personnel while deployed overseas to contribute to the Department's mission.

(7) Information related to the position-specific training received by such personnel before and during placement at a foreign location.

(8) Challenges that may impede the communication of counterterrorism information between Department personnel at foreign locations and Department entities in the United States, including technical, resource, and administrative challenges.

(9) The status of efforts to implement the strategy referred to in subsection (a).

(10) The status of efforts (beginning with the second briefing required under this section) to implement the enhancement plan under section 203.

SEC. 203. OVERSEAS PERSONNEL ENHANCEMENT PLAN.

(a) IN GENERAL.— Not later than 90 days after the first briefing required under section 202, the Secretary shall submit to the Committee on Homeland Security of the House of Representatives and the Committee on Homeland Security and Governmental Affairs of the Senate a plan to enhance the effectiveness of Department personnel at foreign locations.

(b) PLAN REQUIREMENTS.— The plan required under subsection (a) shall include proposals to—

(1) improve efforts of Department personnel at foreign locations, as necessary, for purposes of providing foreign

partner capacity development and furthering the Department's mission;

(2) as appropriate, redeploy Department personnel to respond to changing threats to the United States, consistent with the limits on the resources of the Department;

(3) enhance collaboration among Department personnel at foreign locations, other Federal personnel at foreign locations, and foreign partners;

(4) improve the communication of information between Department personnel at foreign locations and Department entities in the United States, including to address technical, resource, and administrative challenges; and

(5) maintain practices to guard against counter-espionage threats associated with Department personnel.

SEC. 204. TERMINATION.

The briefing requirement under section 202 shall terminate on the date that is 4 years after the submission of the strategy referred to in subsection (a) of such section.

SEC. 205. DEFINITIONS.

In this Act—

(1) the term "Department" means the Department of Homeland Security; and

(2) the term "Secretary" means the Secretary of Homeland Security.

TITLE III— SYNTHETIC OPIOID EXPOSURE PREVENTION AND TRAINING ACT

SEC. 301. [6 U.S.C. 101 note] SHORT TITLE.

This title may be cited as the "Synthetic Opioid Exposure Prevention and Training Act".

SEC. 302. PROTECTION AGAINST POTENTIAL SYNTHETIC OPIOID EXPOSURE WITHIN U.S. CUSTOMS AND BORDER PROTECTION.

(a) IN GENERAL.— Subtitle B of title IV of the Homeland Security Act of 2002 (6 U.S.C. 211 et seq.) is amended by inserting after section 415 the following new section:

"**SEC. 416. [6 U.S.C. 216] PROTECTION AGAINST POTENTIAL SYNTHETIC OPIOID EXPOSURE**

"(a) IN GENERAL.— The Commissioner of U.S. Customs and Border Protection shall issue a policy that specifies effective protocols and procedures for the safe handling of potential synthetic opioids, including fentanyl, by U.S. Customs and Border Protection officers, agents, other personnel, and canines, and to reduce the risk of injury or death resulting from accidental exposure and enhance post-exposure management.

"(b) TRAINING.—

"(1) IN GENERAL.— Together with the issuance of the policy described in subsection (a), the Commissioner of U.S. Customs and Border Protection shall require mandatory and recurrent training on the following:

"(A) The potential risk of opioid exposure and safe handling procedures for potential synthetic opioids, including precautionary measures such as the use of personal protective equipment during such handling.

"(B) How to access and administer opioid receptor antagonists, including naloxone, post-exposure to potential synthetic opioids.

"(2) INTEGRATION.— The training described in paragraph (1) may be integrated into existing training under section 411(l) for U.S. Customs and Border Protection officers, agents, and other personnel.

"(c) PERSONAL PROTECTIVE EQUIPMENT AND OPIOID RECEPTOR ANTAGONISTS.— Together with the issuance of the policy described in subsection (a), the Commissioner of U.S. Customs and Border Protection shall ensure the availability of personal protective equipment and opioid receptor antagonists, including naloxone, to all U.S. Customs and Border Protection officers, agents, other personnel, and canines at risk of accidental exposure to synthetic opioids.

"(d) OVERSIGHT.— To ensure effectiveness of the policy described in subsection (a)—

"(1) the Commissioner of U.S. Customs and Border Protection shall regularly monitor the efficacy of the implementation of such policy and adjust protocols and procedures, as necessary; and

"(2) the Inspector General of the Department shall audit compliance with the requirements of this section not less than once during the 3-year period after the date of the enactment of this section."

.

(b) CLERICAL AMENDMENT.— The table of contents in section 1(b) of the Homeland Security Act of 2002 is amended by inserting after the item relating to section 415 the following new item:

"Sec. 416. Protection against potential synthetic opioid exposure."

.

* * * * * * *

TITLE VI— COUNTER THREATS ADVISORY BOARD ACT OF 2019

SEC. 601. [6 U.S.C. 101 note] SHORT TITLE.

This title may be cited as the "Counter Threats Advisory Board Act of 2019".

SEC. 602. DEPARTMENT OF HOMELAND SECURITY COUNTER THREATS ADVISORY BOARD.

(a) IN GENERAL.— Subtitle A of title II of the Homeland Security Act of 2002 (6 U.S.C. 121 et seq.) is amended by inserting after section 210E the following:

"SEC. 210F. [6 U.S.C. 124m-1] DEPARTMENTAL COORDINATION ON COUNTER THREATS

"(a) ESTABLISHMENT.— There is authorized in the Department, for a period of 2 years beginning after the date of enactment of this section, a Counter Threats Advisory Board (in this section referred to as the 'Board') which shall—

"(1) be composed of senior representatives of departmental operational components and headquarters elements; and

"(2) coordinate departmental intelligence activities and policy and information related to the mission and functions of the Department that counter threats.

"(b) CHARTER.—There shall be a charter to govern the structure and mission of the Board, which shall—

"(1) direct the Board to focus on the current threat environment and the importance of aligning departmental activities to counter threats under the guidance of the Secretary; and

"(2) be reviewed and updated as appropriate.

"(c) MEMBERS.—

"(1) IN GENERAL.—The Board shall be composed of senior representatives of departmental operational components and headquarters elements.

"(2) CHAIR.—The Under Secretary for Intelligence and Analysis shall serve as the Chair of the Board.

"(3) MEMBERS.—The Secretary shall appoint additional members of the Board from among the following:

"(A) The Transportation Security Administration.

"(B) U.S. Customs and Border Protection.

"(C) U.S. Immigration and Customs Enforcement.

"(D) The Federal Emergency Management Agency.

"(E) The Coast Guard.

"(F) U.S. Citizenship and Immigration Services.

"(G) The United States Secret Service.

"(H) The Cybersecurity and Infrastructure Security Agency.

"(I) The Office of Operations Coordination.

"(J) The Office of the General Counsel.

"(K) The Office of Intelligence and Analysis.

"(L) The Office of Strategy, Policy, and Plans.

"(M) The Science and Technology Directorate.

"(N) The Office for State and Local Law Enforcement.

"(O) The Privacy Office.

"(P) The Office for Civil Rights and Civil Liberties.

"(Q) Other departmental offices and programs as determined appropriate by the Secretary.

"(d) MEETINGS.—The Board shall—

"(1) meet on a regular basis to discuss intelligence and coordinate ongoing threat mitigation efforts and departmental activities, including coordination with other Federal, State, local, tribal, territorial, and private sector partners; and

"(2) make recommendations to the Secretary.

"(e) TERRORISM ALERTS.—The Board shall advise the Secretary on the issuance of terrorism alerts under section 203.

"(f) PROHIBITION ON ADDITIONAL FUNDS.—No additional funds are authorized to carry out this section."

.

(b) TECHNICAL AND CONFORMING AMENDMENT.—The table of contents in section 1(b) of the Homeland Security Act of 2002 (Public Law 107-296; 116 Stat. 2135) is amended by inserting after the item relating to section 210E the following:

"Sec. 210F. Departmental coordination on counter threats."

.

(c) REPORT.—Not later than 90 days after the date of enactment of this Act, the Secretary of Homeland Security, acting through the Chair of the Counter Threats Advisory Board established under section 210F of the Homeland Security Act of 2002, as added by subsection (a), shall submit to the Committee on Homeland Security and Governmental Affairs of the Senate and the Committee on Homeland Security of the House of Representatives a report on the status and activities of the Counter Threats Advisory Board.

(d) [6 U.S.C. 124m-1 note] NOTICE.—The Secretary of Homeland Security shall provide written notification to and brief the Committee on Homeland Security and Governmental Affairs of the Senate and the Committee on Homeland Security of the House of Representatives on any changes to or introductions of new mechanisms to coordinate threats across the Department of Homeland Security.

TITLE VII—DHS COUNTERING UNMANNED AIRCRAFT SYSTEMS COORDINATOR ACT

SEC. 701. DHS COUNTERING UNMANNED AIRCRAFT SYSTEMS

COORDINATOR ACT.

(a) **[6 U.S.C. 101 note]** SHORT TITLE.—This title may be cited as the "DHS Countering Unmanned Aircraft Systems Coordinator Act".

(b) COUNTERING UNMANNED AIRCRAFT SYSTEMS COORDINATOR.—

(1) IN GENERAL.—Title III of the Homeland Security Act of 2002 (6 U.S.C. 181 et seq.) is amended by adding at the end the following new section:

"SEC. 321. [6 U.S.C. 195g] COUNTERING UNMANNED AIRCRAFT SYSTEMS COORDINATOR

"(a) COORDINATOR.—

"(1) IN GENERAL.—The Secretary shall designate an individual in a Senior Executive Service position (as defined in section 3132 of title 5, United States Code) of the Department within the Office of Strategy, Policy, and Plans as the Countering Unmanned Aircraft Systems Coordinator (in this section referred to as the 'Coordinator') and provide appropriate staff to carry out the responsibilities of the Coordinator.

"(2) RESPONSIBILITIES.—The Coordinator shall—

"(A) oversee and coordinate with relevant Department offices and components, including the Office of Civil Rights and Civil Liberties and the Privacy Office, on the development of guidance and regulations to counter threats associated with unmanned aircraft systems (in this section referred to as 'UAS') as described in section 210G;

"(B) promote research and development of counter UAS technologies in coordination within the Science and Technology Directorate;

"(C) coordinate with the relevant components and offices of the Department, including the Office of Intelligence and Analysis, to ensure the sharing of information, guidance, and intelligence relating to countering UAS threats, counter UAS threat assessments, and counter UAS technology, including the retention of UAS and counter UAS incidents within the Department;

"(D) serve as the Department liaison, in coordination with relevant components and offices of the Department, to the Department of Defense, Federal, State, local, and Tribal law enforcement entities, and the private sector regarding the activities of the Department relating to countering UAS;

"(E) maintain the information required under section 210G(g)(3); and

"(F) carry out other related counter UAS authorities and activities under section 210G, as directed by the Secretary.

"(b) COORDINATION WITH APPLICABLE FEDERAL LAWS.—The Coordinator shall, in addition to other assigned duties, coordinate with relevant Department components and offices to ensure testing, evaluation, or deployment of a system used to identify, assess, or defeat a UAS is carried out in accordance with applicable Federal laws.

"(c) COORDINATION WITH PRIVATE SECTOR.—The Coordinator shall, among other assigned duties, working with the Office of Partnership and Engagement and other relevant Department offices and components, or other Federal agencies, as appropriate, serve as the principal Department official responsible for sharing to the private sector information regarding counter UAS technology, particularly information regarding instances in which counter UAS technology may impact lawful private sector services or systems."

.

(2) TECHNICAL AND CONFORMING AMENDMENT.—The table of contents in section 1(b) of the Homeland Security Act of 2002 (Public Law 107-296; 116 Stat. 2135) is amended by inserting after the item relating to section 320 the following:

"Sec. 321. Countering Unmanned Aircraft Systems Coordinator."

.

* * * * * * *

TITLE IX— DOTGOV ACT OF 2020

SEC. 901. [6 U.S.C. 101 note] SHORT TITLE.

This title may be cited as the "DOTGOV Online Trust in Government Act of 2020" or the "DOTGOV Act of 2020".

SEC. 902. [6 U.S.C. 665 note] FINDINGS.

Congress finds that—

(1) the .gov internet domain reflects the work of United States innovators in inventing the internet and the role that the Federal Government played in guiding the development and success of the early internet;

(2) the .gov internet domain is a unique resource of the United States that reflects the history of innovation and global leadership of the United States;

(3) when online public services and official communications from any level and branch of government use the .gov internet domain, they are easily recognized as official and difficult to impersonate;

(4) the citizens of the United States deserve online public services that are safe, recognizable, and trustworthy;

(5) the .gov internet domain should be available at no cost or a negligible cost to any Federal, State, local, or territorial government-operated or publicly controlled entity, including any Tribal government recognized by the Federal Government or a State government, for use in their official services, operations, and communications;

(6) the .gov internet domain provides a critical service to those Federal, State, local, Tribal, and territorial governments; and

(7) the .gov internet domain should be operated transparently and in the spirit of public accessibility, privacy, and security.

SEC. 903. [6 U.S.C. 665 note] DEFINITIONS.

In this Act—

(1) the term "Administrator" means the Administrator of General Services;

(2) the term "agency" has the meaning given the term in section 3502 of title 44, United States Code;

(3) the term "Director" means the Director of the

Cybersecurity and Infrastructure Security Agency;

(4) the term "online service" means any internet-facing service, including a website, email, a virtual private network, or a custom application; and

(5) the term "State" means any State of the United States, the District of Columbia, the Commonwealth of Puerto Rico, the Virgin Islands, Guam, American Samoa, the Commonwealth of the Northern Mariana Islands, and any possession of the United States.

SEC. 904. [6 U.S.C. 665 note] DUTIES OF DEPARTMENT OF HOMELAND SECURITY.

(a) PURPOSE.—The purpose of the .gov internet domain program is to—

(1) legitimize and enhance public trust in government entities and their online services;

(2) facilitate trusted electronic communication and connections to and from government entities;

(3) provide simple and secure registration of .gov internet domains;

(4) improve the security of the services hosted within these .gov internet domains, and of the .gov namespace in general; and

(5) enable the discoverability of government services to the public and to domain registrants.

(b) DUTIES AND AUTHORITIES RELATING TO THE .GOV INTERNET DOMAIN.—

(1) IN GENERAL.—Subtitle A of title XXII of the Homeland Security Act of 2002 of 2002[3] (6 U.S.C. 651 et seq.) is amended—

---

[3]   The reference in section 904(b)(1) is so in law. See amendments made by section 1547(b)(1)(B) of division A of Public Law 117–81 and section 7143(a)(1) of division G of Public Law 117–263.

(A) in section 2202(c) (6 U.S.C. 652(c))—

(i) in paragraph (10), by striking "and" at the end;

(ii) by redesignating paragraph (11) as paragraph (12); and

(iii) by inserting after paragraph (10) the following:

"(11) carry out the duties and authorities relating to the .gov internet domain, as described in section 2215; and"

; and

(B) by adding at the end the following:

"**SEC. 2215. [6 U.S.C. 665] DUTIES AND AUTHORITIES RELATING TO .GOV INTERNET DOMAIN**

"(a) DEFINITION.—In this section, the term 'agency' has the meaning given the term in section 3502 of title 44, United States Code.

"(b) AVAILABILITY OF .GOV INTERNET DOMAIN.—The Director shall make .gov internet domain name registration services, as well as any supporting services described in subsection (e), generally available—

"(1) to any Federal, State, local, or territorial government entity, or other publicly controlled entity, including any Tribal government recognized by the Federal Government or a State government, that complies with the requirements for registration developed by the Director as described in subsection (c);

"(2) without conditioning registration on the sharing of any information with the Director or any other Federal entity, other than the information required to meet the requirements described in subsection (c); and

"(3) without conditioning registration on participation in any separate service offered by the Director or any other Federal entity.

"(c) REQUIREMENTS.—The Director, with the approval of the Director of the Office of Management and Budget for agency .gov internet domain requirements and in consultation with the Director of the Office of Management and Budget for .gov internet domain requirements for entities that are not agencies, shall establish and publish on a publicly available website requirements for the registration and operation of .gov internet domains sufficient to—

"(1) minimize the risk of .gov internet domains whose names could mislead or confuse users;

"(2) establish that .gov internet domains may not be used for commercial or political campaign purposes;

"(3) ensure that domains are registered and maintained only by authorized individuals; and

"(4) limit the sharing or use of any information obtained through the administration of the .gov internet domain with any other Department component or any other agency for any purpose other than the administration of the .gov internet domain, the services described in subsection (e), and the requirements for establishing a .gov inventory described in subsection (h).

"(d) EXECUTIVE BRANCH.—

"(1) IN GENERAL.—The Director of the Office of Management and Budget shall establish applicable processes and guidelines for the registration and acceptable use of .gov internet domains by agencies.

"(2) APPROVAL REQUIRED.—The Director shall obtain the approval of the Director of the Office of Management and Budget before registering a .gov internet domain name for an agency.

"(3) COMPLIANCE.—Each agency shall ensure that any website or digital service of the agency that uses a .gov internet domain is in compliance with the 21st Century IDEA Act (44 U.S.C. 3501 note) and implementation guidance issued pursuant to that Act.

"(e) SUPPORTING SERVICES.—

"(1) IN GENERAL.—The Director may provide services to the entities described in subsection (b)(1) specifically intended to support the security, privacy, reliability, accessibility, and speed of registered .gov internet domains.

"(2) RULE OF CONSTRUCTION.—Nothing in paragraph (1) shall be construed to—

"(A) limit other authorities of the Director to

provide services or technical assistance to an entity described in subsection (b)(1); or

"(B) establish new authority for services other than those the purpose of which expressly supports the operation of .gov internet domains and the needs of .gov internet domain registrants.

"(f) FEES.—

"(1) IN GENERAL.—The Director may provide any service relating to the availability of the .gov internet domain program, including .gov internet domain name registration services described in subsection (b) and supporting services described in subsection (e), to entities described in subsection (b)(1) with or without reimbursement, including variable pricing.

"(2) LIMITATION.—The total fees collected for new .gov internet domain registrants or annual renewals of .gov internet domains shall not exceed the direct operational expenses of improving, maintaining, and operating the .gov internet domain, .gov internet domain services, and .gov internet domain supporting services.

"(g) CONSULTATION.—The Director shall consult with the Director of the Office of Management and Budget, the Administrator of General Services, other civilian Federal agencies as appropriate, and entities representing State, local, Tribal, or territorial governments in developing the strategic direction of the .gov internet domain and in establishing requirements under subsection (c), in particular on matters of privacy, accessibility, transparency, and technology modernization.

"(h) .GOV INVENTORY.—

"(1) IN GENERAL.—The Director shall, on a continuous basis—

"(A) inventory all hostnames and services in active use within the .gov internet domain; and

"(B) provide the data described in subparagraph (A) to domain registrants at no cost.

"(2) REQUIREMENTS.—In carrying out paragraph (1)—

"(A) data may be collected through analysis of public and non-public sources, including commercial data sets;

"(B) the Director shall share with Federal and non-Federal domain registrants all unique hostnames and services discovered within the zone of their registered domain;

"(C) the Director shall share any data or information collected or used in the management of the .gov internet domain name registration services relating to Federal executive branch registrants with the Director of the Office of Management and Budget for the purpose of fulfilling the duties of the Director of the Office of Management and Budget under section 3553 of title 44, United States Code;

"(D) the Director shall publish on a publicly available website discovered hostnames that describe publicly accessible agency websites, to the extent consistent with the security of Federal information systems but with the presumption of disclosure;

"(E) the Director may publish on a publicly available website any analysis conducted and data collected relating to compliance with Federal mandates and industry best practices, to the extent consistent with the security of Federal information systems but with the presumption of disclosure; and

"(F) the Director shall—

"(i) collect information on the use of non-.gov internet domain suffixes by agencies for their official online services;

"(ii) collect information on the use of non-.gov internet domain suffixes by State, local, Tribal, and territorial governments; and

"(iii) publish the information collected under clause (i) on a publicly available website to the extent consistent with the security of the Federal information systems, but with the presumption of disclosure.

"(3) NATIONAL SECURITY COORDINATION.—

"(A) IN GENERAL.—In carrying out this subsection, the Director shall inventory, collect, and publish hostnames and services in a manner consistent with the protection of national security information.

"(B) LIMITATION.—The Director may not inventory, collect, or publish hostnames or services under this subsection if the Director, in coordination with other heads of agencies, as appropriate, determines that the collection or publication would—

"(i) disrupt a law enforcement investigation;

"(ii) endanger national security or intelligence activities;

"(iii) impede national defense activities or military operations; or

"(iv) hamper security remediation actions.

"(4) STRATEGY.—Not later than 180 days after the date of enactment of this section, the Director shall develop and submit to the Committee on Homeland Security and Governmental Affairs and the Committee on Rules and Administration of the Senate and the Committee on Homeland Security, the Committee on Oversight and Reform, and the Committee on House Administration of the House of Representatives a strategy to utilize the information collected under this subsection for countering malicious cyber activity."

(2) ADDITIONAL DUTIES.—

(A) OUTREACH STRATEGY.—Not later than 1 year after the date of enactment of this Act, the Director, in consultation with the Administrator and entities representing State, local, Tribal, or territorial governments, shall develop and submit to the Committee on Homeland Security and Governmental Affairs and the Committee on Rules and Administration of the Senate and the Committee on Homeland Security, the Committee on Oversight and Reform, and the Committee on House Administration of the House of Representatives an outreach strategy to local, Tribal, and territorial governments and other publicly controlled entities as determined by the Director to inform and support migration to the .gov internet domain, which shall include—

(i) stakeholder engagement plans; and

(ii) information on how migrating information technology systems to the .gov internet domain is beneficial to that entity, including benefits relating to cybersecurity and the supporting services offered by the Federal Government.

(B) [6 U.S.C. 665 note] REFERENCE GUIDE.—Not later than 1 year after the date of enactment of this Act, the Director, in consultation with the Administrator and entities representing State, local, Tribal, or territorial governments, shall develop and publish on a publicly available website a reference guide for migrating online services to the .gov internet domain, which shall include—

(i) process and technical information on how to carry out a migration of common categories of online services, such as web and email services;

(ii) best practices for cybersecurity pertaining to registration and operation of a .gov internet domain; and

(iii) references to contract vehicles and other private sector resources vetted by the Director that may assist in performing the migration.

(C) SECURITY ENHANCEMENT PLAN.—Not later than 1 year after the date of enactment of this Act, the Director shall develop and submit to the Committee on Homeland Security and Governmental Affairs and the Committee on Rules and Administration of the Senate and the Committee on Homeland Security, the Committee on Oversight and

Reform, and the Committee on House Administration of the House of Representatives a .gov internet domain security enhancement strategy and implementation plan on how to improve the cybersecurity benefits of the .gov internet domain during the 5-year period following the date of enactment of this Act, which shall include—

(i) a modernization plan for the information systems that support operation of the .gov top-level internet domain, such as the registrar portal, and how these information systems will remain current with evolving security trends;

(ii) a modernization plan for the structure of the .gov program and any supporting contracts, and how the program and contracts can remain flexible over time so as to take advantage of emerging technology and cybersecurity developments; and

(iii) an outline of specific security enhancements the .gov program intends to provide to users during that 5-year period.

(3) TECHNICAL AND CONFORMING AMENDMENT.—The table of contents in section 1(b) of the Homeland Security Act of 2002 (Public Law 107-196; 116 Stat. 2135) is amended by inserting after the item relating to section 2214 the following:

"Sec. 2215. Duties and authorities relating to .gov internet domain."

·

(c) HOMELAND SECURITY GRANTS.—Section 2008(a) of the Homeland Security Act of 2002 (6 U.S.C. 609(a)) is amended—

(1) in paragraph (13), by striking "and" at the end;

(2) by redesignating paragraph (14) as paragraph (15); and

(3) by inserting after paragraph (13) the following:

"(14) migrating any online service (as defined in section 3 of the DOTGOV Online Trust in Government Act of 2020) to the .gov internet domain; and"

·

SEC. 905. REPORT.

Not later than 1 year after the date of enactment of this Act, and every 2 years thereafter for 4 years, the Director shall submit a report to or conduct a detailed briefing for the Committee on Homeland Security and Governmental Affairs and the Committee on Rules and Administration of the Senate and the Committee on Homeland Security, the Committee on Oversight and Reform, and the Committee on House Administration of the House of Representatives on the status of—

(1) the outreach strategy described in section 904(b)(2)(A);

(2) the security enhancement strategy and implementation plan described in section 904(b)(2)(C);

(3) the inventory described in 2215(f) of the Homeland Security Act of 2002, as added by section 904(b) of this Act;

(4) the supporting services described in section 2215(c)(1) of the Homeland Security Act of 2002, as added by section 904(b) of this Act; and

(5) the development, assessment, and determination of the amount of any fees imposed on new .gov internet domain registrants or annual renewals of .gov internet domains in accordance with section 2215(d) of the Homeland Security Act of 2002, as added by section 904(b) of this Act.

SEC. 906. RESEARCH AND DEVELOPMENT.

Not later than 1 year after the date of enactment of this Act, the Under Secretary for Science and Technology of the Department shall conduct a study and submit to the Director a report on mechanisms for improving the cybersecurity benefits of the .gov internet domain, including—

(1) how information systems support operation of the .gov top-level internet domain, such as the registrar portal, and how these information systems can remain current with evolving security trends;

(2) how the structure of the .gov internet domain program can take advantage of emerging technology and cybersecurity developments; and

(3) additional mechanisms to improve the cybersecurity of the .gov internet domain.

SEC. 907. [6 U.S.C. 665 note] TRANSITION.

(a) There shall be transferred to the Director the .gov internet domain program, as operated by the General Services Administration under title 41, Code of Federal Regulations, on the date on which the Director begins operational administration of the .gov internet domain program, in accordance with subsection (c).

(b) Not later than 30 days after the date of enactment of this Act, the Director shall submit a plan for the operational and contractual transition of the .gov internet domain program to the Committee on Homeland Security and Governmental Affairs and the Committee on Rules and Administration of the Senate and the Committee on Homeland Security, the Committee on Oversight and Reform, and the Committee on House Administration of the House of Representatives.

(c) Not later than 120 days after the date of enactment of this Act, the Director shall begin operationally administering the .gov internet domain program, and shall publish on a publicly available website the requirements for domain registrants as described in section 2215(b) of the Homeland Security Act of 2002, as added by section 904(b) of this Act.

(d) On the date on which the Director begins operational administration of the .gov internet domain program, in accordance with subsection (c), the Administrator shall rescind the requirements in part 102-173 of title 41, Code of Federal Regulations.

(e) During the 5-year period beginning on the date of enactment of this Act, any fee charged to entities that are not agencies for new .gov internet domain registrants or annual renewals of .gov internet domains shall be not more than the amount of the fee charged for such registration or renewal as of October 1, 2019.

TITLE X—REAL ID MODERNIZATION ACT

SEC. 1001. REAL ID MODERNIZATION.

(a) [49 U.S.C. 30101 note] SHORT TITLE.—This title may be cited as the "REAL ID Modernization Act".

(b) REAL ID ACT AMENDMENTS.—

(1) DEFINITIONS.—Section 201 of the REAL ID Act of 2005 (division B of Public Law 109-13; 49 U.S.C. 30301 note) is

amended—

(A) in paragraph (1)—

(i) by striking "The term 'driver's license' means" and inserting the following:"The term 'driver's license'—

"(A) means"

; and

(ii) by striking "Code." and inserting the following:"Code; and

"(B) includes driver's licenses stored or accessed via electronic means, such as mobile or digital driver's licenses, which have been issued in accordance with regulations prescribed by the Secretary."

; and

(B) in paragraph (2)—

(i) by striking "The term 'identification card' means" and inserting the following:"The term 'identification card'—

"(A) means"

; and

(ii) by striking "State." and inserting the following:"State; and

"(B) includes identification cards stored or accessed via electronic means, such as mobile or digital identification cards, which have been issued in accordance with regulations prescribed by the Secretary."

.

(2) MINIMUM REQUIREMENTS FOR FEDERAL RECOGNITION.—Section 202 of the REAL ID Act of 2005 (division B of Public Law 109-13; 49 U.S.C. 30301 note) is amended—

(A) in the section heading, by striking "document";

(B) in subsection (a)—

(i) in paragraph (2), by striking ", in consultation with the Secretary of Transportation,"; and

(ii) by adding at the end the following:

"(3) LIMITATION.—The presentation of digital information from a mobile or digital driver's license or identification card to an official of a Federal agency for an official purpose may not be construed to grant consent for such Federal agency to seize the electronic device on which the license or card is stored or to examine any other information contained on such device."

;

(C) in subsection (b)—

(i) in the subsection heading, by striking "Document" and inserting "Driver's License and Identification Card";

(ii) in the matter preceding paragraph (1), by inserting ", or as part of," after "features on";

(iii) in paragraph (5), by inserting ", which may be the photograph taken by the State at the time the person applies for a driver's license or identification card or may be a digital photograph of the person that is already on file with the State" before the period at the end;

(iv) in paragraph (6), by striking "principle" and inserting "principal"; and

(v) in paragraph (8)—

(I) by striking "Physical security" and inserting "Security"; and

(II) by striking "document" and inserting "driver's license or identification card";

(D) in subsection (c)—

(i) in paragraph (1)(C), by striking "Proof of the" and inserting "The";

(ii) by redesignating paragraph (3) as paragraph (4);

(iii) by inserting after paragraph (2) the following:

"(3) ELECTRONIC PRESENTATION OF IDENTITY

AND LAWFUL STATUS INFORMATION.—A State may accept information required under paragraphs (1) and (2) through the use of electronic transmission methods if—

"(A) the Secretary issues regulations regarding such electronic transmission that—

"(i) describe the categories of information eligible for electronic transmission; and

"(ii) include measures—

"(I) to ensure the authenticity of the information transmitted;

"(II) to protect personally identifiable information; and

"(III) to detect and prevent identity fraud; and

"(B) the State certifies to the Department of Homeland Security that its use of such electronic methods complies with regulations issued by the Secretary."

; and

(iv) in paragraph (4)(A), as redesignated, by striking "each document" and inserting "the information and documentation"; and

(E) in subsection (d)—

(i) in paragraph (7), by striking "document materials and papers" and inserting "materials, records, and data";

(ii) in paragraph (8), by striking "security clearance requirements" and inserting "background checks"; and

(iii) in paragraph (9), by striking "fraudulent document recognition" and inserting "fraud detection and prevention".

(3) REPEAL OF GRANTS TO STATES.—The REAL ID Act of 2005 (division B of Public Law 109-13; 49 U.S.C. 30301 note) is amended by striking section 204.

(4) NOTIFICATION OF REAL ID ACT OF 2005 REQUIREMENTS.—The REAL ID Act of 2005 (division B of Public Law 109-13; 49 U.S.C. 30301 note) is amended by adding at the end the following:

"SEC. 208. NOTIFICATION OF REQUIREMENTS AND DEADLINES

"During the 15-month period beginning 90 days before the date on which Federal agencies will no longer accept, for official purposes, driver's licenses and identification cards that do not comply with the requirements under section 202, aircraft operators and third party reservation entities shall notify passengers about the requirements and enforcement deadlines under this Act."

.

(c) [49 U.S.C. 30301 note] IMMEDIATE BURDEN REDUCTION MEASURES.—Notwithstanding any other provision of law (including regulations), beginning on the date of the enactment of this Act, a State does not need to require an applicant for a driver's license or identification card to provide separate documentation of the applicant's Social Security account number in order to comply with the requirements of the REAL ID Act of 2005 (division B of Public Law 109-13; 49 U.S.C. 30301 note).

TITLE XI—SOUTHWEST BORDER SECURITY TECHNOLOGY IMPROVEMENT ACT OF 2020

SEC. 1101. SHORT TITLE.

This title may be cited as the "Southwest Border Security Technology Improvement Act of 2020".

SEC. 1102. DEFINITIONS.

In this Act:

(1) APPROPRIATE CONGRESSIONAL COMMITTEES.—The term "appropriate congressional committees" means—

(A) the Committee on Homeland Security and Governmental Affairs of the Senate; and

(B) the Committee on Homeland Security of the House of Representatives.

(2) DEPARTMENT.—The term "Department" means the Department of Homeland Security.

(3) SECRETARY.—The term "Secretary" means the Secretary of Homeland Security.

(4) SOUTHWEST BORDER.—The term "Southwest border" means the international land border between the United States and Mexico, including the ports of entry along such border.

SEC. 1103. SOUTHERN BORDER TECHNOLOGY NEEDS ANALYSIS AND UPDATES.

(a) TECHNOLOGY NEEDS ANALYSIS.—Not later than 1 year after the date of the enactment of this Act, the Secretary shall submit, to the appropriate congressional committees, a technology needs analysis for border security technology along the Southwest border.

(b) CONTENTS.—The analysis required under subsection (a) shall include an assessment of—

(1) the technology needs and gaps along the Southwest border—

(A) to prevent terrorists and instruments of terror from entering the United States;

(B) to combat and reduce cross-border criminal activity, including, but not limited to—

(i) the transport of illegal goods, such as illicit drugs; and

(ii) human smuggling and human trafficking; and

(C) to facilitate the flow of legal trade across the Southwest border;

(2) recent technological advancements in—

(A) manned aircraft sensor, communication, and common operating picture technology;

(B) unmanned aerial systems and related technology, including counter-unmanned aerial system technology;

(C) surveillance technology, including—

(i) mobile surveillance vehicles;

(ii) associated electronics, including cameras, sensor technology, and radar;

(iii) tower-based surveillance technology;

          (iv) advanced unattended surveillance sensors; and

          (v) deployable, lighter-than-air, ground surveillance equipment;

      (D) nonintrusive inspection technology, including non-X-ray devices utilizing muon tomography and other advanced detection technology;

      (E) tunnel detection technology; and

      (F) communications equipment, including—

          (i) radios;

          (ii) long-term evolution broadband; and

          (iii) miniature satellites;

   (3) any other technological advancements that the Secretary determines to be critical to the Department's mission along the Southwest border;

   (4) whether the use of the technological advances described in paragraphs (2) and (3) will—

      (A) improve border security;

      (B) improve the capability of the Department to accomplish its mission along the Southwest border;

      (C) reduce technology gaps along the Southwest border; and

      (D) enhance the safety of any officer or agent of the Department or any other Federal agency;

   (5) the Department's ongoing border security technology development efforts, including efforts by—

      (A) U.S. Customs and Border Protection;

      (B) the Science and Technology Directorate; and

      (C) the technology assessment office of any other operational component;

   (6) the technology needs for improving border security, such as—

      (A) information technology or other computer or computing systems data capture;

      (B) biometrics;

      (C) cloud storage; and

(D) intelligence data sharing capabilities among agencies within the Department;

(7) any other technological needs or factors, including border security infrastructure, such as physical barriers or dual-purpose infrastructure, that the Secretary determines should be considered; and

(8) currently deployed technology or new technology that would improve the Department's ability—

(A) to reasonably achieve operational control and situational awareness along the Southwest border; and

(B) to collect metrics for securing the border at and between ports of entry, as required under subsections (b) and (c) of section 1092 of division A of the National Defense Authorization Act for Fiscal Year 2017 (6 U.S.C. 223).

(c) UPDATES.—

(1) IN GENERAL.—Not later than 2 years after the submission of the analysis required under subsection (a), and biannually thereafter for the following 4 years, the Secretary shall submit an update to such analysis to the appropriate congressional committees.

(2) CONTENTS.—Each update required under paragraph (1) shall include a plan for utilizing the resources of the Department to meet the border security technology needs and gaps identified pursuant to subsection (b), including developing or acquiring technologies not currently in use by the Department that would allow the Department to bridge existing border technology gaps along the Southwest border.

(d) ITEMS TO BE CONSIDERED.—In compiling the technology needs analysis and updates required under this section, the Secretary shall consider and examine—

(1) technology that is deployed and is sufficient for the Department's use along the Southwest border;

(2) technology that is deployed, but is insufficient for the Department's use along the Southwest border; and

(3) technology that is not deployed, but is necessary for the Department's use along the Southwest border;

(4) current formal departmental requirements documentation examining current border security threats and

challenges faced by any component of the Department;

(5) trends and forecasts regarding migration across the Southwest border;

(6) the impact on projected staffing and deployment needs for the Department, including staffing needs that may be fulfilled through the use of technology;

(7) the needs and challenges faced by employees of the Department who are deployed along the Southwest border;

(8) the need to improve cooperation among Federal, State, tribal, local, and Mexican law enforcement entities to enhance security along the Southwest border;

(9) the privacy implications of existing technology and the acquisition and deployment of new technologies and supporting infrastructure, with an emphasis on how privacy risks might be mitigated through the use of technology, training, and policy;

(10) the impact of any ongoing public health emergency that impacts Department operations along the Southwest border; and

(11) the ability of, and the needs for, the Department to assist with search and rescue efforts for individuals or groups that may be in physical danger or in need of medical assistance.

(e) CLASSIFIED FORM.—To the extent possible, the Secretary shall submit the technology needs analysis and updates required under this section in unclassified form, but may submit such documents, or portions of such documents, in classified form if the Secretary determines that such action is appropriate.

* * * * * * *

DIVISION W— INTELLIGENCE AUTHORIZATION ACT FOR FISCAL YEAR 2021

SEC. 1. SHORT TITLE; TABLE OF CONTENTS .

(a) SHORT TITLE.— This division may be cited as the "Intelligence Authorization Act for Fiscal Year 2021".

(b) TABLE OF CONTENTS.— The table of contents for this division is as follows:

DIVISION U—HOMELAND SECURITY AND GOVERNMENTAL

AFFAIRS PROVISIONS

* * * * * * *

DIVISION W— INTELLIGENCE AUTHORIZATION ACT FOR FISCAL YEAR 2021

and entities of commercially available cyber intrusion and
surveillance technology.
Sec. 603. Reports on recommendations of the Cyberspace Solarium
Commission.
Sec. 604. Assessment of critical technology trends relating to
artificial intelligence, microchips, and semiconductors and related
supply chains.

* * * * * * *

Sec. 617. Annual reports on worldwide threats.

* * * * * * *

TITLE III— INTELLIGENCE COMMUNITY MATTERS

Subtitle A— General Intelligence Community Matters

SEC. 301. RESTRICTION ON CONDUCT OF INTELLIGENCE ACTIVITIES.

The authorization of appropriations by this division shall not be
deemed to constitute authority for the conduct of any intelligence
activity which is not otherwise authorized by the Constitution or the
laws of the United States.

SEC. 302. INCREASE IN EMPLOYEE COMPENSATION AND BENEFITS AUTHORIZED BY LAW.

Appropriations authorized by this division for salary, pay,
retirement, and other benefits for Federal employees may be
increased by such additional or supplemental amounts as may be
necessary for increases in such compensation or benefits authorized
by law.

SEC. 303. [50 U.S.C. 3316b] CONTINUITY OF OPERATIONS PLANS FOR CERTAIN ELEMENTS OF THE INTELLIGENCE COMMUNITY IN THE CASE OF A NATIONAL EMERGENCY.

(a) DEFINITION OF COVERED NATIONAL EMERGENCY.— In this
section, the term "covered national emergency" means the following:

(1) A major disaster declared by the President under
section 401 of the Robert T. Stafford Disaster Relief and

Emergency Assistance Act (42 U.S.C. 5170).

(2) An emergency declared by the President under section 501 of the Robert T. Stafford Disaster Relief and Emergency Assistance Act (42 U.S.C. 5191).

(3) A national emergency declared by the President under the National Emergencies Act (50 U.S.C. 1601 et seq.).

(4) A public health emergency declared under section 319 of the Public Health Service Act (42 U.S.C. 247d).

(b) IN GENERAL.— The Director of National Intelligence, the Director of the Central Intelligence Agency, the Director of the National Reconnaissance Office, the Director of the Defense Intelligence Agency, the Director of the National Security Agency, and the Director of the National Geospatial-Intelligence Agency shall each establish continuity of operations plans for use in the case of covered national emergencies for the element of the intelligence community concerned.

(c) SUBMISSION TO CONGRESS.—

(1) DIRECTOR OF NATIONAL INTELLIGENCE AND DIRECTOR OF THE CENTRAL INTELLIGENCE AGENCY.— Not later than 7 days after the date on which a covered national emergency is declared, the Director of National Intelligence and the Director of the Central Intelligence Agency shall each submit to the congressional intelligence committees the plan established under subsection (b) for that emergency for the element of the intelligence community concerned.

(2) DIRECTOR OF NATIONAL RECONNAISSANCE OFFICE, DIRECTOR OF DEFENSE INTELLIGENCE AGENCY, DIRECTOR OF NATIONAL SECURITY AGENCY, AND DIRECTOR OF NATIONAL GEOSPATIAL-INTELLIGENCE AGENCY.— Not later than 7 days after the date on which a covered national emergency is declared, the Director of the National Reconnaissance Office, the Director of the Defense Intelligence Agency, the Director of the National Security Agency, and the Director of the National Geospatial-Intelligence Agency shall each submit the plan established under subsection (b) for that emergency for the element of the intelligence community concerned to the following:

(A) The congressional intelligence committees.

(B) The Committee on Armed Services of the Senate.

(C) The Committee on Armed Services of the House of Representatives.

(d) UPDATES.— During a covered national emergency, the Director of National Intelligence, the Director of the Central Intelligence Agency, the Director of the National Reconnaissance Office, the Director of the Defense Intelligence Agency, the Director of the National Security Agency, and the Director of the National Geospatial-Intelligence Agency shall each submit any updates to the plans submitted under subsection (c)—

(1) in accordance with that subsection; and

(2) in a timely manner consistent with section 501 of the National Security Act of 1947 (50 U.S.C. 3091).

SEC. 304. APPLICATION OF EXECUTIVE SCHEDULE LEVEL III TO POSITION OF DIRECTOR OF NATIONAL RECONNAISSANCE OFFICE.

Section 5314 of title 5, United States Code, is amended by adding at the end the following: "Director of the National Reconnaissance Office." .

SEC. 305. NATIONAL INTELLIGENCE UNIVERSITY.

(a) IN GENERAL.— Title X of the National Security Act of 1947 (50 U.S.C. 3191 et seq.) is amended by adding at the end the following:

"Subtitle D—National Intelligence University

"SEC. 1031. [50 U.S.C. 3227] TRANSFER DATE

"In this subtitle, the term 'transfer date' means the date on which the National Intelligence University is transferred from the Defense Intelligence Agency to the Director of National Intelligence under section 5324(a) of the National Defense Authorization Act for Fiscal Year 2020 (Public Law 116-92).

"SEC. 1032. [50 U.S.C. 3227a] DEGREE-GRANTING AUTHORITY

"(a) IN GENERAL.— Beginning on the transfer date, under regulations prescribed by the Director of National Intelligence, the President of the National Intelligence University may, upon the recommendation of the faculty of the University, confer appropriate degrees upon graduates who meet the degree requirements.

"(b) LIMITATION.— A degree may not be conferred under this section unless—

"(1) the Secretary of Education has recommended approval of the degree in accordance with the Federal Policy Governing Granting of Academic Degrees by Federal Agencies; and

"(2) the University is accredited by the appropriate academic accrediting agency or organization to award the degree, as determined by the Secretary of Education.

"(c) CONGRESSIONAL NOTIFICATION REQUIREMENTS.—

"(1) ACTIONS ON NONACCREDITATION.— Beginning on the transfer date, the Director shall promptly—

"(A) notify the congressional intelligence committees of any action by the Middle States Commission on Higher Education, or other appropriate academic accrediting agency or organization, to not accredit the University to award any new or existing degree; and

"(B) submit to such committees a report containing an explanation of any such action.

"(2) MODIFICATION OR REDESIGNATION OF DEGREE-GRANTING AUTHORITY.— Beginning on the transfer date, upon any modification or redesignation of existing degree-granting authority, the Director shall submit to the congressional intelligence committees a report containing—

"(A) the rationale for the proposed modification or redesignation; and

"(B) any subsequent recommendation of the Secretary of Education with respect to the proposed modification or redesignation.

"SEC. 1033. [50 U.S.C. 3227b] REPORTING

"(a) IN GENERAL.— Not less frequently than once each year, the Director of National Intelligence shall submit to the congressional intelligence committees a plan for employing professors, instructors, and lecturers at the National Intelligence University.

"(b) ELEMENTS.— Each plan submitted under subsection (a) shall include the following:

"(1) The total number of proposed personnel to be employed at the National Intelligence University.

"(2) The total annual compensation to be provided the personnel described in paragraph (1).

"(3) Such other matters as the Director considers appropriate.

"(c) FORM OF SUBMITTAL.— Each plan submitted by the Director to the congressional intelligence committees under subsection (a) shall be submitted as part of another annual submission from the Director to the congressional intelligence committees.

"SEC. 1034. [50 U.S.C. 3227c] CONTINUED APPLICABILITY OF THE FEDERAL ADVISORY COMMITTEE ACT TO THE BOARD OF VISITORS

"The Federal Advisory Committee Act (5 U.S.C. App.) shall continue to apply to the Board of Visitors of the National Intelligence University on and after the transfer date."

.

(b) [50 U.S.C. 3227b note] PLAN REGARDING PERSONNEL AT NATIONAL INTELLIGENCE UNIVERSITY.—

(1) INITIAL SUBMISSION.— Not later than 180 days after the date of the enactment of this Act, the Director of National Intelligence shall submit to the congressional intelligence committees the first submission required by section 1033(a) of the National Security Act of 1947, as added by subsection (a).

(2) CERTAIN REQUIREMENT NOT APPLICABLE.— Subsection (c) of section 1033 of the National Security Act of 1947, as added by subsection (a), shall not apply to the submittal under paragraph (1) of this subsection.

(c) CONFORMING AMENDMENTS.— Section 5324 of the National Defense Authorization Act for Fiscal Year 2020 (Public Law 116-92) is amended—

(1) [50 U.S.C. 3334a] in subsection (b)(1)(C), by striking "subsection (e)(2)" and inserting "section 1032(b) of the National Security Act of 1947";

(2) by striking subsections (e) and (f); and

(3) [10 U.S.C. 2161 50 U.S.C. 3334a] by redesignating subsections (g) and (h) as subsections (e) and (f), respectively.

(d) CLERICAL AMENDMENT.— The table of contents of the National Security Act of 1947 is amended by inserting after the item relating to section 1024 the following:

"Subtitle D— National Intelligence University

"Sec. 1031. Transfer date.
"Sec. 1032. Degree-granting authority.
"Sec. 1033. Reporting.
"Sec. 1034. Continued applicability of the Federal Advisory
Committee Act to the Board of Visitors."

.

**SEC. 306. [50 U.S.C. 3334h] DATA COLLECTION ON ATTRITION IN
INTELLIGENCE COMMUNITY.**

(a) STANDARDS FOR DATA COLLECTION.—

(1) IN GENERAL.— Not later than 90 days after the date of
the enactment of this Act, the Director of National Intelligence
shall establish standards for collecting data relating to attrition
in the intelligence community workforce across demographics,
specialities, and length of service.

(2) INCLUSION OF CERTAIN CANDIDATES.— The Director
shall include, in the standards established under paragraph
(1), standards for collecting data from candidates who accepted
conditional offers of employment but chose to withdraw from
the hiring process before entering into service, including data
with respect to the reasons such candidates chose to withdraw.

(b) COLLECTION OF DATA.— Not later than 120 days after the
date of the enactment of this Act, each element of the intelligence
community shall begin collecting data on workforce and candidate
attrition in accordance with the standards established under
subsection (a).

(c) ANNUAL REPORT.— Not later than 1 year after the date of
the enactment of this Act, and annually thereafter, the Director
shall submit to the congressional intelligence committees a report
on workforce and candidate attrition in the intelligence community
that includes—

(1) the findings of the Director based on the data collected
under subsection (b);

(2) recommendations for addressing any issues identified in
those findings; and

(3) an assessment of timeliness in processing hiring applications of individuals previously employed by an element of the intelligence community, consistent with the Trusted Workforce 2.0 initiative sponsored by the Security Clearance, Suitability, and Credentialing Performance Accountability Council.

SEC. 307. LIMITATION ON DELEGATION OF RESPONSIBILITY FOR PROGRAM MANAGEMENT OF INFORMATION-SHARING ENVIRONMENT.

Section 1016(b) of the Intelligence Reform and Terrorism Prevention Act of 2004 (6 U.S.C. 485(b)), as amended by section 6402(a) of the National Defense Authorization Act for Fiscal Year 2020 (Public Law 116-92), is further amended—

(1) in paragraph (1), in the matter before subparagraph (A), by striking "Director of National Intelligence" and inserting "President";

(2) in paragraph (2), by striking "Director of National Intelligence" both places it appears and inserting "President"; and

(3) by adding at the end the following:

"(3) DELEGATION.—

"(A) IN GENERAL.— Subject to subparagraph (B), the President may delegate responsibility for carrying out this subsection.

"(B) LIMITATION.— The President may not delegate responsibility for carrying out this subsection to the Director of National Intelligence."

.

SEC. 308. REQUIREMENT TO BUY CERTAIN SATELLITE COMPONENT FROM AMERICAN SOURCES.

(a) IN GENERAL.— Title XI of the National Security Act of 1947 (50 U.S.C. 3231 et seq.) is amended by adding at the end the following new section:

"SEC. 1109. [50 U.S.C. 3239] REQUIREMENT TO BUY CERTAIN SATELLITE COMPONENT FROM AMERICAN SOURCES

"(a) DEFINITIONS.— In this section:

"(1) COVERED ELEMENT OF THE INTELLIGENCE

COMMUNITY.— The term 'covered element of the intelligence community' means an element of the intelligence community that is not an element of the Department of Defense.

"(2) NATIONAL SECURITY SATELLITE.— The term 'national security satellite' means a satellite weighing over 400 pounds whose principle purpose is to support the national security or intelligence needs of the United States Government.

"(3) UNITED STATES.— The term 'United States' means the several States, the District of Columbia, and the territories and possessions of the United States.

"(b) REQUIREMENT.— Beginning January 1, 2021, except as provided in subsection (c), a covered element of the intelligence community may not award a contract for a national security satellite if the satellite uses a star tracker that is not produced in the United States, including with respect to both the software and the hardware of the star tracker.

"(c) EXCEPTION.— The head of a covered element of the intelligence community may waive the requirement under subsection (b) if, on a case-by-case basis, the head certifies in writing to the congressional intelligence committees that—

"(1) there is no available star tracker produced in the United States that meets the mission and design requirements of the national security satellite for which the star tracker will be used;

"(2) the cost of a star tracker produced in the United States is unreasonable, based on a market survey; or

"(3) such waiver is necessary for the national security interests of the United States based on an urgent and compelling need."

(b) CLERICAL AMENDMENT.— The table of contents in the first section of the National Security Act of 1947 is amended by inserting after the item relating to section 1108 the following new item:

"Sec. 1109. Requirement to buy certain satellite component from American sources."

SEC. 309. LIMITATION ON CONSTRUCTION OF FACILITIES TO BE USED PRIMARILY BY INTELLIGENCE COMMUNITY.

Section 602(a)(2) of the Intelligence Authorization Act for Fiscal Year 1995 (50 U.S.C. 3304(a)(2)) is amended—

(1) by striking " $1,000,000" both places it appears and inserting " $2,000,000"; and

(2) by striking "the Director of National Intelligence shall submit a notification" and inserting "the head of such component, in coordination with and subject to the approval of the Director of National Intelligence, shall submit a notification".

SEC. 310. [50 U.S.C. 3334g note] INTELLIGENCE COMMUNITY STUDENT LOAN REPAYMENT PROGRAMS.

(a) SENSE OF CONGRESS.— It is the sense of Congress that—

(1) student loan repayment programs are a crucial tool in attracting and retaining talented individuals to the intelligence community, particularly individuals from diverse backgrounds;

(2) generous student loan repayment programs help the intelligence community compete with the private sector for talented employees;

(3) departments and agencies containing elements of the intelligence community have authority to establish student loan repayment programs either under section 5379 of title 5, United States Code, or under the delegable authority of the Director of National Intelligence under section 102A(n)(1) of the National Security Act of 1947 (50 U.S.C. 3024(n)(1));

(4) although the Director should use the authority under such section 102A(n)(1) sparingly, and should be exceedingly sparing in delegating such authority to an element of the intelligence community, the Director should approve well-predicated requests for such authority in the student loan repayment context if an element of the intelligence community can articulate an impediment to establishing or enhancing a program under section 5379 of title 5, United States Code; and

(5) student loan repayment programs established by an element of the intelligence community should provide flexibility to intelligence community employees, including employees who pursue loan-financed education in the middle of their careers

or after the day on which they first become intelligence community employees.

(b) STUDENT LOAN REPAYMENT PROGRAM STANDARDS.— Not later than 180 days after the date of the enactment of this Act, the Director of National Intelligence, or a designee of the Director who is an employee of the Office of the Director of National Intelligence, shall establish minimum standards for the repayment of student loans of employees of elements of the intelligence community by such elements of the intelligence community.

(c) REPORT.— Not later than 180 days after the date of the enactment of this Act, the Director shall submit to the appropriate congressional committees a report on the standards established under subsection (b). Such report shall include—

(1) an explanation of why such minimum standards were established; and

(2) how such standards advance the goals of—

(A) attracting and retaining a talented intelligence community workforce;

(B) competing with private sector companies for talented employees; and

(C) promoting the development of a diverse workforce.

(d) FAILURE TO MEET STANDARDS.— Not later than 180 days after the date on which the standards required under subsection (b) are established, the head of an element of the intelligence community that does not meet such standards shall submit to the appropriate congressional committees a report containing an explanation for why such element does not meet such standards and an identification of any additional authority or appropriations required to for the element to meet such standards.

(e) SUBMITTAL OF REGULATIONS AND POLICIES TO CONGRESS.— Not later than 180 days after the date on which the standards required under subsection (b) are established, the head of an element of the intelligence community shall submit to the appropriate congressional committees a copy of all internal regulations and policies governing the student loan repayment program of that element as well as copies of such policies redacted to remove classified information.

(f) APPROPRIATE CONGRESSIONAL COMMITTEES DEFINED.— In this section, the term "appropriate congressional committees" means—

(1) the Permanent Select Committee on Intelligence of the House of Representatives;

(2) the Select Committee on Intelligence of the Senate;

(3) with respect to an element of the intelligence community within the Department of Defense, the Committees on Armed Services of the Senate and House of Representatives;

(4) with respect to an element of the intelligence community within the Department of Justice, the Committees on the Judiciary of the Senate and House of Representatives;

(5) with respect to an element of the intelligence community within the Department of Homeland Security, the Committee on Homeland Security and Governmental Affairs of the Senate and the Committee on Homeland Security of the House of Representatives;

(6) with respect to an element of the intelligence community within the Department of State, the Committee on Foreign Relations of the Senate and the Committee on Foreign Affairs of the House of Representatives;

(7) with respect to an element of the intelligence community within the Department of Energy, the Committee on Energy and Natural Resources of the Senate and the Committee on Energy and Commerce of the House of Representatives; and

(8) with respect to an element of the intelligence community within the Department of the Treasury, the Committee on Finance of the Senate and the Committee on Financial Services of the House of Representatives.

(g) FORM OF REPORTS.— Each of the reports required under subsections (c) and (d) shall be submitted in unclassified form, but may contain a classified annex.

Subtitle B— Reports and Assessments Pertaining to the Intelligence Community

SEC. 321. ASSESSMENT BY THE COMPTROLLER GENERAL OF THE UNITED STATES ON EFFORTS OF THE INTELLIGENCE COMMUNITY

AND THE DEPARTMENT OF DEFENSE TO IDENTIFY AND MITIGATE RISKS POSED TO THE INTELLIGENCE COMMUNITY AND THE DEPARTMENT BY THE USE OF DIRECT-TO-CONSUMER GENETIC TESTING BY THE GOVERNMENT OF THE PEOPLE'S REPUBLIC OF CHINA.

(a) ASSESSMENT REQUIRED.— The Comptroller General of the United States shall assess the efforts of the intelligence community and the Department of Defense to identify and mitigate the risks posed to the intelligence community and the Department by the use of direct-to-consumer genetic testing by the Government of the People's Republic of China.

(b) REPORT REQUIRED.—

(1) DEFINITION OF UNITED STATES DIRECT-TO-CONSUMER GENETIC TESTING COMPANY.— In this subsection, the term "United States direct-to-consumer genetic testing company" means a private entity that—

(A) carries out direct-to-consumer genetic testing; and

(B) is organized under the laws of the United States or any jurisdiction within the United States.

(2) IN GENERAL.— Not later than 180 days after the date of the enactment of this Act, the Comptroller General shall submit to Congress, including the congressional intelligence committees, the Committee on Armed Services of the Senate, and the Committee on Armed Services of the House of Representatives, a report on the assessment required by subsection (a).

(3) ELEMENTS.— The report required by paragraph (2) shall include the following:

(A) A description of key national security risks and vulnerabilities associated with direct-to-consumer genetic testing, including—

(i) how the Government of the People's Republic of China may be using data provided by personnel of the intelligence community and the Department through direct-to-consumer genetic tests; and

(ii) how ubiquitous technical surveillance may amplify those risks.

(B) An assessment of the extent to which the

intelligence community and the Department have identified risks and vulnerabilities posed by direct-to-consumer genetic testing and have sought to mitigate such risks and vulnerabilities, or have plans for such mitigation, including the extent to which the intelligence community has determined—

> (i) in which United States direct-to-consumer genetic testing companies the Government of the People's Republic of China or entities owned or controlled by the Government of the People's Republic of China have an ownership interest; and

> (ii) which United States direct-to-consumer genetic testing companies may have sold data to the Government of the People's Republic of China or entities owned or controlled by the Government of the People's Republic of China.

(C) Such recommendations as the Comptroller General may have for action by the intelligence community and the Department to improve the identification and mitigation of risks and vulnerabilities posed by the use of direct-to-consumer genetic testing by the Government of the People's Republic of China.

(4) FORM.— The report required by paragraph (2) shall be submitted in unclassified form, but may include a classified annex.

(c) COOPERATION.— The heads of relevant elements of the intelligence community and components of the Department shall—

(1) fully cooperate with the Comptroller General in conducting the assessment required by subsection (a); and

(2) provide any information and data required by the Comptroller General to conduct the assessment, consistent with Intelligence Community Directive 114 or successor directive.

SEC. 322. REPORT ON USE BY INTELLIGENCE COMMUNITY OF HIRING FLEXIBILITIES AND EXPEDITED HUMAN RESOURCES PRACTICES TO ASSURE QUALITY AND DIVERSITY IN THE WORKFORCE OF THE INTELLIGENCE COMMUNITY.

(a) IN GENERAL.— Not later than 180 days after the date of the enactment of this Act, the Director of National Intelligence shall submit to the congressional intelligence committees a report on how elements of the intelligence community are exercising hiring flexibilities and expedited human resources practices afforded under section 3326 of title 5, United States Code, and subpart D of part 315 of title 5, Code of Federal Regulations, or successor regulation, to assure quality and diversity in the workforce of the intelligence community.

(b) OBSTACLES.— The report submitted under subsection (a) shall include identification of any obstacles encountered by the intelligence community in exercising the authorities described in such subsection.

SEC. 323. REPORT ON SIGNALS INTELLIGENCE PRIORITIES AND REQUIREMENTS.

(a) REPORT REQUIRED.— Not later than 30 days after the date of the enactment of this Act, the Director of National Intelligence shall submit to the congressional intelligence committees, the majority and minority leaders of the Senate, and the Speaker and minority leader of the House of Representatives a report on signals intelligence priorities and requirements subject to Presidential Policy Directive 28.

(b) ELEMENTS.— The report required by subsection (a) shall cover the following:

(1) The implementation of the annual process for advising the Director on signals intelligence priorities and requirements described in section 3 of Presidential Policy Directive 28.

(2) The signals intelligence priorities and requirements as of the most recent annual process.

(3) The application of such priorities and requirements to the signals intelligence collection efforts of the intelligence community.

(c) CONTENTS OF CLASSIFIED ANNEX REFERENCED IN SECTION 3 OF PRESIDENTIAL POLICY DIRECTIVE 28.— Not later than 30 days after the date of the enactment of this Act, in addition to the report submitted under subsection (a), the Director shall submit to the chairmen and ranking minority members of the congressional intelligence committees, the majority and minority leaders of the Senate, and the Speaker and minority leader of the House of Representatives the contents of the classified annex referenced in

318

section 3 of Presidential Policy Directive 28.

(d) FORM.— The report submitted under subsection (a) shall be submitted in unclassified form, but may include a classified annex.

SEC. 324. ASSESSMENT OF DEMAND FOR STUDENT LOAN REPAYMENT PROGRAM BENEFIT.

(a) IN GENERAL.— Not later than 90 days after the date of the enactment of this Act, the head of each element of the intelligence community shall—

(1) calculate the number of personnel of that element who qualify for a student loan repayment program benefit;

(2) compare the number calculated under paragraph (1) to the number of personnel who apply for such a benefit;

(3) provide recommendations for how to structure such a program to optimize participation and enhance the effectiveness of the benefit as a retention tool, including with respect to the amount of the benefit offered and the length of time an employee receiving a benefit is required to serve under a continuing service agreement; and

(4) identify any shortfall in funds or authorities needed to provide such a benefit.

(b) INCLUSION IN FISCAL YEAR 2022 BUDGET SUBMISSION.— The Director of National Intelligence shall include in the budget justification materials submitted to Congress in support of the budget for the intelligence community for fiscal year 2022 (as submitted with the budget of the President under section 1105(a) of title 31, United States Code) a report on the findings of the elements of the intelligence community under subsection (a).

SEC. 325. ASSESSMENT OF INTELLIGENCE COMMUNITY DEMAND FOR CHILD CARE.

(a) IN GENERAL.— Not later than 180 days after the date of the enactment of this Act, the Director of National Intelligence, in coordination with the heads of the elements of the intelligence community specified in subsection (b), shall submit to the congressional intelligence committees a report that includes—

(1) a calculation of the total annual demand for child care by employees of such elements, at or near the workplaces of such employees, including a calculation of the demand for early

morning and evening child care;

(2) an identification of any shortfall between the demand calculated under paragraph (1) and the child care supported by such elements as of the date of the report;

(3) an assessment of options for addressing any such shortfall, including options for providing child care at or near the workplaces of employees of such elements;

(4) an identification of the advantages, disadvantages, security requirements, and costs associated with each such option;

(5) a plan to meet, by the date that is 5 years after the date of the report—

(A) the demand calculated under paragraph (1); or

(B) an alternative standard established by the Director for child care available to employees of such elements; and

(6) an assessment of needs of specific elements of the intelligence community, including any Government-provided child care that could be collocated with a workplace of employees of such an element and any available child care providers in the proximity of such a workplace.

(b) ELEMENTS SPECIFIED.— The elements of the intelligence community specified in this subsection are the following:

(1) The Central Intelligence Agency.

(2) The National Security Agency.

(3) The Defense Intelligence Agency.

(4) The National Geospatial-Intelligence Agency.

(5) The National Reconnaissance Office.

(6) The Office of the Director of National Intelligence.

SEC. 326. OPEN SOURCE INTELLIGENCE STRATEGIES AND PLANS FOR THE INTELLIGENCE COMMUNITY.

(a) REQUIREMENT FOR SURVEY AND EVALUATION OF CUSTOMER FEEDBACK.— Not later than 90 days a fter the date of the enactment of this Act, the Director of National Intelligence, in coordination with the head of each element of the intelligence community, shall—

(1) conduct a survey of the open source intelligence requirements, goals, monetary and property investments, and

capabilities for each element of the intelligence community; and

(2) evaluate the usability and utility of the Open Source Enterprise by soliciting customer feedback and evaluating such feedback.

(b) REQUIREMENT FOR OVERALL STRATEGY AND FOR INTELLIGENCE COMMUNITY, PLAN FOR IMPROVING USABILITY OF OPEN SOURCE ENTERPRISE, AND RISK ANALYSIS OF CREATING OPEN SOURCE CENTER.— Not later than 180 days after the date of the enactment of this Act, the Director, in coordination with the head of each element of the intelligence community and using the findings of the Director with respect to the survey conducted under subsection (a), shall—

(1) develop a strategy for open source intelligence collection, analysis, and production that defines the overarching goals, roles, responsibilities, and processes for such collection, analysis, and production for the intelligence community;

(2) develop a plan for improving usability and utility of the Open Source Enterprise based on the customer feedback solicited under subsection (a)(2); and

(3) conduct a risk and benefit analysis of creating an open source center independent of any current intelligence community element.

(c) REQUIREMENT FOR PLAN FOR CENTRALIZED DATA REPOSITORY.— Not later than 270 days after the date of the enactment of this Act and using the findings of the Director with respect to the survey and evaluation conducted under subsection (a), the strategy and plan developed under subsection (b), and the risk and benefit analysis conducted under such subsection, the Director shall develop a plan for a centralized data repository of open source intelligence that enables all elements of the intelligence community—

(1) to use such repository for their specific requirements; and

(2) to derive open source intelligence advantages.

(d) REQUIREMENT FOR COST-SHARING MODEL.— Not later than 1 year after the date of the enactment of this Act and using the findings of the Director with respect to the survey and evaluation conducted under subsection (a), the strategy and plan developed under subsection (b), the risk and benefit analysis conducted under such subsection, and the plan developed under subsection (c), the Director shall develop a cost-sharing model that leverages the open source intelligence investments of each element of the intelligence community for the beneficial use of the entire intelligence community.

(e) CONGRESSIONAL BRIEFING.— Not later than 1 year after the date of the enactment of this Act, the Director of National Intelligence, the Director of the Central Intelligence Agency, the Director of the Defense Intelligence Agency, the Director of the National Geospatial-Intelligence Agency, and the Director of the National Security Agency shall jointly brief the congressional intelligence committees on—

(1) the strategy developed under paragraph (1) of subsection (b);

(2) the plan developed under paragraph (2) of such subsection;

(3) the plan developed under subsection (c); and

(4) the cost-sharing model developed under subsection (d).

TITLE IV— MATTERS RELATING TO ELEMENTS OF THE INTELLIGENCE COMMUNITY

SEC. 401. ESTABLISHMENT OF OFFICE OF THE OMBUDSMAN FOR ANALYTIC OBJECTIVITY.

(a) OFFICE OF THE OMBUDSMAN FOR ANALYTIC OBJECTIVITY.— The Central Intelligence Agency Act of 1949 (50 U.S.C. 3501 et seq.) is amended by adding at the end the following:

"SEC. 24. [50 U.S.C. 3525] OFFICE OF THE OMBUDSMAN FOR ANALYTIC OBJECTIVITY

"(a) ESTABLISHMENT.—

"(1) IN GENERAL.— There is established in the Agency an Office of the Ombudsman for Analytic Objectivity (in this section referred to as the 'Office').

"(2) APPOINTMENT OF OMBUDSMAN.— The Office shall be headed by an Ombudsman, who shall be appointed by the Director from among current or former senior staff officers of the Agency.

"(b) DUTIES AND RESPONSIBILITIES.— The Ombudsman shall—

"(1) on an annual basis, conduct a survey of analytic objectivity among officers and employees of the Agency;

"(2) implement a procedure by which any officer or employee of the Agency may submit to the Office a complaint alleging politicization, bias, lack of objectivity, or other issues relating to a failure of tradecraft in analysis conducted by the Agency;

"(3) except as provided in paragraph (4), upon receiving a complaint submitted pursuant to paragraph (2), take reasonable action to investigate the complaint, make a determination as to whether the incident described in the complaint involved politicization, bias, or lack of objectivity, and prepare a report that—

"(A) summarizes the facts relevant to the complaint;

"(B) documents the determination of the Ombudsman with respect to the complaint; and

"(C) contains a recommendation for remedial action;

"(4) if a complaint submitted pursuant to paragraph (2) alleges politicization, bias, or lack of objectivity in the collection of intelligence information, refer the complaint to the official responsible for supervising collection operations of the Agency; and

"(5) continuously monitor changes in areas of analysis that the Ombudsman determines involve a heightened risk of politicization, bias, or lack of objectivity, to ensure that any change in the analytic line arises from proper application of analytic tradecraft and not as a result of politicization, bias, or lack of objectivity.

"(c) REPORTS.— (1) On an annual basis, the Ombudsman shall submit to the intelligence committees a report on the results of the survey conducted pursuant to subsection (b)(1) with respect to the most recent fiscal year.

"(2) On an annual basis, the Ombudsman shall submit to the intelligence committees a report that includes—

"(A) the number of complaints of submitted pursuant to subsection (b)(2) during the most recent fiscal year; and

"(B) a description of the nature of such complaints, the actions taken by the Office or any other relevant element or component of the Agency with respect to such complaints, and the resolution of such complaints.

"(3) On a quarterly basis, the Ombudsman shall submit to the intelligence committees a report that includes—

"(A) a list of the areas of analysis monitored during the most recent calendar quarter pursuant to subsection (b)(5); and

"(B) a brief description of the methods by which the Office has conducted such monitoring.

"(d) INTELLIGENCE COMMITTEES DEFINED.— In this section, the term 'intelligence committees' means the Permanent Select Committee on Intelligence of the House of Representatives and the Select Committee on Intelligence of the Senate."

.

(b) [50 U.S.C. 3525 note] REFERENCE.— Any reference in any law, regulation, map, document, paper, or other record of the United States to the Ombudsman for Analytic and Collection Objectivity of the Central Intelligence Agency shall be deemed to be a reference to the Office of the Ombudsman for Analytic Objectivity of the Central Intelligence Agency established by section 24(a) of the Central Intelligence Agency Act of 1949 (50 U.S.C. 3501 et seq.), as added by subsection (a).

(c) REPORT ON SURVEYS FOR FISCAL YEARS 2018 AND 2019.— Not later than 10 days after the date of the enactment of this Act, the Director of the Central Intelligence Agency shall submit to the congressional intelligence committees any reports previously prepared by the Ombudsman for Analytic and Collection Objectivity with respect to the surveys of analytic objectivity conducted for fiscal years 2018 and 2019.

SEC. 402. EXPANSION OF PERSONNEL MANAGEMENT AUTHORITY TO ATTRACT EXPERTS IN SCIENCE AND ENGINEERING.

Section 1599h of title 10, United States Code, is amended—

(1) in subsection (a), by adding at the end the following new paragraph:

"(7) NGA.— The Director of the National Geospatial-Intelligence Agency may carry out a program of personnel management authority provided in subsection (b) in order to facilitate recruitment of eminent experts in science or engineering for research and development projects and to enhance the administration and management of the Agency."

;

(2) in subsection (b)(1)—

(A) in subparagraph (E), by striking "; and";

(B) in subparagraph (F), by striking the semicolon and inserting "; and"; and

(C) by adding at the end the following new subparagraph:

"(G) in the case of the National Geospatial-Intelligence Agency, appoint individuals to a total of not more than 7 positions in the Agency, of which not more than 2 such positions may be positions of administration or management in the Agency;"

; and

(3) in subsection (c)(2), by striking "or the Joint Artificial Intelligence Center" and inserting "the Joint Artificial Intelligence Center, or the National Geospatial-Intelligence Agency".

SEC. 403. SENIOR CHIEF PETTY OFFICER SHANNON KENT AWARD FOR DISTINGUISHED FEMALE PERSONNEL OF THE NATIONAL SECURITY AGENCY.

The National Security Agency Act of 1959 (50 U.S.C. 3601 et seq.) is amended by adding at the end the following new section:

"SEC. 21. [50 U.S.C. 3619] SENIOR CHIEF PETTY OFFICER SHANNON KENT AWARD FOR DISTINGUISHED FEMALE PERSONNEL

"(a) ESTABLISHMENT.— The Director of the National Security Agency shall establish an honorary award for the recognition of female personnel of the National Security Agency for distinguished career contributions in support of the mission of the Agency as civilian employees or members of the Armed Forces assigned to the Agency. The award shall be known as the 'Senior Chief Petty Officer Shannon Kent Award' and shall consist of a design determined appropriate by the Director.

"(b) AWARD.— The Director shall award the Senior Chief Petty Officer Shannon Kent Award to female civilian employees, members of the Armed Forces, or former civilian employees or members, whom the Director determines meet the criteria under subsection (a)."

.

SEC. 404. DEPARTMENT OF HOMELAND SECURITY INTELLIGENCE AND CYBERSECURITY DIVERSITY FELLOWSHIP PROGRAM.

(a) PROGRAM.— Subtitle D of title XIII of the Homeland Security Act of 2002 (5 U.S.C. 3301 note et seq.) is amended by adding at the end the following new section:

"SEC. 1333. [6 U.S.C. 665a] INTELLIGENCE AND CYBERSECURITY DIVERSITY FELLOWSHIP PROGRAM

"(a) DEFINITIONS.— In this section:

"(1) APPROPRIATE COMMITTEES OF CONGRESS.— The term 'appropriate committees of Congress' means—

"(A) the Committee on Homeland Security and Governmental Affairs and the Select Committee on Intelligence of the Senate; and

"(B) the Committee on Homeland Security and the Permanent Select Committee on Intelligence of the House of Representatives.

"(2) EXCEPTED SERVICE.— The term 'excepted service' has the meaning given that term in section 2103 of title 5, United States Code.

"(3) HISTORICALLY BLACK COLLEGE OR UNIVERSITY.— The term 'historically Black college or university' has the meaning given the term 'part B institution' in section 322 of the Higher Education Act of 1965 (20 U.S.C. 1061).

"(4) INSTITUTION OF HIGHER EDUCATION.— The term 'institution of higher education' has the meaning given that term in section 101 of the Higher Education Act of 1965 (20 U.S.C. 1001).

"(5) MINORITY-SERVING INSTITUTION.— The term 'minority-serving institution' means an institution of higher education described in section 371(a) of the Higher Education Act of 1965 (20 U.S.C. 1067q(a)).

"(b) PROGRAM.— The Secretary shall carry out an intelligence and cybersecurity diversity fellowship program (in this section referred to as the 'Program') under which an eligible individual may—

"(1) participate in a paid internship at the Department that relates to intelligence, cybersecurity, or some combination thereof;

"(2) receive tuition assistance from the Secretary; and

"(3) upon graduation from an institution of higher education and successful completion of the Program (as defined by the Secretary), receive an offer of employment to work in an intelligence or cybersecurity position of the Department that is in the excepted service.

"(c) ELIGIBILITY.— To be eligible to participate in the Program, an individual shall—

"(1) be a citizen of the United States; and

"(2) as of the date of submitting the application to participate in the Program—

"(A) have a cumulative grade point average of at least 3.2 on a 4.0 scale;

"(B) be a socially disadvantaged individual (as that term in defined in section 124.103 of title 13, Code of Federal Regulations, or successor regulation); and

"(C) be a sophomore, junior, or senior at an institution of higher education.

"(d) DIRECT HIRE AUTHORITY.— If an individual who receives an offer of employment under subsection (b)(3) accepts such offer, the Secretary shall appoint, without regard to provisions of subchapter I of chapter 33 of title 5, United States Code, (except for section 3328 of such title) such individual to the position specified in such offer.

"(e) REPORTS.—

"(1) REPORTS.— Not later than 1 year after the date of the enactment of this section, and on an annual basis thereafter, the Secretary shall submit to the appropriate committees of Congress a report on the Program.

"(2) MATTERS.— Each report under paragraph (1) shall include, with respect to the most recent year, the following:

"(A) A description of outreach efforts by the Secretary to raise awareness of the Program among institutions of higher education in which eligible individuals are enrolled.

"(B) Information on specific recruiting efforts conducted by the Secretary to increase participation in the Program.

"(C) The number of individuals participating in the Program, listed by the institution of higher education in which the individual is enrolled at the time of participation, and information on the nature of such participation, including on whether the duties of the individual under the Program relate primarily to intelligence or to cybersecurity.

"(D) The number of individuals who accepted an offer of employment under the Program and an identification of the element within the Department to which each individual was appointed."

.

(b) CLERICAL AMENDMENT.— The table of contents for such Act is amended by inserting after the item relating to section 1332 the following new item:

"Sec. 1333. Intelligence and cybersecurity diversity fellowship program."

.

SEC. 405. CLIMATE SECURITY ADVISORY COUNCIL.

(a) STUDY ON ADVISORY COUNCIL MODEL FOR STRATEGIC OR TRANSNATIONAL THREATS.—

(1) STUDY REQUIRED.— The Director of National Intelligence, in coordination with the heads of other elements of the intelligence community determined appropriate by the Director, shall conduct a study on the effectiveness of the Climate Security Advisory Council as a potential model for future advisory councils that—

(A) focus on optimizing the collection and analysis of intelligence relating to strategic or transnational threats to the national security of the United States (including threats posed by disease outbreaks, pandemics, or other global health threats); and

(B) are composed of elements of the intelligence community and relevant elements of the Federal Government that are not elements of the intelligence community.

(2) REPORT.— Not later than 1 year after the date of the enactment of this Act, the Director shall submit to the congressional intelligence committees a report containing the findings of the study under paragraph (1).

(b) TECHNICAL CORRECTION.— Section 120(c)(4) of the National Security Act of 1947 (50 U.S.C. 3060(c)(4)) is amended by striking "security indicators" and inserting "intelligence indications".

* * * * * * *

TITLE VI— REPORTS AND OTHER MATTERS

* * * * * * *

SEC. 602. REPORT ON THREATS POSED BY USE BY FOREIGN GOVERNMENTS AND ENTITIES OF COMMERCIALLY AVAILABLE CYBER INTRUSION AND SURVEILLANCE TECHNOLOGY.

(a) REPORT REQUIRED.— Not later than 180 days after the date of the enactment of this Act, the Director of National Intelligence shall submit to the congressional intelligence committees, the Committee on Homeland Security and Governmental Affairs of the Senate, and the Committee on Homeland Security of the House of Representatives a report on the threats posed by the use by foreign governments and entities of commercially available cyber intrusion and other surveillance technology.

(b) CONTENTS.— The report required by subsection (a) shall include the following:

(1) Matters relating to threats described in subsection (a) as they pertain to the following:

(A) The threat posed to United States persons and persons inside the United States.

(B) The threat posed to United States personnel overseas.

(C) The threat posed to employees of the Federal Government, including through both official and personal accounts and devices.

(2) A description of which foreign governments and entities pose the greatest threats from the use of technology described in subsection (a) and the nature of those threats.

(3) An assessment of the source of the commercially available cyber intrusion and other surveillance technology that poses the threats described in subsection (a), including whether such technology is made by United States companies or companies in the United States or by foreign companies.

(4) An assessment of actions taken, as of the date of the enactment of this Act, by the Federal Government and foreign governments to limit the export of technology described in subsection (a) from the United States or foreign countries to foreign governments and entities in ways that pose the threats described in such subsection.

(5) Matters relating to how the Federal Government, Congress, and foreign governments can most effectively mitigate the threats described in subsection (a), including matters relating to the following:

(A) Working with the technology and telecommunications industry to identify and improve the security of consumer software and hardware used by United States persons and persons inside the United States that is targeted by commercial cyber intrusion and surveillance software.

(B) Export controls.

(C) Diplomatic pressure.

(D) Trade agreements.

(c) FORM.— The report submitted under subsection (a) shall be submitted in unclassified form, but may include a classified annex.

SEC. 603. REPORTS ON RECOMMENDATIONS OF THE CYBERSPACE SOLARIUM COMMISSION.

(a) APPROPRIATE COMMITTEES OF CONGRESS.— In this section, the term "appropriate committees of Congress" means—

(1) the Committee on Armed Services, the Select

Committee on Intelligence, the Committee on Homeland Security and Governmental Affairs, the Committee on Commerce, Science, and Transportation, and the Committee on Energy and Natural Resources of the Senate; and

(2) the Committee on Armed Services, the Permanent Select Committee on Intelligence, the Committee on Homeland Security, the Committee on Science, Space, and Technology, and the Committee on Energy and Commerce of the House of Representatives.

(b) REPORTS REQUIRED.— Not later than 180 days after the date of the enactment of this Act, each head of an agency described in subsection (c) shall submit to the appropriate committees of Congress a report on the recommendations included in the report issued by the Cyberspace Solarium Commission under section 1652(k) of the John S. McCain National Defense Authorization Act for Fiscal Year 2019 (Public Law 115-232).

(c) AGENCIES DESCRIBED.— The agencies described in this subsection are the following:

(1) The Office of the Director of National Intelligence.

(2) The Department of Homeland Security.

(3) The Department of Energy.

(4) The Department of Commerce.

(5) The Department of Defense.

(d) CONTENTS.— Each report submitted under subsection (b) by the head of an agency described in subsection (c) shall include the following:

(1) An evaluation of the recommendations in the report described in subsection (b) that the agency identifies as pertaining directly to the agency.

(2) A description of the actions taken, or the actions that the head of the agency may consider taking, to implement any of the recommendations (including a comprehensive estimate of requirements for appropriations to take such actions).

SEC. 604. ASSESSMENT OF CRITICAL TECHNOLOGY TRENDS RELATING TO ARTIFICIAL INTELLIGENCE, MICROCHIPS, AND SEMICONDUCTORS AND RELATED SUPPLY CHAINS.

(a) ASSESSMENT REQUIRED.— Not later than 180 days after

the date of the enactment of this Act, the Director of National Intelligence shall complete a detailed assessment of critical technology trends relating to artificial intelligence, microchips, and semiconductors and related supply chains.

(b) ELEMENTS.— The assessment required by subsection (a) shall include the following:

(1) EXPORT CONTROLS.—

(A) IN GENERAL.— An assessment of efforts by partner countries to enact and implement export controls and other technology transfer measures with respect to artificial intelligence, microchips, advanced manufacturing equipment, and other artificial intelligence enabled technologies critical to United States supply chains.

(B) IDENTIFICATION OF OPPORTUNITIES FOR COOPERATION.— The assessment under subparagraph (A) shall identify opportunities for further cooperation with international partners on a multilateral and bilateral basis to strengthen export control regimes and address technology transfer threats.

(2) SEMICONDUCTOR SUPPLY CHAINS.—

(A) IN GENERAL.— An assessment of global semiconductor supply chains, including areas to reduce United States vulnerabilities and maximize points of leverage.

(B) ANALYSIS OF POTENTIAL EFFECTS.— The assessment under subparagraph (A) shall include an analysis of the potential effects of significant geopolitical shifts, including those related to Taiwan.

(C) IDENTIFICATION OF OPPORTUNITIES FOR DIVERSIFICATION.— The assessment under subparagraph (A) shall also identify opportunities for diversification of United States supply chains, including an assessment of cost, challenges, and opportunities to diversify manufacturing capabilities on a multinational basis.

(3) COMPUTING POWER.— An assessment of trends relating to computing power and the effect of such trends on global artificial intelligence development and implementation, in consultation with the Director of the Intelligence Advanced Research Projects Activity, the Director of the Defense

Advanced Research Projects Agency, and the Director of the National Institute of Standards and Technology, including forward-looking assessments of how computing resources may affect United States national security, innovation, and implementation relating to artificial intelligence.

(c) REPORT.—

(1) DEFINITION OF APPROPRIATE COMMITTEES OF CONGRESS.— In this subsection, the term "appropriate committees of Congress" means—

(A) the Select Committee on Intelligence, the Committee on Armed Services, the Committee on Banking, Housing, and Urban Affairs, the Committee on Foreign Relations, and the Committee on Homeland Security and Governmental Affairs of the Senate; and

(B) the Permanent Select Committee on Intelligence, the Committee on Armed Services, the Committee on Financial Services, the Committee on Foreign Affairs, and the Committee on Homeland Security of the House of Representatives.

(2) IN GENERAL.— Not later than 180 days after the date of the enactment of this Act, the Director shall submit to the appropriate committees of Congress a report on the findings of the Director with respect to the assessment completed under subsection (a).

(3) FORM.— The report submitted under paragraph (2) shall be submitted in unclassified form, but may include a classified annex.

* * * * * * *

SEC. 617. ANNUAL REPORTS ON WORLDWIDE THREATS.

(a) IN GENERAL.— Title I of the National Security Act of 1947 (50 U.S.C. 3021 et seq.) is amended by inserting after section 108A the following new section:

"SEC. 108B. [50 U.S.C. 3043b] ANNUAL REPORTS ON WORLDWIDE THREATS

"(a) DEFINITION OF APPROPRIATE CONGRESSIONAL COMMITTEES.— In this section, the term 'appropriate congressional committees' means—

"(1) the congressional intelligence committees; and

"(2) the Committees on Armed Services of the House of Representatives and the Senate.

"(b) ANNUAL REPORTS.— Not later than the first Monday in February 2021, and each year thereafter, the Director of National Intelligence, in coordination with the heads of the elements of the intelligence community, shall submit to the appropriate congressional committees a report containing an assessment of the intelligence community with respect to worldwide threats to the national security of the United States.

"(c) FORM.— Each report under subsection (b) shall be submitted in unclassified form, but may include a classified annex only for the protection of intelligence sources and methods relating to the matters contained in the report.

"(d) HEARINGS.—

"(1) OPEN HEARINGS.— Upon request by the appropriate congressional committees, the Director (and any other head of an element of the intelligence community determined appropriate by the committees in consultation with the Director) shall testify before such committees in an open setting regarding a report under subsection (b).

"(2) CLOSED HEARINGS.— Any information that may not be disclosed during an open hearing under paragraph (1) in order to protect intelligence sources and methods may instead be discussed in a closed hearing that immediately follows such open hearing."

.

(b) CLERICAL AMENDMENT.— The table of contents at the beginning of such Act is amended by inserting after the item relating to section 108A the following new item:

"Sec. 108B. Annual reports on world-wide threats."

.

* * * * * * *

DIVISION FF— OTHER MATTER

* * * * * * *

TITLE XX— PORT SURVEILLANCE

SEC. 2001. [15 U.S.C. 2066 note] PORT SURVEILLANCE.

(a) CPSC SURVEILLANCE PERSONNEL DURING THE COVID-19 PANDEMIC.— For the duration of a public health emergency declared pursuant to section 319 of the Public Health Service Act (42 U.S.C. 247d) as a result of confirmed cases of 2019 novel coronavirus (COVID-19), including any renewal thereof, the Commission shall ensure, to the maximum extent feasible, that investigators are stationed at ports of entry to protect the public against unreasonable risk of injury from consumer products, with the goal of covering no fewer than 90 percent of all consumer products entering the United States that are risk-scored in the Risk Assessment Methodology system. The Commission shall consult with United States Customs and Border Protection, and other relevant agencies, including health and safety agencies, on methods to safely staff ports during the pandemic.

(b) ADDITIONAL CPSC SURVEILLANCE PERSONNEL AT KEY PORTS OF ENTRY.— The Commission shall hire, train, and assign not fewer than 16 additional full-time equivalent personnel to be stationed at or supporting efforts at ports of entry, including ports of entry for de minimis shipments, for the purpose of identifying, assessing, and addressing shipments of violative consumer products. Such hiring shall continue during each fiscal year until the total number of full-time equivalent personnel equals and sustains the staffing requirements identified in the report to Congress required under subsection (c)(2)(F).

(c) REPORT TO CONGRESS.—

(1) IN GENERAL.— Not later than 180 days after the date of enactment of this section, the Commission shall transmit to Congress, and make publicly available, a study and report assessing the risk to consumers associated with the reduction in Commission port inspection activity during the COVID-19 pandemic and the targeting and screening of de minimis shipments.

(2) REPORT REQUIREMENTS.— In the study and report, the Commission shall—

(A) identify—

(i) the risks associated with the reduction in

Commission port inspection activity during the COVID-19 pandemic;

(ii) the extent to which the reduction in port inspection activity is linked to inadequate Commission resources or due to shortages of trained Commission staff due to the COVID-19 pandemic; and

(iii) the steps the Commission has taken and plans to take to mitigate those risks, such as recalls, inspections of product inventory, consumer warnings, and other appropriate measures;

(B) examine a sampling of de minimis shipments at a sufficient and representative sample of all types of ports of entry where de minimis shipments are processed, including express consignment carrier facilities, international mail facilities, and air cargo facilities to assess the extent to which such shipments include violative consumer products;

(C) examine a sampling of shipments coming from countries identified as high-risk for exporting violative consumer products to identify trends associated with the shipment of products containing both intellectual property rights infringements and consumer product safety violations;

(D) detail plans and timelines to effectively address targeting and screening of de minimis shipments to prevent the entry of violative consumer products entering into the commerce of the United States taking into consideration projected growth in e-commerce;

(E) establish metrics by which to evaluate the effectiveness of the Commission efforts to reduce the number of de minimis shipments containing violative consumer products from entering into the commerce of the United States; and

(F) assess projected technology and resources, including staffing requirements necessary to implement such plans based on available and needed Commission resources.

(d) DEFINITIONS.— In this section—

(1) the term "Commission" means the Consumer Product Safety Commission;

(2) the term "de minimis shipments" means articles containing consumer products entering the United States under the de minimis value exemption in 19 U.S.C. 1321(a)(2)(C);

(3) the term "ports of entry for de minimis shipments" means environments where de minimis shipments are processed, including express consignment carrier facilities, international mail facilities, and air cargo facilities; and

(4) the term "violative consumer products" means consumer products in violation of an applicable consumer product safety rule under the Consumer Product Safety Act or any similar rule, regulation, standard, or ban under any other Act enforced by the Commission.

(e) SAVINGS CLAUSE.— Nothing in this section shall be construed to limit, affect, or conflict with any other authority of the Commission or any other statutory requirements governing the Commission.

* * * * * * *

www.ingramcontent.com/pod-product-compliance
Lightning Source LLC
Chambersburg PA
CBHW062115020426
42335CB00013B/973